YALE STUDIES IN ENGLISH

VOLUME 99

PUBLISHED ON
THE KINGSLEY TRUST ASSOCIATION
PUBLICATION FUND
ESTABLISHED BY
THE SCROLL AND KEY SOCIETY
OF YALE COLLEGE

Hawthorne
Critic of Society

BY

LAWRENCE SARGENT HALL

GLOUCESTER, MASS.

PETER SMITH

1966

TO M. H.

"... SHE TAUGHTE OF FYN LOVYNGE,
AND NAMELY OF WIFHOD THE LYVYNGE."

PREFACE

IT WOULD of course be impossible to think of Whitman and his work apart from the social and political circumstances of the America in which he lived. It would be nearly as difficult to separate Mark Twain, Emerson, or even the perverse Thoreau from the social scene of nineteenth-century America. Yet it has always been easy to regard Hawthorne as anything but the product and spokesman of democratic society. The few sympathetic critics who have understood the fallacy here seem hardly to have been heard. Herman Melville insisted, in his remarkable essay on "Hawthorne and His Mosses," that "great geniuses are parts of the times, they themselves are the times, and possess a corresponding colouring." Melville thought that Hawthorne stood almost alone as a truly American writer "bound to carry republican progressiveness into Literature as well as into Life."

Since this book is intended to deal only with those aspects of Hawthorne's life and work which bear directly on his social thought, an initial glance at the biographical background of this thought is perhaps desirable. Hawthorne's career will be found to fall more or less naturally into several well defined periods. Each of these periods is unique because each represents a concentration of experience around a singular circumstance or attitude of mind.

Hawthorne was graduated from Bowdoin in 1825. As a student he had been pleased to consider himself one of a group of radical thinkers who had little use for the conscientious scholarship and conservatism of Longfellow. But his "radicalism," at graduation, was not let loose on the world. It was cast aside, or tucked away, for nearly a decade. The unaccountable years which he spent in the solitude and shadows of his room in Salem comprise the most romantic and perhaps the most incalculable period of his life. The whole effect of this abnormal retirement on his character would be hard to estimate. Without doubt many qualities of the man and his writing are traceable to the sombre whim which caused him to maintain himself in solitary aloofness during what is normally the most exuberant time of youth. Here, however, the importance of this phase of his career is that it had a profound negative influence upon his subsequent social consciousness. It taught him the viciousness of isolation.

Hawthorne was driven from his voluntary confinement by loneliness and by lack of economic and literary accomplishment. Then, from 1836 to 1839 he tried unsuccessfully to earn a living and some professional standing by writing for magazines and gift books, and by editing the bankrupt *American Magazine of Useful and Entertaining Knowledge*. The latter was abominable hackwork and fortunately of brief duration. By 1839 he had entered on his irregular but significant course in political office-holding. But as weigher and measurer in the Boston Custom House he found the business of supporting himself degrading. His distasteful chores left him little energy or impulse to write. In Boston he became acquainted with theorists and theories advocating social and economic reformation. America, like Europe, was seething with them at the turn of the decade. And by the spring of 1841 he had begun another phase of his career—the shortest-lived but possibly the farthest-reaching of all.

The Brook Farm experiment attracted Hawthorne for two reasons. He had been unable to gain a livelihood by writing, and he was unwilling to gain it without writing. He gambled one thousand dollars on the chance that the socialistic community at West Roxbury would enable him to resolve a paradox which the unenlightened competitive economy of the outer world would not. Disappointed in his hope, he withdrew from the community the following fall, having lived critically in the very house of social reform meanwhile.

The period of residence in the Old Manse at Concord, from 1842 to 1846, is an idyll in many respects, though not an interlude. In it Hawthorne had time to become acquainted with Emerson and Thoreau (who had not resided at Brook Farm), to start raising a family, to read that organ of transcendentalism *The Dial,* to publish several pieces in the *Democratic Review,* to write the tales and sketches which struck Melville so forcibly in the *Mosses.* His literary reputation waxed, and though his productivity had not then reached its peak, it revealed him utilizing his extensive leisure in observation and reflection (usually satirical) on the multiform aspects of American life. But the period was one of evasion, in a sense, because he made no effort to come to grips with the practical problems of existence. Having tried and rejected the Utopian schemes of his contemporaries, he put off the alternative of adapting himself to the inevitable conditions of his age until he was eventually driven by poverty and parenthood into everyday society once more.

The job which he chose was again a political appointment, the Surveyorship of the Port of Salem. This post—which he held comatosely enough except at the very end—proved to be an inauspicious but invigorating expedient. It was inauspicious because he was prematurely rejected, charged unfairly with the very political partisanship which was the real motive for ousting him. It was invigorating because it awoke in him the uncompromising spirit of economic individualism which was so contrary to the major thesis of the Brook Farmers, yet so absolute elsewhere in his materialistic country.

The removal to Lenox at about the half-century, following the sordid affair at Salem, was not a retreat but an interval of intense creative energy. By 1851 Hawthorne had written three of his four great romances in about the same number of years. *The Scarlet Letter, The Blithedale Romance,* and *The House of the Seven Gables* represent an artistic drive which he never again achieved, except during the few months in Rome when he was writing *The Marble Faun.* They were conceived and written under a maturing evaluation of the democratic world which up to that point he had tried alternately to evade and to exploit.

Indicative of the new and materialistic individualism with which Hawthorne confronted society is the fact that, the moment the opportunity presented itself, undaunted by previous disillusionment and on his own initiative he set out to obtain another political preferment. This time, as Consul at Liverpool, he got one of the juiciest plums in the foreign service, and he dedicated the four years of his incumbency under the Pierce administration to squeezing it for all it would yield.

The lucrative business of the consulate and the perspective gained by observing America from a foreign land made Hawthorne more sympathetic toward New World dynamics than he had formerly been. The comparison of a growing democratic country with one still clinging to a few remnants of feudalism ultimately convinced him of the ascendancy of American modes. This comparison broadened his point of view and ripened his criticism. But by the time he had returned home the integrity of American democracy, which was the premise on which his social philosophy had to rest, was disrupted by civil war. His sense of values bogged down in the midst of the dilemmas and confusion which were everywhere.

Although Hawthorne was quite aware of the moral issue which slavery involved, his awareness, like that of many of his countrymen, was somewhat overwhelmed by his concern with the international aspect of the predicament—the fact that America's inward turmoil (far more than slavery itself) was discrediting democracy as a system and way of life in the eyes of the world at large. This, he rightly felt, might prove damaging and possibly even fatal to the fortunes of democratic institutions. He died perturbed by a social and political anomaly which has not been regulated yet.

Hawthorne's death was timely in the sense that it coincided with the passing of the confident, ambitious, proselytizing republicanism which was the product of his lifetime. His social consciousness had

developed with American society from the agrarian democracy of
Andrew Jackson and the Brook Farmers to the philosophy of progress
which was instinctive in the equalitarianism of Lincoln, as it had been
implicit in his career. The rise of realism which followed the war had
much in its method and slant that Hawthorne might have found
agreeable. But it represented a different stage in American life altogether, and its dearth of ethical intelligence and social vision would
only have added to his exasperation.

Hawthorne belonged to an excitable, irrepressible, altruistic generation which took for granted the validity and importance of democracy as a social faith, and the mission of the United States as the
champion of that faith. And he went in for social thinking more
thoroughly than many of his contemporaries. He joined Brook Farm,
for one thing, while Emerson preferred to stay a householder in Concord and Thoreau retired to the woods. Hawthorne's social consciousness has been less obvious to critics than that of his fellow writers because it was less blatant. And a surreptitious habit of thought and
expression has caused him to be improperly set forth for years as a
romancer in art, and in life a reticent spook.

It has been truly said that Hawthorne wrote tragedy of a genuinely classical type. And the creation of tragedy, as Matthiessen has
pointed out, requires that a writer have insight into the social order
and the moral forces at work there. For the tragic theme consists of
the maladjustment of the individual to the behavior patterns regulating his relations with fellow individuals. These considerations alone
should make evident the fact that a social sense is—and had to be—
a fundamental ingredient of Hawthorne's art. Actually, the portrayal
of life in the tales and romances is as democratic as anything which
nineteenth-century America produced.

ACKNOWLEDGMENTS

To the following I wish to express my appreciation for permission to quote from unpublished material in their personal collections: H. W. L. Dana for the Hawthorne-Longfellow correspondence in the Craigie House, Cambridge, Massachusetts; Richard C. Manning of Kenyon College for letters in the Manning Collection of the Essex Institute in Salem, Massachusetts; the Marquis of Crewe, K. G., for Hawthorne's letter to Richard Monckton Milnes in his personal collection; and Miss Marian Bridge Maurice for letters by Hawthorne to Bridge and Pike. Similarly I wish to make acknowledgment to the Henry Huntington Library, San Marino, California, for sundry letters of Hawthorne and fragments of the unfinished romance; also the Massachusetts Historical Society for other fragments of this incomplete romance in the Washburn Papers; the New York Public Library for letters of Hawthorne in the Berg Collection; the Widener Library at Harvard for letters by Hawthorne to Charles Sumner and Emerson; the National Archives for Hawthorne's Consular Dispatches in the Records of the Department of State; the Pierpont Morgan Library for letters of Hawthorne; the New Hampshire Historical Society for Hawthorne-Pierce correspondence; the Library of Congress for letters in the Pierce Papers and Marcy Papers; and Stanley T. Williams of Yale University, Randall Stewart of Brown University, Norman Holmes Pearson of Yale University, and Manning Hawthorne of the University of Maine for Hawthorne's Official Correspondence from Liverpool and for access to the files of the Hawthorne Correspondence Project.

For permission to make quotations from copyrighted material I am indebted to the following publishing houses: Harcourt, Brace and Company for T. S. Eliot's essays; Houghton Mifflin Company for *The Correspondence of Thomas Carlyle and Ralph Waldo Emerson,* for Edward Stanwood's *A History of the Presidency,* and for the works of Emerson, Cooper, Burns, and Hawthorne; Yale University Press for Hawthorne's *American Notebooks,* edited by Randall Stewart, and the *Correspondence of James Fenimore-Cooper,* edited by J. F. Cooper; G. P. Putnam's Sons for *The Social Contract,* edited by Edward L. Walter and translated by R. W. Harrington, and for Whitman's *Complete Prose Works;* Charles Scribner's Sons for the works of Carlyle; the Oxford University Press for F. O. Matthiessen, *American Renaissance;* and the Modern Language Association of America for Hawthorne's *English Notebooks,* edited by Randall Stewart.

Certain passages from Chapter VIII appeared in the New England issue of *The Saturday Review of Literature* on 22 May 1943, under the title "Hawthorne: Critic of Society—The Making of an American Philosophy."

I should like to express my grateful thanks for the generosity and kindness of many friends: the staffs of the libraries at Yale University, Harvard University, the Massachusetts Historical Society, the New York Public Library and the Library of Congress; Edward H. Davidson of Ohio University for the use of his dissertation on *The Last Phase of Nathaniel Hawthorne* (Yale, 1940); Norman Holmes Pearson of Yale University for valuable editorial advice and for placing his knowledge of Hawthorne and his edition of the French and Italian journals at my disposal; Randall Stewart of Brown University for generously allowing me to use his manuscript of the indispensable English Notebooks before the printed edition was available; Edward P. Lilly of Catholic University for keeping me in line historically; J. H. Hagstrum of Northwestern University for his interpretation of the theological aspects of Hawthorne's social ethic; Anna Chapman Kirby for her assistance in assembling material in the National Archives; and my colleagues J. B. Heidler and J. Homer Caskey of Ohio University for encouraging and facilitating my work. Above all I owe a renewal of gratitude to Stanley T. Williams, whose advice and consideration have been of inestimable advantage to me. Grateful as I am for this help, I nevertheless assume entire responsibility for whatever may be the limitations that the work contains. Finally, I wish to express my obligation and appreciation to the English Department of Yale University, to the Yale University Press, and Benjamin C. Nangle, editor of the Yale Studies in English, for making possible the publication of this study, which in its original form was a dissertation submitted to the Graduate School of Yale University in partial fulfilment of the requirements for the doctoral degree.

L. S. HALL
Lieutenant (j.g.) U.S.N.R.

United States Naval Academy,
15 April 1943.

NOTE ON DOCUMENTATION

References to Hawthorne's works unless otherwise stipulated are to the Standard Library Edition of *The Works of Nathaniel Hawthorne, with Introductory Notes by George Parsons Lathrop,* Boston and New York, 1891, in 13 volumes. For convenience I have made use of readily recognizable abbreviations of the titles of the volumes: e. g., *Tales, Sketches, and Other Papers* is cited in the notes as *Sketches, The House of the Seven Gables* as *Seven Gables.* In cases where the title of an individual work is not included in the title appearing on the volume in which the work is to be found, the name of the work is given, followed by the number of the volume. Abbreviations are also used for primary biographical sources. Julian Hawthorne's biography *Nathaniel Hawthorne and His Wife* is regularly cited as *Hawthorne and His Wife;* Horatio Bridge's *Personal Recollections of Nathaniel Hawthorne* as *Personal Recollections;* and *The Letters of Hawthorne to William D. Ticknor* and *The Love Letters of Nathaniel Hawthorne* as *Ticknor Letters* and *Love Letters* respectively. Care should be taken to distinguish between *Passages from the American Note-Books,* which is Volume IX of the Standard Library Edition, and *The American Notebooks by Nathaniel Hawthorne, Based upon the Original Manuscripts in the Pierpont Morgan Library,* edited by Randall Stewart. A similar distinction exists in regard to the English Journals. In either instance the Standard Library Edition is differentiated from Professor Stewart's by the word *Passages.*

CONTENTS

I

The Critical Temper

The work of Hawthorne is truly a criticism—true because a fidelity of the artist and not a mere conviction of the man—of the Puritan morality, of the Transcendentalist morality, and of the world which Hawthorne knew.
T. S. ELIOT.

NATHANIEL HAWTHORNE is a conspicuous example of a writer whose work and whose career, at least in the first half of both, were determined by a social maladjustment. In the latter part they were determined by the partial disappearance of that maladjustment.

To pass through the main gallery of portraits in Hawthorne's fiction is to review a preponderant number of men and women who in one way or another seldom seem to be at ease in life. The weary little knot of travellers on their way to Canterbury village, the regenerate Donatello, frail figures like Peter Goldthwaite, old Esther Dudley, the Artist of the Beautiful, the tortured Dimmesdale, the saddened Hester, the thwarted Zenobia, the cynical Holgrave and Coverdale are a few of the throng of human beings who tragically or pathetically or criminally are out of step with the world in which they live.

Outside this throng Hawthorne envisioned a few who find the pattern of their own existence in harmony with the arrangement of society and the variegated nature of the people and institutions that comprise it. If any, they must be the Priscillas, the Hildas, the Phoebes, the Sophias, whose delicate sensibilities are miraculously instinct with good and impervious to evil. It is their angelic function to dispel from the lives of others the dark humors of imagination or the exasperations of fact.

Maladjustment inevitably begins as soon as a discrepancy appears between what society is and what the individual would like it to be. This discrepancy between the ideal and the actual is, of course, the cause of progress. But when the discrepancy grows to the point of grotesqueness, one finds maladjusted persons like Hollingsworth, the rabid reformer, or Septimius Felton, who sought the clue to immortality. Their fanaticism rendered them sterile.

On the other hand, when there is no difference at all between what the world is and what a man would like to have it, one mingles with people like the practical Silas Foster, or Peter Hovenden and Robert

Danforth, whose heavy-handedness is a torment to the Artist of the Beautiful. These men are equally unproductive in the realm of spirit, and quite as monstrous in their grossness as the others were in their fanaticism. It is hard to tell which is the greater anomaly—Aylmer, whose insane desire for perfection symbolizes the excess spirituality of men, or Aminadab, in his "indescribable earthiness."[1]

The maladjustment from which Hawthorne himself suffered was neither so enormous at the one extreme nor so negligible at the other. It was a productive maladjustment. That is to say, it contained enough idealism to render him acutely critical of society, but not so much as to make him reject it. For at the base of Hawthorne's social criticism lay a principle which held that the proper course of human progress, somewhat like that of his favorite pilgrim, lay between the sloughs of skepticism on one hand and the shortcuts of wishful thinking on the other. This poised criticism of society was what made possible Hawthorne's writing of real tragedy, for it enabled him to portray that hard necessity which men feel to reconcile what is and what is desired. And the effort of this reconciliation is the crucial phase of tragic action.

After his graduation from Bowdoin Hawthorne's emergence into the America of his contemporaries was delayed by the ten years of solitude spent in an attic room of the house on Herbert Street in Salem. Consequently, the last two decades of his life, those years lying between 1842 and 1862, are the ones that are richest in his criticism of society. Next to his threats of joining the community of Shakers at Canterbury in the early thirties,[2] his first overt judgment of society was implied by his participation in the communal reform at Brook Farm, whither he was propelled by a maladjustment which he shared at that time with thousands of his fellow Americans.

There ensued after the panic of 1837 a depression of six years. During this period thoughtful citizens in the United States became harassed by a sense of insecurity and concerned over the newly apparent wastefulness of a competitive national economy. They began to speculate upon the advantages of a planned economy where the intense application of the outer world to the mere means of subsistence could be replaced by a system less racking to the nerves and less stultifying to the spirit. As one contemporary critic descriptively overstated it: "The writings of Thomas Carlyle, and the addresses of Ralph Waldo Emerson, had completely unsettled the public mind,

1. *Mosses*, p. 55.

2. See his letter to Louisa, 4 November 1831, in the Manning Collection in the Essex Institute at Salem, Massachusetts. In sharp contrast to his early attitude is the tirade he directed in 1851 against "these foolish Shakers" (*American Notebooks*, p. 230).

and there had arisen a Young America, ready to be moulded into the first form that seemed to promise a new order of society."[3]

To the quick eye of Hawthorne himself the people who came to Brook Farm were there because, in the battle of craft and strength in the industrial world, they had found none less shrewd than themselves from whom to wrest a living.[4] In society at large they were misfits, either incapable of the cruelty and selfishness of competition, or unwilling to castigate their souls utterly by sordid maneuvering for worldly goods. They were, according to George Ripley, who founded Brook Farm, hastened into an unperfected social experiment through distaste for the prevailing "worship of Mammon."[5] For the most part they were individuals who, to quote Hawthorne, "had gone through such an experience as to disgust them with ordinary pursuits," though they had not yet lost faith in "the better time to come."[6] And thus they had set out to construct a method of living which would free them of the crassness of materialism and afford them the leisure and environment for courting spirituality through the writings of Carlyle or Emerson.[7] If they were not all transcendentalists of a sort, they perhaps resembled Hawthorne in nourishing at least some vague antagonism to society at large. "We had individually found one thing or another to quarrel with in our past life," Hawthorne wrote, "and were pretty well agreed as to the inexpediency of lumbering along with the old system any further."[8] Dissatisfied with the old living which they had been able to procure, they simply desired to contrive a new one that would prove more agreeable.

What was extravagantly conceded in the thirties to be the minimum which an American should secure as a living was, in fact, considerably above what was actually necessary for existence. Every man had set his cap for the aristocracy's way of life; it seemed the one due him as an equalitarian. Hawthorne, Jacksonian Democrat that he was, proved to be no exception to the rule here. Even while he was at Bowdoin this strange democratic snobbery appears in his character. He wrote in a letter to his uncle: "My Chum is the Son of the Hon. Mr. Mason of Portsmouth. He has money enough, which is per-

3. Moncure D. Conway, "Concerning Hawthorne and Brook Farm," *Every Saturday*, VII (2 January 1869), 14.

4. *Blithedale*, p. 342.

5. George Ripley, "The Commencement of Association," *The Harbinger*, I (16 August 1845), 159.

6. *Blithedale*, pp. 389–90.

7. There are echoes of Carlyle from several residents of Brook Farm. Hawthorne read *Heroes and Hero Worship* during his stay at the community. (See *Passages from the American Note-Books*, p. 233, and *Blithedale*, p. 379.) Georgianna Bruce Kirby wrote of a friend at the Farm: "Now she was deep in 'Sartor Resartus,' claiming his sympathy with this last gospel . . ." (*Overland Monthly*, v [July, 1870], 14).

8. *Blithedale*, p. 391.

haps unfortunate for me, as it is absolutely necessary that I should make as good an appearance as he does."[9] This impulse to realize as a democrat the refinements and grace of the aristocracy—so difficult to indulge if one must waste energy in the struggle for mere sustenance—is the key to Hawthorne's early maladjustment.

"I saw mankind, in this weary old age of the world," Hawthorne wrote in a tale published when he was only twenty-nine, "either enduring a sluggish existence amid the smoke and dust of cities, or, if they breathed a purer air, still lying down at night with no hope but to wear out to-morrow, and all the to-morrows which make up life, among the same dull scenes and in the same wretched toil that had darkened the sunshine of to-day."[1] Before he had entered Brook Farm he had suffered under the miserable burdens of his job in the Boston Custom House. In a letter to his friend O'Sullivan he avowed his intention, if God would grant him endurance, of remaining in his position as Measurer until he had drawn two thousand dollars in salary. At the end of that time he meant to throw himself upon fortune. "There is a most galling weight upon me—an intolerable sense of being hampered and degraded," he complained. He had had little time or energy for writing, and no opportunity for purging the grime from his spirit as he felt the constant impulse to do.[2] His work was neither inspiring nor very lucrative, and for a man who needed inspiration and who wanted to be married there could hardly have been a greater tribulation. So it was that he became affiliated by late November, 1840, after the onerous Custom House position had been resigned, with "Mr. Ripley's Utopia"[3]—a scheme which Emerson not incorrectly but rather too harshly stigmatized in the name of "arithmetic and comfort." It was, he observed with true Yankee shrewdness, "a rage in our poverty and politics to live rich and gentlemanlike."[4]

To live like a gentleman farmer, cultivating the mind as well as the soil, was indubitably one of Hawthorne's ideas in joining the people of Brook Farm. With the thousand dollars he had saved out of his emoluments as Measurer he purchased two shares of stock in the enterprise.[5] He entered the community on 12 April, 1841, in the hope

9. This letter, dated 9 October 1821, is in the Manning Collection in the Essex Institute at Salem, Massachusetts.

1. *Twice-Told Tales*, p. 408.

2. See *Passages from the American Note-Books*, p. 216.

3. *Love Letters*, I, 229. This letter is dated 27 November 1840.

4. E. W. Emerson and Waldo Emerson Forbes, eds. *The Journals of Ralph Waldo Emerson* (Boston, 1909–14), V, 473.

5. He purchased shares 18 and 19. (See Lindsay Swift, *Brook Farm* [New York, 1900], p. 18; also the original records of Brook Farm in the library of the Massachusetts Historical Society.) Robert F. Metzdorf errs in saying that Hawthorne invested an additional sum in excess of $500. ("Hawthorne's Suit Against Ripley and Dana," *Ameri-*

of finding there a home for himself and his future bride, and he resigned from the association the following October in the bitter suspicion that he and Sophia would never be able to "lean upon the
community" for their future livelihood and happiness.[6]

But if Brook Farm fell short of Hawthorne's practical demands, it
proved even more delinquent in respect to his ideal ones. The young
man who confessed to his beloved that he had demonstrated no talent
whatever which might avail to gather gold[7] had exchanged the
world where gold was mandatory for one which had to do with a no
less brutifying commodity. What he failed to realize at first was that
the gold mine of Mammon and the "gold mine" of Mr. Ripley[8]—as
the manure pile at Brook Farm was affectionately called—differed
from each other only superficially. The pastoral encomiums of manure
which he sent to Sophia are extraordinary proof of how deluded he
was at the start. "It defiles the hands, indeed, but not the soul," he
assured her. "This gold ore is a pure and wholesome substance; else
our Mother Nature would not devour it so readily."[9]

But these rhapsodic outbursts were quickly curtailed. For a time
Hawthorne cajoled himself into thinking that because he was engaged in "a righteous and heaven-blessed way of life" he had deeper
reserves of patience than he had formerly possessed in the Custom
House.[1] But for this misapprehension he was finally chastened. "That
abominable gold mine!" he expostulated at last in a letter to Sophia.
"Thank God, we anticipate getting rid of its treasures . . . It is my
opinion . . . that a man's soul may be buried and perish under a
dung-heap or in a furrow of the field, just as well as under a pile of
money."[2] The master allegorist had discovered in the inexhaustible
manure pile at Brook Farm a symbol of the fact that the everyday
world is not so easily put aside as he had once imagined. He wrote

can Literature, xii [May, 1940], 239–40). Examination of his letters between the years
1842 and 1846 shows an impecuniousness in the face of which it would have been
impossible for him to have made such an investment. It is altogether more probable
that the $524.05 he later tried to recover by law represented one of his two original
shares which he had probably been persuaded to leave at interest when he withdrew
his membership in the association.

6. *Love Letters*, ii, 32.   7. *Ibid.*

8. The designation "gold mine" by which the manure heap at Brook Farm became
known originated in all probability not with Hawthorne, as has nearly always been
supposed (see for example Clarence Gohdes, "Getting Ready for Brook Farm," *Modern Language Notes*, xlix [January, 1934], 38), but with George Ripley. See George
P. Bradford, "Reminiscences of Brook Farm," *The Century Magazine*, xlv, n.s. xxiii
(1892), 142. Bradford, along with Hawthorne, served his apprenticeship in the barn-
yard and should have known. (See Ora Gannet Sedgwick, "A Girl of Sixteen at Brook
Farm," *Atlantic Monthly*, lxxxv [March, 1900], 396.) Ripley's extensive economic
calculations were based almost entirely upon the supply of manure, so that he had
more motive than anyone else for deriving the euphemism. (See his *Commonplace
Book*, pp. 66 ff., in the Widener Library at Harvard.)

9. *Love Letters*, ii, 17.   1. *Ibid.*, p. 19.   2. *Ibid.*, p. 20.

again to Sophia, jubilant at the prospect of his release: "Even my Custom-House experience was not such a thraldom and weariness; my mind and heart were freer. Oh, belovedest, labor is the curse of the world, and nobody can meddle with it, without becoming proportionably brutified. . . . Thank God, my soul is not utterly buried under a dung-heap."[3]

Under the existing state of society Hawthorne had found that men must sacrifice spiritual values to making a living, or in striving for those values they must neglect the business of making a living, and starve. It was the belief of the Brook Farmers that through coöperative brotherhood men could nourish the spirit at the same time that they kept themselves materially comfortable.[4] To do both was theoretically the purpose of a democratic state. Because he was "national," as an early reviewer put it, "national in subject, in treatment and in manner,"[5] Hawthorne shared this belief.

The dissatisfaction with society, which rose whenever there was a discrepancy between such a belief and reality, was what sent Hawthorne to Brook Farm. From then on it kept him constantly making appraisals. In this way he was more responsive to the social currents of his day than was Emerson, who preferred to invent his own fetishes rather than examine others, or than Thoreau, who in many ways rejected the trend of the age, or sought to escape it by living in a strictly private Utopia. Instead of adding his own fanaticism or fad to the others, Hawthorne merely allowed himself to scrutinize the thousands already in existence. For this reason he represents his age more faithfully than many of his contemporaries. In his role of critic he was panoramic. He wore no blinders like a prophet, apostle, or hermit, devoting himself to one great creed alone. He reacted to many and confined himself to none.

Even in seclusion Hawthorne was receptive to the various impulses from the world about him. Yet the old myth of the recluse still enshrouds him now and then in spite of our enlightened scholarship. "A ghost-story about an old castle," one writer remarks of his years in England, "a tree with a hollow trunk, a spider in the British Museum were of more importance to his mind than the foreign policies of the American or English governments." This is patently false.[6] For it was particularly during the years he spent in England, under the influence of his long delayed material success and a perspective of three thousand miles, that the maladjustment which had characterized

3. *Ibid.*, p. 25.

4. See Orestes A. Brownson, "Brook Farm," *Democratic Review*, XI (November, 1842), 489.

5. Charles Wilkins Webber, "Hawthorne," *The American Review, A Whig Journal*, IV (September, 1846), 304.

6. See below, chapter V.

him through poverty and the humiliating experience of his political office in Salem almost entirely fell away. Those phases of American democracy that had struck him as so inglorious in the satire of early tales like "The New Adam and Eve" and "The Celestial Railroad" suddenly took on the aspect of propriety, vigor, and progressiveness, in contrast to the outworn institutions of Europe. He himself commenced not only to repeat but to enjoy hearing "the national watchword, 'Go ahead!' "[7] which had often sounded so blatant to him back home. It is a little tragic that in the end this sound was destined to be drowned out by the rising crescendoes of "John Brown's Body" and "The Battle Hymn of the Republic," just at the moment when it was beginning to seem harmonious.

7. *Mosses*, p. 283.

II

Humanitarian Reform

A person to be in the possession of something as perfect as mortal man has a right to demand; he tries to make it better, and ruins it entirely.

American Notebooks.

TO comprehend fully the intricate reasoning on the basis of which Hawthorne rejected Brook Farm necessitates thorough consideration of his relation to the whole subject of reform. The result of such consideration will ultimately be to elucidate further his social criticism, through an analysis of it in its more active phase. For there is no better indication of a man's judgment of society than his estimate of the practical extent to which it requires and is susceptible of reformation.

Lloyd Morris includes the following generalization in his portrait of Hawthorne. "His was not the temperament of a reformer," he says flatly of his subject, "and he had no interest and but small sympathy with reform in any sphere."[1] This statement is typical of a misconception that has prevailed altogether too long. Probably it is based on a hurried retrospect of *The Blithedale Romance,* and a literal perusal of excerpts from Hawthorne's writings which treat caustically the subject of reformers and their work. But Hawthorne's numerous strictures are not enough to signify that he had no concern and only slight sympathy with the business of reform at bottom. They simply mean that he was usually dissatisfied with its aims and its methods, as these were revealed in the manifold enthusiasms of the early nineteenth century.

The very frequency of Hawthorne's references to reform is sufficient to refute the argument that he was indifferent to it, suspicious and skeptical though he may have been. And for the rest, there exists throughout his work and in hitherto unpublished letters which he wrote to men like Secretary of State William L. Marcy, Senator Charles Sumner, and Richard Monckton Milnes, M. P., documentary evidence not only of his sympathy with reform but also of a temperament which, though hardly that of a fanatic, was indisputably a heritage from the deep reformative instinct of puritan New England.

Hawthorne's relation to the reform impulses of his time is closer than that of almost any other major American writer of the mid-

1. Lloyd Morris, *The Rebellious Puritan* (New York, 1927), p. 121.

century. One of his sisters-in-law, Elizabeth Peabody, was ostentatiously involved during her lifetime in various schemes for educational reform, abolition, and homeopathy.[2] Another sister-in-law married Horace Mann, who among his many more illustrious activities made a fetish of phrenology and a pet aversion of tobacco. Many of these reformers—men and women in whose natures the puritanical strain still predominated—were people who wished merely to purify the living conditions of their country, not to replace them. In this respect they differed, if only in the matter of degree, from the more freakish who, dissatisfied with the very superstructure of contemporary society, sought to build life over from the cellar-hole up, in accordance with their own particular aspirations or caprice. Hawthorne cannot be aligned with the extreme position of those who would have remodelled the whole social architecture; yet it must be recognized that he was at one time both personally and financially committed to one of the most famous of their experiments in rehabilitation.

The commitments Hawthorne made, whether they tend toward or away from reform, are essential to an understanding of the man in his relation to the society of his day. For one thing they serve to establish his position with regard to the wave of humanitarianism which swept America during his lifetime. But of far broader significance than this is the fact that they also trace the history of his efforts to come to some sort of terms with the world about him. They specify what he considered to be the responsibility of government and community in a democratic society, and the obligations they might be expected properly and effectually to discharge toward the individual. Above all they indicate what he thought to be the degree both of men's collective perfectibility and of their power to assist toward its realization themselves.

The nineteenth century was an era of reform if of nothing else. The humanitarians in this century worked hard at their rôle. "We are all a little wild here with numberless projects of social reform," Emerson wrote to Thomas Carlyle. "Not a reading man but has a draft of a new Community in his waistcoat pocket. . . . One man renounces the use of animal food; and another of coin; and another of domestic hired service; and another of the State; and on the whole we have a commendable share of reason and hope."[3]

Literature was as quick to capitalize upon these movements as

2. Hawthorne ridiculed homeopathy. See *The Blithedale Romance*, p. 366, and *The Letters of Hawthorne to William D. Ticknor* (Newark: printed by The Cartaret Club, 1910), II, 78.

3. Emerson to Carlyle, 30 October 1840, *The Correspondence of Thomas Carlyle and Ralph Waldo Emerson 1834–1872* (Boston, 1888), I, 334–35.

the movements themselves were to grow fat upon the nation's vices. About the question of temperance particularly there arose a whole cult of sentimental literature like Lewis Sargent's *Temperance Tales,* or Mrs. Sigourney's poems upholding the sanctity of the American Home with a style that was corseted to propriety. Most outstanding, of course, was Timothy Shay Arthur's immortal *Ten Nights in a Bar-Room.*

As early as 1835 the subject of reformers and their work appears in Hawthorne's journals as matter for fiction. An unusually austere humor is evident in the first plot of a sketch in which a reformer, on the point of making many converts to his extreme doctrines, is discovered to be a fugitive from a madhouse.[4] In time Hawthorne's satire became more frequent and obvious, although its acerbity gave place to something more airy and fanciful. One of the "improbables" of "A Select Party," for example, was "a Reformer untrammelled by his theory."[5] The voyager of "The Celestial Railroad" observes with bemused tolerance an ingenious scheme at Vanity Fair whereby a man had only to throw his "quota of virtue" into the common stock of a society and the directors, it was presumed, invested the aggregate to the subsequent profit of every shareholder.[6] Brook Farm lay close to Hawthorne's heart, so that when he touched it at all he did so, as in this instance, with a gently derisive pen. His harshest stricture occurs in an unidentified fragment of a letter which was probably written about 1843, or shortly after, when he boasted to Emerson that he had belonged to the community during its "heroic age."[7] "Brook Farm," he wrote, ". . . is soon to see worse times that it ever has yet—at least, so men of business appear to think. Let it sink, say I;—it has long since ceased to have any sympathy from me, though individually I wish well to all concerned."[8]

Throughout *The Blithedale Romance* there runs the deep vein of sarcasm which, in its most humorless moments, closely resembles the grimmest satire of Swift, for whose writing Hawthorne had a

4. *Passages from the American Note-Books,* pp. 20–21.
5. *Mosses,* p. 78.   6. *Ibid.,* p. 226.
7. *The Journals of Ralph Waldo Emerson,* vi, 441–42.
8. This fragment is in the Yale Collection of American Literature. The date and addressee are unknown. By 1843 and 1844 it was generally believed that Brook Farm was insolvent, and that whatever ruse its directors might resort to would only postpone its eventual doom. Thus on 31 October 1844, Charles A. Dana, in his financial report, asserted that the community would go on paying only the interest of five per cent per annum indefinitely. (See John T. Codman, *Brook Farm . . .* [Boston, 1894], pp. 118–19.) Partly to stave off desolation the community was incorporated as a Phalanx, 1 May 1845. Hawthorne's antagonism at this time may therefore have been caused by the fact that he still had money, which he could not afford to lose, invested in the community (see above, p. 4, n. 5), and by the fact that the Fourierites were taking over, applying the prescriptions of a theorist for whom he had no use (see *Hawthorne and His Wife,* i, 269).

natural taste. But this sarcasm is directed not toward the community
—which receives its hardest blows in the mild joking of the first chap-
ters—but toward philanthropists, and toward Hollingsworth in particular.[9] Hawthorne seldom found philanthropists attractive to contemplate. However genial by nature, they grew less personable in
the exact ratio in which they became reformative. At Brook Farm
he had had excellent facilities for studying such men. And in en-
countering individuals like Orestes Brownson he was struck above
all by their pig-headedness and want of manners. Brownson was not
"the prince of gentlemen in a debate," according to one of the Brook
Farmers who knew him. "He raised his voice and pounded a table,
if one was at hand, and when worsted, declared that his opponent
could not place him- or herself on his standpoint."[1] All this must
have been shrewdly observed by Hawthorne; for in "The Hall of
Fantasy" the guide proves his familiarity with mannerisms like
Brownson's by crying out: "Pray Heaven he do not stamp his foot
or raise his voice . . . !"[2]

A certain quality of nuisance eventually became apparent to Hawthorne in the activities and personalities of reformers. The prandial
habits of sects like the Grahamites, the teetotalism of temperance
societies, the anti-tobacconism of men like Horace Mann he called
"theoretical nonsense."[3] His own personal habits were entirely if not
spectacularly at variance with the practice of these Malvolios. He
was an inveterate smoker of cigars, and seldom or never made a practice of abstinence where liquor was concerned. In a letter to James
Russell Lowell, dated 26 May 1863, he candidly admitted drinking
and smoking too much at the dinners of the Saturday Club, and
filling the pipe too often in Lowell's study. All his life, in fact, he
remained a devotee of these aids to conviviality. He sat an entire day
observing character and enjoying the genial atmosphere in a bar-
room at North Adams in 1838.[4] Later he made personal use of the
bar at Parker's in Boston as a rendezvous at which to meet his
friends.[5] So that it is impossible to ascertain whether George Stillman Hillard was simply misinformed or indulging in wishful thinking when he wrote: "He cared nothing for wine or tobacco or strong
coffee or strong tea."[6] Certainly Hawthorne was poking fun when
he described the keeper of the temperance hotel at Hartford as "reading a Hebrew bible in the bar, by means of a Lexicon and an English

9. For example, see pp. 345, 384.
1. Georgianna Bruce Kirby, *Years of Experience: An Autobiographical Narrative*
(New York and London, 1887), p. 147.
2. *The Pioneer*, February, 1843, p. 53.
3. For a gibe at the vegetarians, see *Mosses*, p. 210.
4. See *American Notebooks*, p. 50.   5. *Ibid.*, pp. 248, 332 n., 617.
6. George Stillman Hillard, "The English Note-Books of Nathaniel Hawthorne," *The
Atlantic Monthly*, xxvi (September, 1870), 266.

version."[7] In "A Rill from the Town Pump" he wrote sardonically of water as "the grand reformer of the age," with the cow as its confederate,[8] at the same time challenging the decency of those who get "tipsy with zeal for temperance, and take up the honorable cause of the Town Pump in the style of a toper fighting for his brandy bottle."[9] For his own part, he frankly admitted his "affection" for the whisky-bottle,[1] and he confessed on the occasion of an English banquet at which the wines were of noteworthy excellence, "I was about half-seas over when I got up to speak . . ."[2]

His personal objection to temperance reform was that it abetted the prevailing cheerlessness of life. Emerson, lamenting the absence of geniality and picturesqueness in an inn he and Hawthorne passed on their walking trip to the village of Harvard, said: "The Temperance Society emptied the bar-room. It is a cold place. Hawthorne tried to smoke a cigar, but I observed he was soon out on the piazza."[3] It was in spite of legal restrictions that Hawthorne hoped, as he told Ticknor, to keep himself "pretty jolly."[4] And with his stock of Ticknor's claret that had already, he said, given him "a great deal of comfort"—not to mention other gifts of sauterne, champagne, and sherry, plus a supply of "first rate brandy" he himself had laid in against the Maine Liquor Law—he must have maintained a tolerable state of jollity.

In England Hawthorne found rather saturnine the position of Mr. Ireland, editor of the *Manchester Examiner*, who "talked earnestly in favor of the Maine Liquor law, while quaffing sherry, champagne, hock, port, and claret."[5] And he wrote to Ticknor, remarking, "Massachusetts must be a very uncomfortable place, just now, with your liquor laws and other nonsense."[6] In fact his comments upon temperance legislation were far less non-committal than they had been while he still lived in the United States.[7] The Scotch, he found, were improved by their liquor; it made them less dour, better-natured and more sociable.[8] "It is delightful to see how little progress tee-totalism has yet made in these parts . . . ," he observed enthusiastically. "It is like returning to times twenty years gone by, for a New Englander to witness such simplicity of manners."[10] In *The*

---

7. *American Notebooks*, p. 71.   8. *Twice-Told Tales*, p. 170.

9. *Ibid.*, p. 172. For additional satire upon temperance people, see pp. 212, 518, and *Mosses*, pp. 86, 186, 435–36.

1. *Ticknor Letters*, I, 20.   2. *Ibid.*, II, 14.

3. *Journals*, VI, 259–60.   4. *Ticknor Letters*, I, 4–5.

5. *English Notebooks*, p. 351.   6. *Ticknor Letters*, I, 98.

7. See his purely narrative account of the blacksmith at North Adams, who threatened to cock his rifle in the cause of repealing a license law that had become effective in Massachusetts on 1 July 1838. *American Notebooks*, p. 38. Cf. *ibid.*, pp. 38–71, *passim*.

8. *English Notebooks*, p. 339.   10. *Ibid.*, p. 345.

Blithedale Romance he had sympathetically defended men's use of liquor.

> But the true purpose of their drinking—and one that will induce men to drink, or do something equivalent, as long as this weary world shall endure—was the renewed youth and vigor, . . . with which, for about a quarter of an hour, the dram permeated their systems. And when such quarters of an hour can be obtained in some mode less baneful to the great sum of man's life, . . . we temperance people may ring out our bells for victory![1]

He could not find it in his heart to deprive the "sad revellers" of Liverpool's slums of their gin, though death were in the draught. For it was only by this means that they became elevated in spirit a little way above the "smothering squalor" of their lives, or caught befogged vistas of something spiritual beyond the suffering to which they were accustomed.[2]

Not long before his death Hawthorne is reported by Fields to have asked plaintively: "Why has the good old custom of coming together to get drunk gone out? Think of the delight of drinking in pleasant company and then lying down to sleep a deep strong sleep."[3] This inebriety and the consequent relaxation seem seriously to have constituted in his mind "simplicity of manners." At all events he remarked with not very oblique sarcasm: "The temperance-reformers unquestionably derive their commission from the Divine Beneficence, but have never been taken fully into its counsels. All may not be lost though those good men fail."[4]

Now, all these comments are fairly representative of Hawthorne's more open and lively attacks upon the philanthropists. But there is another aspect of the man which ought to be even more carefully considered. Regardless of what seems at times a preponderant disinclination toward reform, Hawthorne was himself a product of New England. If he rallied it for its foibles he still partook of its essence. And part of New England's essence was the puritanical instinct that engenders reformation wherever the puritan is found. George Lathrop remarked something akin to this instinct in Hawthorne when he spoke inaccurately and obsequiously of his "inexorable demand for perfection in all things."[5]

Hawthorne's critics and biographers are unfortunately disposed as a rule to overlook such reforming acts as his sermon to an intemperate and half-mad Doctor of Divinity,[6] or his reputed conversion to

---

1. *Blithedale*, pp. 521–22. 2. *Our Old Home*, p. 328.
3. M. A. DeWolfe Howe, *Memories of a Hostess* . . . (Boston, 1922), p. 63.
4. *Our Old Home*, p. 328.
5. See *Passages from the French and Italian Note-Books*, pp. 119–20.
6. *English Notebooks*, 24 May 1855. Cf. *Our Old Home*, pp. 44–45.

total abstinence of a dissipated sea captain,[7] or his paternalistic effort to restrict his friend Burchmore's dipsomaniacal habits to Sunday. To be sure he was a trifle self-conscious in each of these instances. And yet there is no mistaking the fact that he recognized and deplored the excesses of these men. His objection was not to intoxication but to debauchery. He hated to see a man mentally and physically ruined by wholly unrestrained application to the bottle. And if he would not inveigh against the use of liquor, he was ready enough publicly to condemn its abuse.

In the same way, while holding no brief for the fantastic schemes of Utopians to reconstruct the materialistic society of the world at large, he nevertheless clung doggedly to his dissatisfaction with that society. Though he abandoned Brook Farm, he did not in the next twenty years relinquish the humanitarian impulses or the hankerings for improvement and progress which had helped bring him there for a few disillusioning months.

In "The Christmas Banquet" Hawthorne wrote: "There was a modern philanthropist, who had become so deeply sensible of the calamities of thousands and millions of his fellow-creatures, and of the impracticableness of any general measures for their relief, that he had no heart to do what little good lay immediately within his power . . ."[8]

It was doubtless because he had no mind to see himself placed in a category with this modern philanthropist that Hawthorne engaged, during his consulship at Liverpool, in the most active reform of his career. He had discovered through his office the deplorable condition in the American merchant marine at the mid-century. But unlike his modern philanthropist he set out almost immediately to do what he could to correct a situation that during years of criminal negligence had grown steadily worse. "There is a most dreadful state of things aboard our ships," he soliloquized in his journals in 1855. "Hell itself can be no worse than some of them; and I do pray that some New Englander with the itch of reform in him, may turn his thought this way."[9] However, no such New Englander appeared. Hawthorne tried, and failed, to put Charles Sumner on the trail. He wrote a letter, as he later informed Ticknor, urging Sumner to bring the matter before Congress. "Had he busied himself about this, instead of Abolitionism," he told his publisher, "he would have done good service to his country and have escaped Brooks's cudgel. I offered to supply him with any amount of horrible facts; but he never noticed my letter."[1]

7. Hawthorne to Ticknor, 31 August 1855. *Ticknor Letters*, I, 105–06.
8. *Mosses*, p. 343.   9. *English Notebooks*, p. 267.
1. *Ticknor Letters*, II, 39. This letter is dated 31 January 1857.

Hawthorne first took the initiative in the spring of 1855. He entered in his journals for May 11 and 15 of that year the harrowing case of an American by the name of Daniel Smith, who had been kidnapped at Charleston and pressed into service aboard an American vessel bound for Liverpool. During the voyage Smith, a landlubber, was brutally beaten for his ineptitude as a sailor and then abandoned in a dying state upon the ship's arrival in port. Profoundly shocked that a free citizen of the United States should thus be literally abducted, "carried to a foreign country, treated with savage cruelty . . . and left to die on his arrival,"[2] Hawthorne reinforced his official certificate with the following address to Secretary of State Marcy:

Consulate of the United States
Liverpool 18th May 1855

Sir

I have the honor to transmit herewith my certificate, the affidavit of Joseph Bone a Police officer, the certificate of the surgeon of the Liverpool Hospital and a copy of a certificate of the Coroner of this Borough, all relating to a seaman named Daniel Smith being left destitute in this Port by the ship George A. Ropley of Charleston Captain Dan¹ Molony.

The circumstances are narrated in my certificate and shew the case to be one of great cruelty, and I submit whether it is not one in which an example ought to be made of the offender.

In transmitting these papers I take the liberty of again earnestly calling your attention to the mode of shipping seamen in our seaports, & to the evils arising from the payment of the months advance wages; under that system our citizens are stolen & expatriated from their country, & put on board vessels to do duties they know nothing of, to their great suffering and the endangering of Life and property. I on a former occasion suggested a commission to ascertain the merits or rather demerits of the system & the best mode of reform, & I still think that would be the best course to adopt.

With high respect
I have the honor to be
Your obed Servant
NATH^L HAWTHORNE [3]

This was the second communication which Hawthorne had sent the Secretary of State earnestly recommending reform and taking it upon himself to suggest the most efficacious means of bringing it about. But he was not content to let the matter rest here, after seeing how ineffectual had been his earlier advice. Five days later he wrote to Sumner a letter which sheds so much light upon his reformative impulses that it is given below intact.

2. *English Notebooks*, p. 112.

3. This and the following unpublished letters of Hawthorne to William Learned Marcy are taken from the Records of the Department of State, *Consular Despatches, Liverpool*, volumes 12 and 13, in the National Archives, Washington, D. C.

U. S. Consulate, Liverpool, May 23ᵈ 1855.

My dear Sumner,

For some time past I have been thinking of asking you to interest yourself in bringing the condition of our mercantile marine before Congress. Matters are really in a very terrible state between shipmasters and seamen; and having been thrust by Providence (and Pierce) into this consulate, I ought not to leave it without an attempt to do some little good. Every day, some miserable cruelty and carnage is brought under my notice. For instance, a month or two ago, I took the deposition of a free white citizen, a farmer of South Carolina, who had been absolutely kidnapped by a shipping-master at Charleston, and, without ever intending to go to sea, had been sent off to Liverpool as a seaman, and so abused by the captain and officers, during the voyage, that when I saw him he was half-dead. He has since died in the Hospital. In three instances, which came before me, sailors have been shot dead by their officers; and the most perplexing part of the matter is, that all this bloodshed and cruelty seems to be strangely justifiable, and almost inevitable under the circumstances. It certainly is not the fault, so much as it is the fate, of our shipmasters to do these abominable deeds. They are involved in a wrong system, which renders it impossible for them to do right; and they themselves become morally deteriorated by it, and continually grow worse and worse. As for the seamen, they are no better than pirates. The truth is, we have no seamen of our own, our ships being manned almost entirely by the offscourings of the British merchant service, and by Germans and other foreigners whom the shipping-masters entrap. I should like to know what is to become of us, at sea, in case of a war—but *that* you don't care about.

If you will let slavery alone, for a little while, and attend to this business (where much good may, and no harm can possibly, be done) I think you will be doing our country a vast service. The shipping-masters in the American ports seem to be at the bottom, or near the bottom, of the mischief. You would have to make inquiries into their system, on your side of the water; and I could help you to many atrocities which come to my knowledge through the statements of seamen. These shipping-masters should be annihilated at once;—no slave-drivers are so wicked as they, and there is nothing in slavery so bad as the system with which they are connected.

I see no way to secure a supply of good seamen, unless by establishing a system of apprenticeage, compelling each vessel to take a certain number of apprentices. England, however, has given up this plan, so that it probably has its defects. For my part, I only see what is bad, and do not pretend to any faculty of suggesting what may be better.

Do think seriously of the above.

Truly yours,

Nathᴸ Hawthorne.

P.S. I had a most agreeable little bit of a visit from your brother George, last Saturday and Sunday.

P.S. 2ᵈ You must not suppose that I wish to represent the American shipmasters as worse than the system of manning their ships inevitably makes them. As a body, they are men of admirable qualities, and far superior to the same class of Englishmen;—capable, many of them, of acting on high moral considerations, and sincerely desirous (were it only for their own sakes) of finding a remedy for the evils to which I allude. Still, they are human, and therefore apt to become devilish, under evil influences.

N. H.

P.S. 3ᵈ A law went into effect on the first of this month, regulating the British merchant-service. I have not seen it; but it may suggest some available ideas.[4]

Hawthorne now redoubled his own official efforts to bring those who practised these criminal tactics to justice in the hope that, as he had said to Marcy, an example might be made of the offenders.[5] On the last day of November he forwarded to the New York District Attorney depositions taken at an inquest on the body of a murdered sailor, in an attempt to cause the murderer to be remanded as soon as he arrived unwittingly in New York upon the return voyage.[6] The following month he sent similar depositions to the District Attorney of the Southern New York District, enclosing a letter on the subject which had been addressed to the American Ambassador, James Buchanan, and which Buchanan had forwarded to Liverpool.[7]

But little or no improvement resulted. Hawthorne was persistent enough, but he was handicapped by two things—an injudicious selection of champions and a hiatus in international judicature. Marcy was busy with affairs of state which were deemed to take precedence over the shipping question, and Sumner was exposing his skull to the cudgels of Southern senators in a cause which he continued to think more important than Hawthorne's, despite the latter's candor in telling him otherwise.

Meantime it was almost impossible to apprehend the perpetrators of the savagery aboard what Hawthorne called the "floating hell"[8] which was an American merchantman. English and American maritime law failed to provide adequate reciprocal jurisdiction covering crimes committed in mid-ocean. The seat of the trouble lay in the fact that American vessels were incompetently manned. Their crews were made up largely either of men not at all qualified to be sailors, or of able seamen whose incentive to work had been removed by the payment of wages in advance. The ships' officers who were under the necessity of getting work out of such reluctant and inefficient crews were driven to employ constant punishment which, in moments of

4. The original of this letter is in The Widener Library at Harvard.
5. Compare a letter by Hawthorne to the District Attorney, New York, 10 July 1857. *Official Correspondence.*
6. This letter is dated 30 November 1855. Compare, also, a letter to the same, 10 July 1857. *Ibid.*
7. *Ibid.* The letter bears the date 21 December 1855.
8. *English Notebooks,* p. 267.

carelessness or exasperation, easily became aggravated to brutality.

Matters had been growing progressively worse for more than a year when all at once the citizens of Liverpool took a hand in the business. On the last day of January, 1857, Hawthorne informed his publisher of more than the usual amount of trouble in his consulate. "The Liverpool philanthropists are aroused about the enormities on board of our ships," he related, "and would like to have me run a-muck with them against the American ship-masters."[9]

A special report of the managing committee to the Members of The Liverpool Society of Friends of Foreigners in Distress, adopted at a meeting held on the fourth of February, stated that out of 106 cases examined by the committee sixty-nine seamen were discovered to have been brought over against their will and eighty-two had been obliged upon their arrival to be taken to the hospital or to receive medical treatment. The report cited the deposition of a surgeon performing the autopsy upon a Dutchman, who had been the victim in one of these "ferocious assaults." His head, according to the examiner, "presented an enormously contused mass; the face was completely battered in, and there were from 70 to 80 contused wounds upon the feet, legs, thighs and the back."[1]

At a meeting six days earlier, on January thirtieth, the American shipmasters in their turn unanimously adopted a set of resolutions revealing their concerted wish for reform. They laid the blame for existing conditions at the door of the American shipping masters, and testified that both masters and seamen were the "dupes of *Land Sharks*." They particularly recommended that all shipping agents be government officers with a professional knowledge of nautical affairs. They argued for a treaty of reciprocity between England and the United States to provide for criminal action on the high seas and cases of desertion in foreign ports. They pointed out that the system of giving advance wages was a detriment to property, since the sailor, having received what was coming to him at the beginning of the voyage, made a minimum of exertion on behalf of property from which he expected to derive nothing further. They stated likewise: "We would urge our employers to form Shipowners' Societies, that they may examine into the existing abuses so that a system of marine laws shall be enacted that will efficiently protect their interest as well as the seamen who sail their ships."[2] And they requested the

9. *Ticknor Letters*, II, 38.
1. See the Special Report of the Managing Committee issued from 16, Sir Thomas's Buildings, Liverpool, to "The Liverpool Society of Friends of Foreigners in Distress Founded in 1851." The Report was signed by F. Prance, vice-president, and E. Pictet, honorary secretary. *Consular Despatches*, XIII, encl.
2. Resolutions drawn up by a committee of five appointed by the American Shipmasters, *Consular Despatches*, XIII, encl.

American Consul, Nathaniel Hawthorne, to forward their resolutions to the United States Government.

Now prepared to treat the matter in considerable detail, Hawthorne once more wrote to Marcy, forwarding these testimonials of the absence of effective jurisdiction. This time he again ventured to suggest a method of procuring a better state of affairs.

Consulate of the United States
Liverpool 13th February 1857

Sir,

I have the honor to forward herewith a special report of a society established in Liverpool for the relief of Foreigners in distress. The society is composed of the most influential, & intelligent Foreigners residing in Liverpool, & their opinions are entitled to great consideration

I also enclose a copy of Resolutions adopted at a meeting of American Shipmasters, lately held in Liverpool.

I have on several previous occasions, called your attention to the system of shipping seamen for our merchant service, and the evils resulting; & am constrained to do so again, by the enclosed papers having been forwarded to me—the first mentioned having been also published in the London Times, & the Local newspapers—& by the frequent occurrence of late, of cases of gross cruelty occurring on board our vessels, during the voyage from the United States. Scarcely a vessel arrives from New York, or any of the southern ports of the U S, the Crew of which does not almost entirely consist of persons totally ignorant of the duties for which they shipped— or rather were shipped—mere landsmen. And these persons are subjected to the most revolting treatment at the hands of the officers, and, in very many cases, at the hands of their init[i]ated shipmates They arrive here almost naked, & in a state of great debility, the result of exposure & illtreatment combined.

Latterly I have been almost daily called upon to investigate complaints made by such persons, of assaults committed upon them by the inferior officers or their shipmates, or of their being plundered of the little clothing they brought on board. A Despatch which accompanies this, will inform you of a recent case of a man (by trade a grocer, never before at sea but once as passenger to America) dying in the Liverpool Hospital, from the effect of ill usage from the 2nd & 3rd Mates & Boatswain of his vessel.[3] And unless this fatal result occurs, & in Liverpool, the perpetrators go unpunished, the authorities having no jurisdiction; & the Treaty giving me none,

---

3. This dispatch (*Consular Despatches*, xiii, 82) plainly illustrates how inadequate were the legal facilities for bringing offenders to justice.

Consulate of the United States
Liverpool February 14 1857

Sir,

On the 16th Ult^o a Coroners Jury found a verdict of Manslaughter against the 2nd and 3rd Mates and Boatswain of the American Ship Guy Mannering in the case of a man name unknown who died in the Liverpool Hospital from the ill usage received during the voyage from New York to Liverpool

On this verdict the 3rd Mate Henry D. Cutting and the Boatswain John Lewis were

unless I can make out a case of murder, assault with intent to commit murder, or Robbery.

It is not easy to remedy the evil of inefficient manning of our vessels, of which all the other evils are but branches—& when I speak of inefficient manning I include the entire for I am sorry to say the officers need improvement, almost as much as seamen, & are becoming rapidly worse; but if what I have before suggested were done—a competent commission of enquiry instituted—I am sure a remedy would be found. The abolition of the pernicious advance system, & of the Law requiring two thirds Americans; the adoption of a better mode of shipping seamen; & an apprentice system—seem to be obvious.

Something must be done, as our National character & commerce are suffering great damage. I have had it from good authority that the rates of Insurance by American vessels have been materially increased, because of the inefficient crews they are known to have.

To carry out an apprentice system, an International arrangement would be necessary to reclaim deserters; For this no Treaty would be needed, as the merchant shipping act,[4] which I had the honor to forward at the time of its passage, contains a provision similar to our own Reciprocity Act—that on satisfactory evidence being given of facilities being granted for the arrest of deserters from British ships in any foreign country, Her Majesty may issue proclamation for like facilities being granted in England in favor of that country.

committed to Gaol and are to be tried at the next Liverpool Assizes to be holden in March

The 2nd Mate escaped and cannot be found

The Magistrates have always been of opinion that they had no Jurisdiction in such cases and were confirmed in that view by the English Secretary of State in a letter in reply some time since addressed to the Mayor of Liverpool

The Coroner however contends that the death occurring in Liverpool gives jurisdiction and is supported in that view by the Judges.

The case particularly as against the Boatswain at present seems a very bad one in which the perpetrators should not escape punishment If the authorities here have no Jurisdiction they must certainly escape as I could not obtain their surrender to send them to the United States for trial the Treaty not including Manslaughter

In a despatch accompanying this I have ventured to make some suggestions on the subject of Jurisdiction in such cases

With high respect
I have the honour to be
Your Obedient Servant
NATH^L HAWTHORNE

4. Hawthorne later sent the following correction (*Consular Despatches*, XIII, 5).

Consulate of the United States
Liverpool 27th Februy 1857

Sir,

The present is to correct an error in my Despatch 83 dated 14 Febry. On the subject of reclaiming deserters, I refer to the "Merchant Shipping Act" it should be "The Foreign Deserters Act 1852"

Herewith I have the honor to enclose two pamphlets Board's orders. Pages 16.17.18 of that for Febry–March 1856 contains an order in Council extending the benefit of the Act to Chilian Vessels. On 28 July (pamphlet for August pgs 11–12) another order is promulgated in lieu of the preceding, the only difference being the omission in the latter of the words "not being British subjects" No doubt it was found that the Crews of Chilian Vessels coming here, like our own, were composed principally of persons

To put a stop to the violence & thieving on board ships on the high seas; and to remedy the mode of shipping seamen on this side, a Treaty would be necessary. In the first case to give the Magistrates jurisdiction in all offences below those provided for in the Treaty. In the other to compel the seaman when shipped, to fulfil his contract, which would enable captains to dispense with shipping masters. And I submit whether there can be any national objection to giving the English local courts jurisdiction in minor offences, on the written application of the National Representative, & with the proviso that the accused should have the right of being tried by a Jury of his own Country men. It would certainly be vastly beneficial to our Commerce.

> With high respect
> I have the honor to be
> Your obed Servant
> NATHᴸ HAWTHORNE [5]

That the British and Americans were at last fully resolved to interfere in the matter is clear from the two letters of Hawthorne which follow. The first is to an English firm. ·

> Consulate of the United States
> Liverpool 13 Feby. 1857

Gentlemen,

I am painfully conscious of the evils of the present system of shipping seamen for the American Merchant Service, from the cases almost daily coming before me, of men, who, having been put on board vessels as seamen, have been subjected to the most cruel treatment at the hands of their irritated officers and shipmates, & plundered of their clothing.

I am glad the subject has enlisted your attention, & that you have determined to use your influence in procuring a remedy. American ship owners can do much, as the prime source of the evil lies in the advance system of shipping seamen, & the want of a nursery for seamen.

At the same time it must be admitted the Laws on the subject want revising, & this will no doubt be attended to by our Government.

To put an end to the violence committed by officers & seamen, & now so painfully common, some international arrangement is necessary, to give the magistrates jurisdiction—such an arrange is also needed to reclaim desserters, and to compel seamen shipped here to fulfil the contract they enter into; this would enable masters to dispense with the services of unlicensed shipping masters This would also enable seamen to be shipped through the Sailors Home.

> I am very Respectfully
> Your faithful Servant
> NATHᴸ HAWTHORNE [6]

who, according to the English notion, are British subjects, & that the order was consequently practically inoperative. The omission might be obtained in favor of American Vessels, with such a late precedent.

> With Hight Respect
> Your obed Servᵗ
> NATHᴸ HAWTHORNE

5. *Ibid.*, xɪɪɪ, 83.
6. Hawthorne to Messrs. Rathbone Bros. & Co. *Official Correspondence.*

The second letter was addressed to Marcy.

Consulate of the United States
Liverpool 27 March 1857

Sir,

On the 14th Ulto I had the honor to forward copies of the Resolutions adopted at a meeting of American Shipmasters, and a Report of the Society for the relief of distressed foreigners in Liverpool, with reference to the mode of shipping seamen in American vessels and their treatment on board.

I have now the honor to forward a Report on the same subject since made by the American chamber of Commerce, with the view of inducing American shipowners to move in the matter.[7]

I also enclose copies of depositions made before me, relating to the death of a man named Daniel McKay on board the ship Wandering Jew, which occurred the day after crossing the Bar of the Mississippi, & was no doubt accelerated, if not occasioned, by the brutal treatment received from the first & third mates of the vessel, Kingsbury N Miller & W[m] W Owen, who both absconded as soon as the vessel entered the Mersey.

The evidence not being such as would sustain a charge of murder, the two persons could not be given up under the provision of the Treaty, but on being assured by the Police authorities that they would not object, if I chose to arrest the accused and send them back on my own responsibility, I employed officers to capture and put them on board a vessel, but up to this time they have not been found.

I am satisfied the Police could have found them had they been very desirous of so doing, but acting without any evidence of legal authority made them lukewarm.

The case strongly shews the necessity for, either an extension of the provisions of the Treaty to all criminal offences, or an International arrangement, as I have before suggested, for their trial in this country.

I am with high respect
Your obedient Servant
NATH[L] HAWTHORNE [8]

These letters state plainly the points Hawthorne considered important. He continued to feel that the root of the evil lay in the system of manning American vessels through unscrupulous shipping

7. The American Chamber of Commerce at Liverpool urged (12 March 1857) that steps be taken to correct the situation. It concurred with the American Shipmasters' Resolutions in placing the cause of the trouble with the shipping masters, who benefited more by the system of advanced wages than either the owners or the sailors themselves. It also demanded the coöperation of the Chamber of Commerce in New York and other American ports. The subcommittee advocating international reciprocity asked to have the authorities of Great Britain given jurisdiction over seamen on American vessels in cases of criminal offense committed upon the high seas (or in cases of desertion) to the same extent that they already had jurisdiction over British seamen. This proposed jurisdiction was to be subject to the sanction of the American Minister or Consul, and similar jurisdiction was to be conferred on the authorities in the United States. See *Consular Despatches*, XIII, encl.

8. *Ibid.*, XIII, 86.

masters, and that reform was to be sought chiefly by means of domestic and international law. The corrupt method of shipping seamen would then be done away with at home, and the vicious effects of it on the high seas would be put down through some kind of reciprocal treaty with England. Having previously seen many more inane reforms translated into law in Massachusetts and in New England, he was confident that the Federal Government would legislate promptly in a case of such international notoriety as this. But he was disappointed.

Early in April Lord Napier, Her Majesty's Minister at Washington, acting on instructions from the Earl of Clarendon, presented to the United States government a representation relating to the treatment of seamen on board vessels in the American merchant marine. The reply of Lewis Cass, Marcy's successor in the State Department, which was never intended to be made public,[9] elicited from Hawthorne about the longest letter he ever wrote in his life.[1]

The complacence with which Cass coolly absolved the law of any deficiency and bluntly intimated that the fault, if fault there was, might possibly devolve upon the consuls whose duty it was to execute such laws as existed,[2] roused an unwonted excitement in Hawthorne. He may have been somewhat piqued, it is true, by the oblique reflection on himself. Yet it was not his custom to waste energy in defending himself against the misunderstandings of others.[3] His primary motive throughout the long and closely argued reply to General Cass, in defending his own conduct and that of the consuls at large, was rather more impersonal. He wanted to prevent Cass, whose serene ignorance of the subject he later made public,[4] from dismissing the matter on erroneous grounds or shifting the blame from the law to its executors, where blame did not belong. Consequently he was eager to exonerate the consuls, since by so doing he would leave it apparent that the seat of the trouble rested in the law alone and any measures for reform must be brought to bear there. "I believe that no man, practically connected with our commercial navy, whether as owner, officer, or seaman," he told Cass, "would affirm that the present marine laws of the United States are

9. A copy of Cass's note, dated 28 April 1857, was published in England by the *Shipping and Mercantile Gazette* and reprinted by the *Times*, 13 June 1857, in an article entitled "Treatment of Seamen on Board American Ships." In answer to a letter by Hawthorne, Cass asserted that the publication of his note was carried out without the cognizance of the State Department. See *Hawthorne and His Wife*, II, 161.

1. See *Hawthorne and His Wife*, II, 153–61.

2. See The London *Times*, 13 June 1857, p. 12.

3. See Hawthorne to Delia Bacon, 24 October 1856. "Indeed, when people misunderstand me, I seldom take the trouble (and never should, on my own account) to attempt to set them right." Theodore Bacon, *Delia Bacon, A Biographical Sketch* (Boston and New York, 1888), p. 270.

4. *Our Old Home*, p. 49.

such as the present condition of our nautical affairs imperatively demands."[5]

Hawthorne employed at this time almost every means at his disposal for focusing attention upon the dire need of reform, even pointing out the *modus operandi*. One thing he did not avail himself of was his public pen. The crux of the matter came just as he was about to resign his consulship, and so the pamphlet which he projected was never written.[6] But later on he did devote several eloquent paragraphs of *Our Old Home* to the subject.[7] Also, in response to Henry Bright's request[8] he wrote immediately to Richard Monckton Milnes, who in 1859 finally brought the question before the House of Commons.[9]

Redcar, July 30th '59.

My dear Mr Milnes,

Our friend Henry Bright has given me great pleasure by telling me that you mean to bring the subject of the cruelty on board ships in the English and American trade, before Parliament. A better or more necessary thing could not be done—nor one in which the legislators of the two countries ought more heartily to combine. It is impossible to imagine unless compelled (as I often was, in my office of American Consul at Liverpool) to investigate the matter, what an immense mass of cruelty and brutality falls into the ocean, between your laws and our own, and remains absolutely unpunishable. Finding myself almost utterly powerless either to protect the victims or punish the offenders, I frequently addressed my own Government on the subject; but there are such international difficulties in the way of a reform, that the voice of an individual can never have sufficient emphasis.

You will please to observe, that I acknowledge these evils a little more readily, because I do not consider the character of my own sea-faring countrymen as solely or principally involved in them. In a vast majority of the cases that came under my notice, the perpetrator of the cruelties was not an American; and very frequently it turned out that the single American among the officers of the ship (that is to say, the captain) was the only person against whom no cruelty could be proved. These men, as a class, were fully capable of appreciating and deploring the evils of the system under which they acted, and I feel confident that none would more rejoice at the prospect of a better state of things.

---

5. *Hawthorne and His Wife*, II, 154. Cf. *ibid.*, p. 158.
6. See *Our Old Home*, p. 49.   7. *Ibid.*, pp. 48–50.
8. Bright to Hawthorne, 29 July 1859, quoted by Caroline Ticknor, *Hawthorne and His Publisher* (Boston, 1913), p. 226.
9. Richard Monckton Milnes, later Lord Crewe, mentioning Hawthorne's name in the House (see The London *Times*, 3 August 1859, p. 6), reported that the number of sufferers reputed to have been in the Liverpool hospital was 135 between June, 1857, and June, 1858; between June, 1858, and January, 1859, the number was 80; and in the Liverpool workhouse from June, 1858, to the following March there were no less than 23. (*Ibid.*) The situation was reflected on the American side by the New York *Times*, 27 July, 28 July, 1 August, 2 August, 15 August.

It seems to me entirely practicable that England and America should confer together on this matter, in a friendly and generous spirit.

Wishing that I could do anything to promote so excellent an object, I am
Very sincerely yours
NATH^L HAWTHORNE.[1]

Thus it was that Hawthorne became launched upon a crusade of his own, the importance of which in his opinion far overbalanced that of slavery, as he was at no pains to conceal from Charles Sumner. On the other hand, the importance to his biographers of his venture into reform lies in the fact that it exposes again the favorite myth of Hawthorne the escapist. It shows him as no inconsiderable man of affairs, active in the interest of the contemporary world, and participating more frankly and efficiently than most of the other prominent New England writers of his day in the actual business of reformation.

What has now happened to the man who loudly decried the behavior of philanthropists in *The Blithedale Romance?* "Such prolonged fiddling upon one string," he had exclaimed there, "—such multiform presentation of one idea!"[2] At Brook Farm Orestes Brownson had seemed an unusually noxious example of a failing for which Hawthorne chided all reformers—the inability to extend their thoughts beyond the circumscriptions of their single dominant idea.

When a good man has long devoted himself to a particular kind of beneficence—to one species of reform—he is apt to become narrowed into the limits of the path wherein he treads, and to fancy that there is no other good to be done on earth but that selfsame good to which he has put his hand, and in the very mode that best suits his own conceptions. All else is worthless.[3]

And yet, in the supercilious manner with which he required Sumner to put away anti-slavery for the particular philanthropy which he underwrote, and in his extravagant claim that the latter was nothing short of "a national emergency,"[4] Hawthorne himself presents as good a picture as his own abolitionist of a reformer "brandishing his one idea like an iron flail."[5]

What was the line of reasoning that led Hawthorne to condemn certain kinds of reform and espouse certain others? This is a question which is best answered by returning for the moment to an analysis of his connection with the Brook Farm experiment, which represents his most direct contact with reformers and the reform movements.

1. The original of this letter is in the possession of the Marquis of Crewe, K.G.
2. *Blithedale*, p. 383. 3. *Mosses*, pp. 246–47.
4. *Hawthorne and His Wife*, II, 159. 5. *Mosses*, p. 205.

It is quite foolish to presume, as critics have, either that Hawthorne felt a negligible interest in the West Roxbury Community as a social trial, or that he remained singularly untouched by the motivation and spirit that vitalized it.[6] Actually he regarded it as a valuable object lesson in the amelioration of society, a lesson presenting such "singular moral aspects" that there was "great desirability that its progress and developments should be observed, and its history written."[7] If it was a failure, it was an instructive one.

In the eyes of several of its best known friends Brook Farm failed notably in its main intent. To Hawthorne the manure pile had proved an exacting taskmaster, and he had learned a hard lesson from his apprenticeship. "The peril of our new way of life," he remarked almost a decade later, "was not lest we should fail in becoming practical agriculturalists, but that we should probably cease to be anything else."[8] Hawthorne's judgment was not the only one of its kind. Elizabeth Peabody, one of the community's most ardent well-wishers,[9] wrote to John S. Dwight that the experiment was making evident little else beyond the fact that "gentlemen, if they will work as many hours as boors, will succeed even better in cultivating a farm."[1] Emerson's statement ran in the same vein: ". . . labor may easily exceed. . . . The Irish population in our towns is the most laborious, but neither the most moral nor the most intelligent: the experience of the colleagues of Brook Farm was unanimous, 'We have no thoughts.'"[2]

The great paradox demonstrated by the Brook Farmers was that in endeavoring to avoid the sordid competition of the material world they were driven to do labor which proved equally if not more brutifying. "It struck me as rather odd," wrote Hawthorne in *The Blithedale Romance*, "that one of the first questions raised, after our separation from the greedy, struggling, self-seeking world, should relate to the possibility of getting the advantage over the outside barbarians in their own field of labor."[3] This predicament represents what one of the Brook Farmers themselves would have called "the necessary shortcomings of the *actual*" which, as John S. Dwight's sister once explained in a letter, it was the "tact" and talent of the

6. Lloyd Morris calls Hawthorne's reasons for enrolling in the colony "exclusively practical" (*The Rebellious Puritan*, p. 122).

7. *American Notebooks*, p. 176.

8. *Blithedale*, pp. 393-94.

9. See her articles "A Glimpse of Christ's Idea of Society," *The Dial*, October, 1841; "A Plan of the West Roxbury Community," *ibid.*, January, 1842.

1. E. P. Peabody to John S. Dwight, 24 June 1841. See Zoltán Haraszti, "Brook Farm Letters," *More Books: The Bulletin of the Boston Public Library*, XII (February, 1937), 62.

2. Emerson, *Journals*, VI, 34.   3. *Blithedale*, p. 343.

group to idealize.[4] But something went cruelly wrong with the Brook Farmers' idealization of the actual.

"My hope was," Hawthorne openly confessed in *The Blithedale Romance*, "that, between theory and practice, a true and available mode of life might be struck out . . ."[5] He interpreted Brook Farm's disintegration in terms of its inability to achieve that delicate balance between theory and practice, actuality and ideality. No better allegory is to be had of this tragic discrepancy than the fact that, unable to witness the sale of the estate in 1847, the few remaining residents took refuge in the Pine Woods, where with William Ellery Channing they sought comfort from an oral reading of Browning's *Paracelsus*.[6] Afterward, a special committee investigating the actuality they had left behind found that the enterprise had failed only through an insufficiency of those two things which even the transcendentalists could not successfully idealize—labor and manure![7]

Sometime before joining the West Roxbury Community Hawthorne had entered in his journals the following remarks concerning an ant hill:

Here is a type of domestic industry—perhaps, too, something of municipal institutions—perhaps, likewise (who knows) the very model of a community, which Four[i]erites and others are stumbling in pursuit of. Possibly, the student of such philosophies should go to the ant, and find that nature has given him his lesson there.[8]

In the light of such reflections the lesson inculcated in Hawthorne's mind by Brook Farm was plain enough. This eminently noble social experiment proved in the end a perfect example of the revenge which nature takes upon those who set up their ideas to rival hers. It stood as a warning to all kinds of reformers thinking to rearrange the normal course of human affairs, of the "excruciating agonies which Nature inflicts" on those impractical visionaries "who break her laws"[9] and irrespective of her try to intrude their own. Like Beatrice Rappaccini, Brook Farm proved to be "the poor victim of man's ingenuity and of thwarted nature, and of the fatality that attends all such efforts of perverted wisdom."[1]

Hawthorne believed thoroughly in the ethical necessity of all things to equalize themselves according to the instincts with which nature had endowed them. He was convinced likewise of the practical

4. Marianne Dwight to Anna Q. T. Parsons, 1844. See Amy L. Reed (ed.), *Letters From Brook Farm 1844–1847: by Marianne Dwight* (Poughkeepsie, 1928), pp. 6–7.
5. *Blithedale*, p. 391.
6. See Amy L. Reed, *Letters From Brook Farm* . . . , p. xv.
7. Haraszti, "Brook Farm Letters," *loc. cit.*, p. 113.
8. *American Notebooks*, p. 10.
9. *Passages from the American Note-Books*, p. 80.　　1. *Mosses*, p. 147.

wisdom of letting them do so wherever possible. Therefore he disapproved of the over zealous and often damaging interference with
this natural moral process on the part of reformers. Yet he was not
hostile to the reformer; he was critical of him. To the Christmas
Banquet came "a theorist who had conceived a plan, by which all the
wretchedness of earth, moral and physical, might be done away,
and the bliss of the millennium at once accomplished."[2] This man's
fault was that he was in too much of a hurry. There is a difference
between him and "the deep philosophers who think the thought in
one generation that is to revolutionize society in the next."[3] This
was the difference between Hawthorne and the fanatical people of
Liverpool, who wanted him to "run amuck" with them against the
American shipmasters.

The reformer so often overreached himself[4] in building his kind
of world, without first taking his cue from nature, that he was likely
to bring down in ruins not only his own edifice but those he wished
to improve upon as well. "He seeks to burn up our whole system of
society, under pretence of purifying it from its abuses!"[5] Hawthorne
complained. Like Hollingsworth, the philanthropist had too much
conscientiousness and too little conscience. He lacked breadth of
view. He had little regard for fact and almost no respect for reality.
In the end, the victim of his own arrogance, he must take his place
among the indeterminate figures in "The Hall of Fantasy," all of
whom in one way or another have failed to strike the balance between theory and practice.[6]

On such a basis Hawthorne condemned Abolitionism. In the case
of John Brown, most criminal of reformers, there was, as he put it,
"a certain intellectual satisfaction" in seeing him hanged by way of
requital for his "preposterous miscalculation of possibilities."[7] The
Civil War itself—a reform war—would at best, he told Elizabeth
Peabody, "only effect by a horrible convulsion the self-same end that
might and would have been brought about by a gradual and peaceful change."[8] In their antislavery agitation reformers proceeded with
destructive single-mindedness, he outspokenly reminded his sister-
in-law.[9]

2. *Ibid.*, p. 342.   3. *Ibid.*, p. 239.   4. See *English Notebooks*, p. 267.
  5. *Our Old Home*, p. 296. Compare the passage from which the theme of "The
Birthmark" grew: "A person to be in possession of something as perfect as mortal man
has a right to demand; he tries to make it better, and ruins it entirely." (*American Notebooks*, p. 183.)
  6. "But, alas!" Hawthorne wrote in "The Hall of Fantasy", "if reformers would understand the sphere in which their lot is cast they must cease to look through pictured
windows. Yet they not only use this medium, but mistake it for the whitest sunshine."
(*Mosses*, p. 206.)   7. *Sketches*, p. 328.
  8. Hawthorne to Elizabeth Peabody, 20 July 1863. Printed in the Boston *Post*, 18
April 1887.
  9. Hawthorne to E. P. Peabody, 13 August 1857, in the Berg Collection.

Astringent remedies like those prescribed and put into effect by the Abolitionists were completely discredited in Hawthorne's eyes. For to the best of his belief they were "beyond the scope of man's discretionary rights."[1] By the same logic he recommended no harsh cure for the ills which he thought he saw in the English social system. Drastic methods, he surmised, were proper only to Divine Providence, and would even so be held in abeyance "until the opportunity of milder reformation shall have been offered us again and again, through a series of future ages."[2]

Yet in this milder reformation where the aim was sound and the means consistent with nature and good sense he was more than ready to participate. His own venture into reform seemed to him absolutely commensurate with orderliness and sanity. For he remarked of it significantly to Lewis Cass that "the now wasted or destructive energy of our philanthropists might here be most beneficially employed."[3]

Though he had a strong faith in the salutary tendencies of nature if allowed to pursue her normal course, he nevertheless showed by his conduct that there were intervals when he felt man should supplement these tendencies. There were instances which required, as he told Cass, "the intervention of Government with all its wisdom and all its power."[4] In his conviction he was quite in line with New England in general, and Massachusetts in particular, where a sense of "community responsibility" has always been evident.

But how did Hawthorne reconcile this concept of paternalistic government with the policy of *laissez faire;* for his affinity with the principles of Jacksonian Democracy cannot be overlooked? As a matter of fact the reconciliation came about simply enough. Hawthorne believed in letting things go their own way until it was quite certain that they were going badly. After that he believed in the operation of social and civil authority, subject, however, to all the judgment, perspective, and restraint of an agency whose function is to assist and protect, not supersede. Since he by no means sanctioned too strict an intervention,[5] the efforts of government and community to improve social conditions had to be, in his allegorical way of thinking, like a gardener's attempts to enhance landscape. Wherever the art of man has "*conspired* with Nature, as if he and the great mother had taken counsel together how to make a pleasant scene,"[6] the outcome proves fortunate. It is not so where nature has been contra-

1. *Our Old Home,* p. 357.   2. *Ibid.*
3. *Hawthorne and His Wife,* ii, 159–60.   4. *Ibid.,* p. 159.
5. For his bitter resentment of all governmental attempts to superintend the management of his consulate, see his letters written between June, 1853, and August, 1857, to George Ticknor.
6. *Our Old Home,* p. 266.

verted, or ignored, or too hard pressed, as she had been at Brook Farm. Effectual philanthropy, according to Hawthorne, could be achieved only through a sober pressure of the ideal, which every man desires, upon the actuality which nature has put ready to his hand.

It is possible in the absence of a better phrase to call Hawthorne an empirical puritan. This he was not only in the major aspects of morality, intellectuality, and art, but even in such minor matters as style, tobacco, or wine. Whether in painting, literature, or the improvement of society, he sought always for what he considered "the better truth etherialized out of the prosaic truth of Nature."[7] And in spite of all the to-do to the contrary, he possessed a strong predilection for the kind of reform which was based on the broadest human experience. He hung back quizzically in all matters of "theoretical nonsense." But he was ready enough to subjoin himself to a reform that was "natural and sensible," a reform that took into account in its program of improvement the motley and contradictory realities of men's existence. Such reform was not likely to cause with its cure effects which might prove more deleterious to the general happiness of mankind than the original disease.

"If we consider the lives of the lower animals," Hawthorne once wrote with something Aeschylean in his feeling, "we shall see in them a close parallelism to those of mortals;—toil, struggle, danger, privation, mingled with glimpses of peace and ease; enmity, affection, a continual hope of bettering themselves . . ."[8] In view of his personal conduct, it would be impossible to think that he ever meant such hope to be inoperative.

Certainly he believed in social progress and to a degree in man's perfectibility. He bestirred himself actively for reform, and not only in the instance of American shipping problems. His satire,[9] his criticism of society, his very strictures upon philanthropy itself are reformatory—the result of his share in men's continual and active hope of bettering themselves. He praised the humanitarianism of reformers as eloquently as he condemned their foolishness.

The prison, the insane asylum, the squalid chamber of the almshouse, the manufactory where the demon of machinery annihilates the human soul, and the cotton field where God's image becomes a beast of burden; to these and every other scene where man wrongs or neglects his brother, the apostles of humanity have penetrated.[1]

7. *English Notebooks*, p. 614.   8. *American Notebooks*, p. 133.
9. Hawthorne's rather extensive satirical writings are treated by H. P. Miller, *Hawthorne as a Satirist* (Yale, 1936), unpublished dissertation.
1. *Mosses*, p. 245.

Whatever their theory or method, Hawthorne had faith in the motives of these men who represented, he said, "the struggle of the race after a better and purer life than had yet been realized on earth."[2]

These words could hardly have issued from the pen of a man whose heart was hardened against philanthropy. On the contrary, they came from a New Englander who, like almost every other New Englander, had felt keenly what he himself once referred to as the "itch" of reform. Then in contradiction to what many have thought, Hawthorne is neither a pessimist nor a defeatist. For behind the gloomy trend of his fiction and the agonized careers of his characters, there is the true tragedian's intimation of the necessity for human striving.

2. *Ibid.*, p. 205.

III

The Decade between Theory and Practice

*For it is my creed . . . that a man has no claim upon his fellow creatures,
beyond bread and water, and a grave, unless he can win it by his own
strength or skill.*

HAWTHORNE *to* HILLARD, *9 December 1853.*

Theory

IN Hawthorne's judgment Brook Farm had missed its mark, not
because it was a reform, but because it was a defective reform
that had proved incapable of achieving the all-important liaison
between theory and practice. It had aimed, in the words of one commentator, "at the physical and mental elevation of the poorer classes
. . . because it believed in their natural capacity for elevation as
children of God."[1] But American democracy had an almost identical
goal, and was based on a similar belief. In addition it rested upon a
very broad and normal basis that artificial societies did not. And that
is why it one day became for Hawthorne the great natural, practicable reform by whose impetus alone social conditions could be advanced over an enlightened earth.

Hawthorne's reconciliation between the theoretical and the practical in his social philosophy, which led him to reject Brook Farm and
ultimately to accept democracy as the one magnanimous and work-
able reform, was brought about largely through certain factors in his
own experience. What took place during the decade and more that
followed his departure from Brook Farm was the accomplishment
of this very reconciliation of theory and practice in terms of everyday life.

After leaving the West Roxbury community, Hawthorne continued
to face America like an idealist. He wrote in his journals not long
after his marriage in 1842: "The fight with the world—the struggle
of a man among men—the agony of the universal effort to wrench
the means of life from a host of greedy competitors—all this seems
like a dream to me."[2] For several years he went on attaching opprobrium to the politicians and men of affairs, in whom he saw an incarnation of all the materialism and utilitarianism with which the age
was rampant. But driven by the uncertain and sadly impecunious

1. O. B. Frothingham, *George Ripley* (Boston, 1882), p. 120.
2. *American Notebooks*, p. 154.

state of authorship, he himself took up the same career as the very politicians whom he had castigated, and for somewhat the same materialistic reasons as those he had formerly stigmatized.[3]

And then there happened to him something which was to prove, if not the most important incident in his life, at least the most energizing one. He was removed from the Surveyorship of the Salem Custom House under the very stigma he had earlier branded on others. The result of this ironic twist of affairs is of inestimable significance. It served in the capacity of what Carlyle would have called his "Baphometic, or Fire-Baptism." In a state of penury, he was deprived of his means of livelihood through the false accusations of political rivals. Instead of retiring to Lenox embittered, he moved there to start anew under revised standards. The period of his most uncompromising idealism, and hence of his greatest maladjustment to American society, was at that time giving way to another stage of his career—one that seems to the critic a little more amiable, certainly, and more normal.

This newest period is marked by his literary fame and by his service abroad as United States Consul at Liverpool. It is a period in which he demonstrated an astonishing hard-headedness in the unconscionable, methodical way that he resorted to most of the wiles of the politicians and materialists he had once reviled, in order to accumulate a fortune for himself.

Without a full and clear comprehension of Hawthorne's personal enlistment in the ranks of the materialists, it would be difficult to account for the final phase of his social criticism. For that final phase represents an almost unconditional endorsement of the democratic society of America, against whose materialistic ways and utilitarian spirit his most bitter criticism had at one time been directed. The materialism characterizing the entire business of the consulship testifies, as hardly anything else could, to the transition which took place in Hawthorne between the illiberal, exacting critic who maintained perennial dissatisfaction with the society of his country, and the man of wider experience who committed himself to America's mode of existence as being, in any event, the best the world had to offer at the time.

3. Politically Hawthorne was no more than he claimed to be, "a faithful Democrat in principle" (*Scarlet Letter,* p. 29). For his admiration of Jackson, see *Sketches,* p. 105; *Passages from the French and Italian Note-Books,* pp. 363–64; and James T. Fields, *Yesterdays With Authors* (Boston, 1884), p. 66. He was occasionally linked with the socialistically minded Democrats called "Locofocos" (see Longfellow to G. W. Greene, 23 July 1839, quoted by Randall Stewart, *American Notebooks,* pp. 288–89; and *Scarlet Letter,* p. 23). For an evaluation of his political practices while Surveyor of the Port of Salem, see Winfield S. Nevins, "Nathaniel Hawthorne's Removal from the Salem Custom House," *The Essex Institute Historical Collections,* LIII (April, 1917), 97–132.

The interlocutor of "The Hall of Fantasy" had been correct in his surmise respecting the author. Hawthorne's faith in the ideal was indeed deeper than he had been aware.[4] For though he had repudiated the visionaries of Brook Farm he retained, in his retreat from their Utopia, much of the recalcitrance which had caused him to undertake the experiment in the first place. For several years he remained, in regard to the realities of American life at large, almost as maladjusted and as censorious as he had ever been. In a sense he and his young wife strongly resembled his own Shaker lad and maid who abandoned their home in the community, trusting that they could earn their daily bread "among the world's people as well as in the Shaker village."[5] But it was at best a dismal commentary which was offered by the hopeless refugees from society who passed them, retiring to the community in a desperate effort to find sanctuary there from the ills of the everyday world.[6]

Life in America during the thirties and forties presented, as one historian has it, "one of the outstanding instances in history of the working of individuals trammeled by a minimum of law and convention." The temper of society in general was opportunistic. William H. Seward wrote to his wife from New York:

Thus far on my way to Washington, I find myself floating on a strongly-increasing tide of people, who hinder, annoy, and embarrass each other. The world seems almost divided into two classes, both of which are moving in the same direction; those who are going to California in search of gold, and those going to Washington in quest of office. How many adventurers are preparing themselves for disappointment, revenge, and misanthropy.[7]

America's aspirations were cast in a materialistic mould, and her creed during these decades, so far as there was one, was prevailingly utilitarian. Of the speculators, whether political or economic, Hawthorne was never oblivious. Ultimately, he himself subscribed in a measure to the doctrine of opportunism. But at first he rejected it. He sought to escape from it into a tiny group which had set up society in opposition to it. And after his subsequent emergence from their rather indefensible stronghold, he subjected it to a running fire of scathing, satirical criticism.

Before his own conversion he turned his attack upon the world-lings and the common Mammon-worshippers of society. One of the most lugubrious of the Canterbury Pilgrims *en route* to the Shaker village is a mighty speculator who, though he has been finally and devastatingly ruined, still pursues his will-o'-the-wisp. He cannot help the last paltry hope that the Shakers will make him business-manager

4. *Mosses*, p. 204.   5. *Snow Image*, p. 526.   6. *Ibid.*, pp. 526–28.
7. F. W. Seward, *Seward at Washington* (New York, 1891), I, 100.

of their concerns; in which case he solemnly pledges himself to double their capital in four or five years.[8] Of a similar resilient disposition and indomitable hope is the bankrupt at the Intelligence Office. Having heard of a scheme for rehabilitation at the Intelligence Office, he is "resolved to live out this one other experiment of better fortune."[9] Of all the wishes registered by the clerk at this office his had recurred with the most tedious monotony.

Hawthorne severely scrutinized the passionate wish of his countrymen to enjoy the "outward world," and it required little penetration on his part to realize what a premium they had put upon the commodity Wealth, as the "golden essence" of the world and the condition of its enjoyment.[1] Without doubt the yellow metal so casually and naïvely treated by the New Adam and Eve was "the mainspring, the life, the very essence of the system that had wrought itself into the vitals of mankind, and choked their original nature in its deadly gripe."[2] Hawthorne took pleasure in the fate which he had meted out in fiction to the capitalists—those "shrewd men of traffic who had devoted so many years to the most intricate and artificial of sciences, and had barely mastered it when the universal bankruptcy was announced by peal of trumpet!"[3]

The satire of these men is conveyed through a variety of forms. It may appear in not too subtle allegory, as in the case of the close-fisted materialist who was assured that the snake concealed in his vitals was "a copper-head, and had been generated by the immense quantities of that base metal, with which he daily defiled his fingers."[4] Or it may have the brilliant and caustic irrationality of Swift, as in Clifford Pyncheon's perverse defense of bank-robbers on the grounds that they differed from the conventional capitalist only in keeping more unconventional office-hours.[5] With the same vicious propriety, a forger from the state prison walks arm in arm in the Procession of Life with a distinguished financier.[6] Hawthorne's exegesis follows:

Statesmen, rulers, generals . . . are most liable to be deluded in this way; they commit wrong, devastation, and murder on so grand a scale, that it impresses them as speculative rather than actual; but in our procession we find them linked in detestable conjunction with the meanest criminals . . .[7]

These portraits of hapless materialists comprise a large gallery, ranging from the meanest miser to men at whose failure the national economic structure could be felt to tremble. There is Ichabod Pigsnort, who was "accustomed to spend a whole hour after prayer time,

8. *Snow Image*, pp. 525–26. 9. *Mosses*, p. 374. 1. *Ibid.*, pp. 376–77.
2. *Ibid.*, p. 295. 3. *Ibid.*, pp. 294–95. 4. *Ibid.*, p. 311.
5. *Seven Gables*, pp. 313–14. 6. *Mosses*, pp. 242–43. 7. *Ibid.*, p. 244.

every morning and evening, in wallowing naked among an immense quantity of pine-tree shillings, which were the earliest silver coinage of Massachusetts."[8] (This is the one vulgarity in Hawthorne.) On a little larger scale was an English Doctor by the name of Jephson, who discovered the virtues of the well that had made Leamington into a watering place, and whom Hawthorne described as "just the man to build up the fortunes of his native village, or perhaps to ruin all its inhabitants by his speculations."[9] On a still larger scale was the ruined financial despot whose "imperious, and, in many respects, noble, lofty nature, might have entitled him to a place . . . among the peers of Pandemonium."[1] Such a man was Nicholas Biddle, who, together with his bank, was long and inexorably persecuted by Andrew Jackson. Good Jacksonian Democrat that he was, Hawthorne returned to Biddle many years later for his model of "a man whose great designs made him a sort of potentate, whose schemes became of national importance, . . . a man who sought to do great things, and like many who have had similar aims, disregarded many small rights, strode over them, on his way to effect a gigantic purpose."[2]

In the business of money-making to which Americans devoted themselves almost exclusively, there was involved a moral issue. As Hawthorne one day remarked to Ticknor, it was a pursuit that was "too apt to draw a man's thoughts from better things."[3] While he was in England he remarked of the sea captains, whom he met officially at his consulate and socially at Mrs. Blodgett's boarding house, that it was "pleasant to see Americans who are not stirred by such motives as usually interest our countrymen—no hope or desire of growing rich, but planting their claims to respectability on other grounds, and therefore acquiring a certain nobleness, whether it is inherent in their nature or no."[4] He had directed his efforts throughout the previous decade not only to attacking the materialists, but to demonstrating their spiritual shortcomings and—through pathetic characters in his fiction like old Moodie, in *The Blithedale Romance*[5]—the sordid fatality of their lives.

By his own sense of being rather a misfit in a society which required men to perform duties like those of a measurer in the Boston Custom House, Hawthorne was thoroughly awakened to the basic utilitarianism of American civilization. But he ridiculed it rather gently, even tenderly, for he realized that upon it America had to rely for speed and strength in her advancement. And the unimaginative, materialistic democrat was satirized at times so delicately and affectionately

8. *Twice-Told Tales*, p. 175.   9. *English Notebooks*, p. 566.
1. *Mosses*, pp. 342–43.
2. *The Ancestral Footstep* (Works, xi), p. 458. See also, *ibid.*, p. 485.
3. *Ticknor Letters*, I, 95.
4. *English Notebooks*, p. 496.   5. *Blithedale*, pp. 527 ff.

that he was no doubt too dull of wit to appreciate the implied criticism of himself. Such a man, though otherwise the salt of the earth and the soul of dependability, was Mr. Lindsey. In contrast to his wife, whose nature had "a strain of poetry in it," he is described as an "exceedingly matter-of-fact" dealer in hardware, who belonged to the common-sense school, and who had a head as "impenetrable, and therefore, perhaps as empty" as one of his own iron pots.[6] By his sluggish credulity he brings about the Snowchild's untimely demise. Fellow members of his school were the Michigan traders who, though impressed by Niagara's water-power, would have journeyed twice the distance for a look at the masonry works at Lockport, which locked the Grand Canal down a drop of sixty feet.[7] And on a somewhat higher plane were the American artists Hawthorne encountered in Rome. If they were not "wholly confined within the sordid compass of practical life,"[8] they were generally a set of smart "practical men" who lacked a proper reverence either for their work or for the marble in which they wrought.

It was merely a sort of white limestone from Carrara, cut into convenient blocks, and worth, in that state, about two or three dollars per pound; and it was susceptible of being wrought into certain shapes (by their own mechanical ingenuity, or that of the artisans in their employment) which would enable them to sell it again at a much higher figure.[9]

Hawthorne realized justly that, in addition to being simply the products of the new democratic society, these artists were the victims of an absence of a national aesthetic. Of the democratic taste they themselves had no very high opinion. For Kenyon said, in reply to a query as to what Americans would do to the Fountain of Trevi, as magnificent a piece of work "as ever human skill contrived:"[1]

"The good people would pull down those rampant marble deities, . . . and, possibly, they would give me a commission to carve the one-and-thirty (is that the number?) sister States, each pouring a silver stream from a separate can into one vast basin, which should represent the grand reservoir of national prosperity."[2]

At that he was more charitable in his guess than his colleague who intimated that he could see the fountain harnessed to an American cotton mill. To the true artist like Owen Warland the "unimaginative sagacity"[3] by which the modern American industrialist converted every slight impracticality into a dream was deadly. His own work was "refined from all utilitarian coarseness"[4] and his very talents were "doomed to inutility as regarded the world."[5]

6. *Snow Image*, p. 391.   7. *Sketches*, p. 49.   8. *The Marble Faun*, p. 164.
9. *Ibid.*, p. 163.   1. *Ibid.*, pp. 172–73.   2. *Ibid.*, p. 174.
3. *Mosses*, p. 514.   4. *Ibid.*, p. 507.   5. *Ibid.*, p. 514.

Of all the hard-headed utilitarians the politicians were the ones in whom Hawthorne's critical shafts sank deepest and most often in the early part of this decade of the forties. They were as shrewd and as materialistic as the financiers, and usually more far-reaching in their corruption. Hawthorne was, and he remained, doubtful even of the best of them. Though quite won over by the charm of his once intimate friend Jonathan Cilley, he characterized him, with that inexorable candor which always pervades his sketches in the journals, as "crafty" and "insinuating," a man who avoided major rascalities principally for reasons of expedience, who deceived in the manner of the best political tacticians by telling half of the truth, yet who possessed withal a quality *approaching* high-mindedness.[6] Later on while he himself was making the most of a consular appointment, he continued to cast aspersions upon the professional politician. But there was a notable difference. The category at that moment fitted him, and his asperity became significantly mollified to the point where it resembled condescension rather than moral indignation.

In politics he was, of course, a sensitive man out of his natural element, although not so completely miscast as he liked to fancy. And he was inclined to patronize men like his friend O'Sullivan, whom he believed to have deteriorated under the influence of "the foul companions with whom necessity and politics have brought him acquainted."[7] He touches his hero Edward Redclyffe more lightly when he credits him with a "disposition naturally somewhat too sensitive for the career which he had undertaken," and represents him as seeking respite from "the virulence of party animosity" and "the abusiveness of the press."[8]

He had little confidence in the sharpness or intelligence of legislative assemblies, whether British or American. The members of the House of Commons impressed him as being "dull, in their aldermanic way,"[9] when he had a chance to observe them during a visit to Parliament. "I suppose," he remarked superciliously, "there are not ten men in the entire six hundred, who would be missed."[1] Moreover, his reference to Congressmen in a letter to Ticknor some two years earlier as "those jackasses at Washington"[2] leaves it obvious that he cherished no better sentiment toward the majority of the members of his own government.[3] "Speaking of American politi-

6. See *American Notebooks*, pp. 19–20. Compare his reference to Daniel Webster in a letter to his sister Elizabeth, dated 25 January 1836, in the Manning Collection.

7. *Love Letters*, II, 241.   8. *Doctor Grimshawe's Secret*, p. 180.

9. *English Notebooks*, p. 324.   1. *Ibid.*

2. *Ticknor Letters*, I, 39. The letter is dated 30 April 1854.

3. On the other hand, American politicians impressed Hawthorne rather favorably compared with the British. See *The Ancestral Footstep* (Works, XI), p. 478. For projected criticism of members of Congress during the Civil War, see *Sketches*, pp. 305–06, n. 1. These remarks upon congressmen in the sketch "Chiefly About War Matters" were

cians," he wrote once, "I remarked that they were seldom anything but politicians, and had no literary nor other culture, beyond their own calling"[4] This statement was made to Richard Monckton Milnes, the man who had been obliged to tell Sir Robert Peel about James Sheridan Knowles and Alfred Tennyson, since, in Hawthorne's scandalized italics, Peel had *"never heard"* of either.[5]

James Buchanan, American Ambassador to England during the first part of Hawthorne's consulship, was one of the few professional politicians whom he was unwilling to dismiss summarily as, for example, "an outrageous tobacco-chewer, and atrocious spitter on carpets."[6] "I like Mr. Buchanan," he wrote, ". . . he may be as crafty as other diplomatists are said to be; but I see only good sense and plainness of speech."[7] But though he found Buchanan venerable and seasoned with the wisdom of wide experience, he could not give himself over to unreserved approval. Buchanan's career was against him, the more so because it had been successful. "I always feel as if he were a man of heart, feeling, and simplicity," Hawthorne confessed, "and certainly it would be unjust to conclude otherwise, merely from the fact (very suspicious it is true) of his having been a life-long politician."[8]

But in his later attitude there was almost nothing left of the quixotism of his earlier criticism. American foreign officials, he told Ticknor in a very off-hand manner, "are (but don't whisper it) a set of swindlers generally."[9] And in fact, he could not at that time have excoriated these politicians as he had before, without shaving dangerously close to his own skin.

The case was altogether different during the early forties. He missed no opportunity to decry the American politician, his nature, his talents, and his practice. At Vanity Fair he observed members of Congress recruiting their pockets by selling their constituents, and he was assured, in his own words, "that public officers have often sold their country at very moderate prices."[1] The serpent which an "ambitious statesman" nourished at his bosom was presumed to be a boa constrictor, "since its appetite was enormous enough to devour the whole country and constitution."[2] Of the Intelligence Office, Hawthorne wrote:

not deleted by the editor as Randall Stewart supposed ("Hawthorne and the Civil War," *Studies in Philology*, xxxiv [January, 1937], 96, n. 30). It is evident from Hawthorne's manuscript, a photostat of which Mr. Norman Holmes Pearson has permitted me to examine, that those "omitted" paragraphs never existed outside the author's fancy.

4. *English Notebooks*, p. 89.   5. *Ibid.*
6. *Ibid.*, p. 36. This is from Hawthorne's description of Mr. Lilly, an Ohioan, "a politician, such as one meets with at home, often enough, without particular notice, but who stands out in strong relief here."
7. *Ibid.*, p. 99. Cf. p. 234.   8. *Ibid.*, p. 221.
9. *Ticknor Letters*, I, 24.   1. *Mosses*, p. 227.   2. *Ibid.*, p. 311.

The ambitious desires of public men, elsewhere so craftily concealed, were here expressed openly and boldly, side by side with the unselfish wishes of the philanthropist for the welfare of the race, so beautiful, so comforting, in contrast with the egotism that continually weighed self against the world.[3]

Among these ambitious materialists those that proved successful presented the ambiguous spectacle of men whom "some malicious contingency of affairs has thrust into conspicuous station, where, while the world stands gazing at them, the dreary consciousness of imbecility makes them curse their birth hour."[4]

But Hawthorne's politicians were seldom stupid. More often their outstanding attribute was a criminal shrewdness. After all, they had as archetype George Bancroft, whose behavior toward Hawthorne at the Boston Custom House was baldly referred to by the latter as that of "an astounding liar."[5] One of the wicked spirits who had waited on Doctor Faustus, seeking employment at the Intelligence Office, was on the verge of departing unsatisfied when the editor of a political newspaper entered the office in search of a "scribbler of party paragraphs." The former employee of Doctor Faustus was offered the job in spite of the fact that some doubt was voiced concerning his "sufficiency of venom."[6] "Next appeared, likewise seeking a service, the mysterious man in Red, who had aided Bonaparte in his ascent to imperial power. He was examined as to his qualifications by an aspiring politician, but finally rejected, as lacking familiarity with the cunning tactics of the present day."[7]

Hawthorne was soon to know more intimately the wide-spread influence for evil of the "Hang-whangers" and "Jack Slades," the "thick-skulled and no-hearted ruffians,"[8] and their "political bloodhounds."[9] With the exception of one or two of his personal acquaintances, a scrupulous politician was a contradiction in terms. Although "an incorruptible Patriot"[1] was numbered among the virtually unreal guests at the Select Party, Hawthorne did manage to eulogize Thomas Green Fessenden as a model of an honest, though consequently impecunious political writer. Fessenden himself had pointed out the fact which Hawthorne maliciously repeated, that he " 'need not have been accused of the crime of poverty, could he have prostituted his principles to party purposes, and become the hireling assassin of the dominant faction.' "[2]

---

3. *Ibid.*, p. 376.   4. *Ibid.*, p. 249.
   5. Hawthorne to Pike, 10 February 1840. Printed by Randall Stewart, "Hawthorne and Politics," *The New England Quarterly*, v (April, 1932), 246.
   6. *Mosses*, p. 373.   7. *Ibid.*
   8. Hawthorne to Hillard, 5 March 1849. Printed in the Autograph Edition, xvii, 427–29.
   9. Hawthorne to Longfellow, 5 June 1849, in the Craigie House.
   1. *Mosses*, p. 78.   2. *Sketches*, p. 256.

The two party system was never more in vogue than during the decade of the forties. Often the animosity of separate factions ran so high that Hawthorne had felt obliged to preface his obituary of Jonathan Cilley with the exhortation: "May no bitterness of party prejudices influence him who writes, nor those, of whatever political opinions, who may read!"[3] The philosophy behind such attitudes— if it can be called a philosophy—became known as the spoils system.

All in all, Hawthorne never entertained a very high opinion of the system of spoils, despite the fact that he was involved in it profitably through three different public offices. Even as late as 1863 he said to Ticknor in reference to the changes with which American institutions were threatened, "I trust that one result will be, to prevent upright and capable men from being sacrificed merely on account of honest political opinions."[4] America wronged itself, he thought, by permitting each revolution of the political wheel to remove a man for no other cause than that he belonged to the other party, and must therefore rely upon its auspices for his personal fortune.[5]

In America, people seem to consider the government merely as a political administration; and they care nothing for the credit of it, unless it is the administration of their own political party. In England, all people, of whatever party, are anxious for the credit of their rulers. Our government, as a knot of persons, changes so entirely, every four years, that the institution itself has come to be considered a temporary thing.[6]

Thus it was that the disappointed office-seekers were entitled to participate, at a side table, in the Christmas Banquet, since they were in "especial need" of a square meal.[7] Less fortunate than these, his brethren, was the "hack politician" who, being deprived of food through his removal from office, cast his teeth into Earth's Holocaust —a gesture made possible by the symbolical fact that they, like everything else about him, were false.[8]

His own bitter experience taught Hawthorne all he needed to know of the system of spoils, in which were united the tactics of politicians and the philosophy of materialists. Father of a family and in straitened circumstances, he was turned resourceless from the Salem Custom House, for nothing but the most "truculent"[9] party reasons and under a barrage of slanderous accusations. His disillusion crept into his restrained defense of himself in the Custom House chapter of *The Scarlet Letter*.

3. *Ibid.*, p. 264.
4. *Ticknor Letters*, II, 121. This letter is dated 8 February 1863.
5. *Our Old Home*, p. 53.
6. *English Notebooks*, p. 97.
7. *Mosses*, p. 344.   8. *Ibid.*, p. 438.
9. Hawthorne to Hillard, 5 March 1849. This letter appears in the Autograph Edition, XVII, 427–29.

Nevertheless, vixenly as she looks, many people are seeking, at this very moment, to shelter themselves under the wing of the federal eagle; imagining, I presume, that her bosom has all the softness and snugness of an eider-down pillow. But she has no great tenderness, . . . and, sooner or later,—oftener soon than late,—is apt to fling off her nestlings, with a scratch of her claw . . .[1]

He had been accused of carrying on strictly partisan business under cover of his official position, a charge he vehemently denied. He pointed out that the Whigs, who had remained in office throughout his Surveyorship, were living testimony to the fact that he had not ascended the Custom House steps in the capacity or spirit of "the exterminating angel" of the Democratic party. "According to the received code in such matters," he elucidated, "it would have been nothing short of duty, in a politician, to bring every one of those white heads under the axe of the guillotine."[2] In the long run he can hardly be blamed for seeing in the action of the Whigs a spirit of malice and revenge which, he thought, had seldom darkened the triumphs of his own party. "The Democrats take the offices, as a general rule, because they need them, and because the practice of many years has made it the law of political warfare, which, unless a different system be proclaimed, it were weakness and cowardice to murmur at."[3]

When Hawthorne spoke of the existing system as something which "it were weakness and cowardice to murmur at," he gave public indication of a change which had been going on within him ever since his first despairing and futile imprecations against those who ousted him from office. In taking home the lesson and the blame, he allied himself with the inflexible individualism of the age. He wrote to Hillard, apropos of the monetary gift which it was the most humiliating duty of his life to receive:

It is something else besides pride that teaches me that ill-success in life is really and justly a matter of shame . . . The fault of a failure is attributable —in a great degree at least—to the man who fails. I should apply this truth in judging of other men; and it behooves me not to shun its point or edge in taking it home to my *own* heart. Nobody has a right to live in the world, unless he be strong and able, and applies his ability to good purpose.[4]

In repaying the money which he alone had chosen to regard as a loan rather than a gift, Hawthorne reiterated his philosophy to Hillard. "For it is my creed . . ." he wrote then, "that a man has no claim upon his fellow creatures, beyond bread and water, and a grave, unless he can win it by his own strength or skill."[5]

1. *The Scarlet Letter*, p. 20.   2. *Ibid.*, p. 29.   3. *Ibid.*, p. 61.
4. This letter, dated 20 January 1850, is printed in the Autograph Edition, xvii, 432–33.
5. *Ibid.*, pp. 436–38. This letter, dated 9 December 1853, is in the Morgan Library.

This change of heart is of marked significance. Ten years prior to his letter to Hillard, which first elucidated his creed regarding the relationship of the individual to society, Hawthorne had written to Sophia Peabody:

It pleased thy husband to think that he also had a part to act in the material and tangible business of this life, and that a part of all this industry could not have gone on without his presence. Nevertheless, my belovedest, pride not thyself too much on thy husband's activity and ultilitarianism; he is naturally an idler, and doubtless will soon be pestering thee with bewailments at being compelled to earn his bread by taking some little share in the toils of mortal man.[6]

In the end, Hawthorne's unhappy experience in the Salem Custom House shattered almost completely the old impudence with which he had criticized the materialistic, utilitarian ways of his countrymen. With the utilitarian creed of his society—"pig-philosophy" Carlyle called it—Hawthorne came to terms, as an older, wiser, more tolerant American. As a younger man and an uncompromising idealist he had recoiled from hearing his countrymen promulgate their doctrine of a conscience of expediency—one whose susceptibilities were not so refined and sensitive as to make it a nuisance to everybody, including its owner. He once wrote to Sophia Peabody:

And I want nothing to do with politicians—they are not men; they cease to be men, in becoming politicians. . . . Their consciences are turned to India-rubber—or to some substance as black as that, and which will stretch as much. One thing, if no more, I have gained by my Custom-House experience—to know a politician.[7]

Throughout his fiction he had conjured up the utilitarian conscience in the shape of a moral bugbear. It hardened Judge Pyncheon's heart and dimmed his understanding;[8] it gave a bad title to the estate of a beleaguered materialist, trying to dispose of his worldly goods in the frantic hope that the "evil conscience" tied up with them might be made over to the purchaser simultaneously.[9] It appeared on the exchange at Vanity Fair.

There was a sort of stock or scrip, called Conscience, which seemed to be in great demand, and would purchase almost anything. Indeed, few rich commodities were to be obtained without paying a heavy sum in this particular stock, and a man's business was seldom very lucrative unless he knew precisely when and how to throw his hoard of conscience into the market.[1]

This was the kind of conscience Hawthorne had encountered everywhere, and he was finally shocked by a painful sense of per-

6. *Love Letters*, I, 164. This letter is dated 3 April 1840.
7. *Ibid.*, p. 149. This letter is dated 15 March 1840.
8. *Seven Gables*, pp. 282–83.
9. *Mosses*, pp. 372–73.   1. *Ibid.*, p. 227.

sonal inadequacy into recognizing that such consciences had a singular propriety and perhaps a necessary function in the social circumstances of the day. No doubt in his self-reproach and his growing consciousness during the late forties of financial failure, he felt how fussy and minute had been his former sentiments. Like his character, Colcord, in *Doctor Grimshawe's Secret*, he had been too full of scruples. And now, like Redclyffe, the hero of the same tale, it struck him that this was too much conscience, "morbid, sick, a despot in trifles, looking so closely into life that it permitted nothing to be done."[2]

Hawthorne was among the Americans who, at the mid-century, had difficulty in suppressing the bright visions of "manifest destiny" that thronged so many democratic heads. He too had found it hard to be convinced that the ideas of cities built as if by magic, of highways laid down in place of the ocean, and of "mighty rivers to be stayed in their courses in order to turn the machinery of a cotton mill," were "as much a matter of fantasy as the old dream of Eldorado, or as Mammon's Cave."[3] Hawthorne had formerly demurred at the coarse, brutal strength of the blacksmith, which had so repelled the Artist of the Beautiful. But at the mid-century he was preparing himself for something quite the opposite in his appreciation of nineteenth century utilitarianism as it appeared at its brutal and industrial worst in the iron foundry at Mersey, England. "I had a respect," he wrote, "for these stalwart workmen, who seemed to be near kindred of the machines amid which they wrought—mighty men, sure enough, smiting stoutly, and looking at the fierce eyes of the furnace fearlessly, and handing the iron when it would have taken the skin off from ordinary fingers."[4]

With a future of unparalleled illustriousness ahead for democracy and every man of it who proved himself equal to the pace, and with a purblind faith that the way of American progress was the way of modern civilization, it is no wonder that a hard and frequently unscrupulous pragmatism should have crept into the national philosophy. Nor is it surprising to find Hawthorne surrendering at last to the preachments of the ethic of efficiency. As was the case with his hero, Redclyffe, it was a doctrine not naturally his, perhaps, but the inculcation of a life mixed up with politics,[5] where a man's behavior had to be set for utility, or remain hopelessly ineffectual. Something more overweening than a fastidious conscience must equip a man who would leave his ineradicable mark on such a world. It must be, as Hawthorne wrote, "an invincible determination to effect something,"[6]

2. *Doctor Grimshawe's Secret*, p. 239.
3. *Mosses*, p. 201.   4. *English Notebooks*, p. 279.
5. *Doctor Grimshawe's Secret*, p. 242.   6. *Ibid.*

a determination that will overwhelm all smaller and more insignificant considerations of right and wrong, of propriety and impropriety. There should be no minor deterrent to the success of democratic America, nor to those participating in it.

One would expect Walt Whitman to celebrate the utilitarianism, the industrialism, the materialism which imbued American society. It must be remembered, though, that Whitman himself was happy with a road, a friend, an unlaundered shirt. His own impulses and energies found satisfactory vent in circumstances quite removed from the febrile materialism which he endorsed in his fellow Americans. And while he perhaps escaped bohemianism, owing to a certain strain of Dutch industry in his blood that kept him usually busy at something, he showed clearly, in blandly living off his friends, that there was not in his make-up the Yankee pride which drove Hawthorne to repay Hillard's gift so meticulously. Whitman did not have what every true Yankee has—what Hawthorne had—a sense of materialistic responsibility, of the ethic of property. If Whitman's ancestors had been the Puritans of New England, he would perhaps have known that grim need for complete personal independence, physical and material as well as spiritual, without which, after all, American civilization might now be a very different thing.

Hawthorne lived in this tradition. Consequently, he had to adjust himself to it as Whitman, living in a tradition and according to a code that was more or less his own, did not. Whitman could look at materialistic America from the outside as a poet, because unlike Hawthorne he was not compelled to be a part of it, with all its virtues and all its mischief, as a man. His endorsement of "money-making"[7] is poetic and romantic; while Hawthorne's adoption of the practice and doctrine of utilitarianism where his consulship was concerned represents criticism of the most empirical sort. In a certain sense Hawthorne's money-making marks the turning point in the development of his social theory from a youthful, unworldly idealism, to something that was clinical and realistic.

Practice

It is not exactly clear how Hawthorne came to write the life of Pierce, in the summer of 1852. He had recently concluded his labors on *The Blithedale Romance,* and according to his custom would have been quite willing to lay aside his pen for a brief season. On his part he always maintained that his services were drafted. But what confuses the issue here is the fact that he himself, not Franklin Pierce, broached the possibility of his doing the campaign biography.

7. See Newton Arvin, *Whitman* (New York, 1938), pp. 85 ff.

On the very next day after hearing the news of Pierce's nomination he wrote to him as follows:

It has occurred to me that you might have some thought of getting me to write the necessary biography: Whatever service I can do you, I need not say, would be at your command, but I do not believe that I should succeed in this matter so well as many other men. . . . I say this with perfect frankness; and (supposing you have even had the subject in your thoughts) submit my honest opinion to your consideration. Do you know Mr. Hazewell,[8] now, I believe, the editor of the Boston Times? He is a man of excellent ability, and extensive information on political and other subjects; a ready and very effective writer. There could not be a better man for the purpose in question. If you should think favorably of it, I would give him all the assistance in my power, and have no doubt that he would acquit himself ten times better than I should. I am not personally acquainted with Mr. Hazewell; (or Haswell; for I don't know how he spells his name) but could easily become so, as he is a resident of this town.[9]

If Hawthorne was a politician, he was not a hypocrite; though one may perhaps rightly wonder how far the two are distinguishable, even in such a man. For hardly a week had elapsed before he wrote to Fields that there would be no more fiction for some time; something new had intervened.[1] In the meantime Pierce had been in Boston, the recipient of another letter from Hawthorne which the latter had entrusted to Ticknor because it was too urgent for the mails.[2] By 17 June, eight days after he had first called the biography to Pierce's attention and had expressed his reluctance to undertake the writing of it, his assumption of the responsibility was a *fait accompli*.

It was a rather sudden capitulation in the face of such disinclination as he had professed. If he had sincerely desired not to be burdened with the biography, why had he thrown himself directly across Pierce's path? He must have known how concerned all his friends had been over his welfare, after his ejection from the Salem Surveyorship. Hillard had solicited in his behalf. Bridge had written to Pierce himself:

8. Charles Creighton Hazewell (1814–83) was a journalist, and a member of the Massachusetts Senate. During part of his life he was employed in an editorial capacity by the "Atlas," the "Times," and the "Traveller" in Boston.

9. This letter, dated Concord (Mass.), 9 June 1852, is in the Franklin Pierce Collection of the New Hampshire Historical Society.

1. This letter, dated Concord (Mass.), 17 June 1852, is printed in part in James T. Fields, *Yesterdays*, pp. 71–72. The manuscript is in the Huntington Library.

2. Hawthorne wrote Ticknor from Concord, June 13: "I take the liberty, although you are a bitter whig, to enclose a letter which I wish to be conveyed to Gen¹ Pierce; because it is of importance that it should reach him immediately, and were I to send by mail, I fear it will not reach him so soon. He intended to return to Boston on Monday (tomorrow) and I suppose will be at the Tremont. Possibly, they may keep him at home till Tuesday." *Ticknor Letters*, I, 3. I have been unable to locate the enclosure.

Hawthorne has gone to Lenox [*sic*], where I fear he will settle down for three or four years. Perhaps he may remain there unless at the end of Whig Administration, he should have a good office tendered him. . . . I trust that this change will be beneficial to Hawthorne in two ways—first by making him work with his pen; and then by giving him an office which will enable him to lay up something beyond a bare support. The Democrats will be sure to remember him for his removal showed how popular and how deserving he is.[3]

Hawthorne had carefully explained to Pierce his unreadiness for the part of biographer, adding that his method of composition and his style were both unsuited to the task. Moreover, he suggested another man for the rôle—a man personally unknown to him—and what is more offered to approach him with regard to the matter in question. At the same time, he must have been aware that however generally successful Hazewell had been as a biographer and historian, his work, if not precisely that of a professional hack, was at least not much above the level of literary jobbing. Hawthorne, meanwhile, had been assured by Fields of his own growing success and reputation. Mrs. Kemble reported from Europe that *The Scarlet Letter* and *The House of the Seven Gables* had made "a greater sensation than any book since Jane Eyre."[4] And the widely celebrated Longfellow had notified him that *The Scarlet Letter* had even been translated into German.[5] Beside such a giant of literary fame poor Hazewell was indeed pygmean. For sheer advertising value, as Hawthorne surely realized, Pierce would have found no comparison between a biography by Hazewell and one by Hawthorne. These powerful and immediate considerations could hardly have failed to elicit from Pierce the response which Hawthorne himself must have anticipated.

But Hawthorne always ascribed his taking the assignment to friendship, and he also managed to convey the impression—quite false—of passive acceptance. He wrote to Bridge:

I was terribly reluctant to undertake this work, and tried to persuade Pierce, both by letter and *viva voce*, that I could not perform it so well as many others; but he thought differently, and of course, after a friendship of thirty years, it was impossible to refuse my best efforts in his behalf, at the great pinch of his life.[6]

In the same letter to Fields in which he made note of his intention to comply with what seemed to be Pierce's importunate request, he

3. Bridge to Pierce, 4 November 1849. The original is in the Pierce Papers, vol. 3, in the Library of Congress.

4. Hawthorne to Fields, 15 July 1851. The original is in the Gardiner Museum, Boston, Massachusetts.

5. Longfellow to Hawthorne, 8 August 1851. In the Berg Collection of the New York Public Library.

6. Hawthorne to Bridge, 13 October 1852. Cf. *Personal Recollections*, p. 131.

wrote: "I seek nothing from him, and therefore need not be ashamed to tell the truth of an old friend."[7]

It is impossible not to be suspicious of this protestation in view of the fact that, less than a year before, Hawthorne and Burchmore had talked of "foreign consulships or other official stations," and of the likelihood of going to Rio together.[8] Pierce had assured his biographer as early as July that " 'no contingency could now happen to defeat his election.' "[9] If Hawthorne had entertained the notion of some preferment in case events corroborated Pierce's judgment, he would of course have had to keep a strict silence. Otherwise the validity of the biography would have been so seriously questioned as to render it virtually ineffective.[1] On the other hand, if he actually had such preferment in mind he has left to posterity, in the letter to Pierce where he first mentioned his unwillingness to write "the necessary biography," and in subsequent letters to friends, an example of dissembling such as few utilitarians have had the art or the consistency of mind to equal.

In any event, by October Hawthorne's part in the affair became appreciably clearer. The biography was completed late in August, and on the thirtieth of that month he left for the Bowdoin Commencement at Brunswick. The evening of 1 September he spent with Pierce and a prominent Jacksonian Democrat named Parris,[2] in Portland, returning to Portsmouth in company with Pierce on the following

7. Hawthorne to Fields, 17 June 1852. Printed in part in *Yesterdays*, pp. 71–72. The original is in the Huntington Library.

8. Hawthorne to Burchmore, 10 July 1852. Printed in the *Saturday Evening Gazette*, 2 September 1883.

9. H. Wilson to Charles Sumner, Natick, 22 July 1852. An unpublished letter in the Sumner Collection at Harvard. Wilson speaks of the statement as having been made "a few days ago."

1. Mrs. Hawthorne stoutly affirmed to her mother, after the publication of the Life, that no word of office had passed between Pierce and her husband. Actually no word was necessary, and her defensive statement to the effect that if Hawthorne saw fit to accept an office, he would not be deterred by the calumnious suspicions of others, somewhat weakens her original assertion. (See *Hawthorne and His Wife*, I, 484.) The Life was suspected anyhow. Hawthorne's friend Dike refused to be convinced that he had told the truth in it. In one of the newspapers it was referred to as his "new Romance." These apostasies were reported to Hawthorne by his sister Elizabeth in a letter from Salem, 23 September 1852, though she herself says of the opinions contained in the work, ". . . it is just what I have always heard you say." (See *ibid.*, I, 465.) Mrs. Hawthorne, with her usual impassioned gentility, upheld its "perfect truth and sincerity." (*Ibid.*, I, 464.) Hawthorne had sought to avoid any excesses of praise and lapses from frankness which might have invalidated the work. (See his letter to Pierce, 5 July 1852, in the Library of Congress; also, Mrs. Hawthorne's statement that he had written "with the most careful sobriety, because he did not wish to seem eulogistic and extravagant." [*Hawthorne and His Wife*, I, 482].) Hawthorne's own best comment on the biography is contained in a letter to Bridge, 13 October 1852. (See Lathrop, *Biographical Sketch of Nathaniel Hawthorne* [Works, XII], 509–10.)

2. Albion Keith Parris (1788–1857) was governor of Maine (1821–26), senator from Maine (1826–28), and Mayor of Portland (1852–53).

day. On the next morning he sailed for the Isles of Shoals, where he was joined only for overnight three days later by Pierce and a party which included Mrs. Pierce and Judge Upham.[3]

Now it is highly probable that on one or all of these golden occasions there took place some discussion of an appointment for Hawthorne in the event that Pierce should be elected, with possibly specific reference to the Liverpool Consulate. For on 13 October Hawthorne wrote to Bridge as follows:

Before undertaking it [i. e., the biography of Pierce], I made an inward resolution that I would accept no office from him,[4] but, to say the truth, I doubt whether it would not be rather folly than heroism to adhere to this purpose, in case he should offer me anything particularly good. We shall see. A foreign mission, I could not afford to take;—the consulship at Liverpool, I might; . . . I have several invitations from English celebrities to come over there; and this office would make all straight. He certainly owes me something; for the biography has cost me hundreds of friends, here at the north, who had a purer regard for me than Frank Pierce or any other politician ever gained, and who drop off from me like autumn leaves, in consequence of what I say on the slavery-question. But they were my real sentiments, and I do not now regret that they are on record.[5]

That Hawthorne's point of view has shifted is now obvious. While reasserting his former declarations regarding the purity of his motives in writing the Life, and insisting upon the integrity of the opinions expressed in it, he has nevertheless adopted a new tone toward the whole situation. He now speaks as though Pierce owed him something for his services, and he has even begun to speculate upon the payment. Moreover, it seems almost inevitable that his remarks in this letter should have been preceded by some discussion between him and Pierce, or those close to Pierce. That he would have hit so specifically upon the consulship at Liverpool otherwise is not likely.

The Liverpool consulship eventually came to Hawthorne, not, however, until there had been some discussion of the ambassadorship to Portugal. Hawthorne wrote abroad to Fields requesting information

3. Julian Hawthorne erroneously supposes Pierce and his father to have spent "about a fortnight" together on the Isles of Shoals (*Hawthorne and His Wife*, I, 466).

4. This statement is borne out by Mrs. Hawthorne in a letter to her mother, dated 10 September: "Mr. Hawthorne did not feel as if he could refuse a boon to an old friend, and one whom he could so safely praise. . . . He knew he never should ask for an office; and not one word on the subject has ever passed between General Pierce and Mr. Hawthorne." See *Hawthorne and His Wife*, I, 484. Inasmuch as Mrs. Hawthorne had not seen her husband since his departure on the thirtieth of August, and had in the meantime received no hint of the matter by letter, her testimony may be considered valid as of that date.

5. This letter, dated Concord (Mass.), 13 October 1852, is printed in part in *Personal Recollections*, pp. 130–34; and also in George P. Lathrop, *Biographical Sketch*, pp. 509–11. The original is in the collection of Miss Maurice.

about that post and about foreign countries in general.[6] It had therefore been somewhat possible to balance one office against another, with the result that Hawthorne accepted the consulship with a materialistic baldness and simplicity which is at first somewhat startling.

Two things which Hawthorne wanted were to be had from the lucrative post at Liverpool—money and the European residence so coveted by many Americans of the day.[7] And in accepting the appointment he was determined to get from it as much as he could of both. His official career as consul was a four-year term that is marked by an assiduous and single-minded devotion to the accumulation of wealth. That is not to say that his life in England had no other phases equally important, nor is it meant to imply that he did not permit himself at least a minimum of conscientiousness in the discharge of his duties. But so far as those duties themselves were concerned, they were made pleasant in the beginning mainly by the solid clink of gold,[8] and their significance in the end was estimated largely in terms of the private earnings which the consul had invested for himself.[9] These earnings were threatened a number of times with diminution, and no better record can be had of Hawthorne's constant efforts to make money than the history of his attempts to insure his profits by vigorously contesting any move on the part of the American Government to curtail his emoluments.

Hawthorne's nomination for the Liverpool consulship took place on 23 March, and it was confirmed by the Senate three days afterward. He was not to take up office, however, until the first of August, a fact which set him calculating at once the financial loss represented should his term be cut short to the extent of four months. Before the end of March he wrote to Pike, reporting Pierce's decision to grant the request of his predecessor, Crittenden, to be allowed to remain at the Consulate until his full four years should have expired. "The same favor," concluded Hawthorne, "must be granted to me at the end of my term, or I shall be woefully out of pocket by Pierce's complaisance."[1]

6. Hawthorne to Fields, 11 December 1852. Printed in part in Fields, *Yesterdays,* p. 72. The original is in the Huntington Library.

7. Hawthorne himself recognized this national yearning. See *Doctor Grimshawe's Secret,* p. 180: ". . . he had resolved, . . . to seize the opportunity for a visit to England, whither he was drawn by feelings which every educated and impressible American feels, in a degree scarcely conceivable by the English themselves."

8. See *English Notebooks,* p. 3.

9. Hawthorne frankly admitted his mercenary attitude toward his official activities. On 11 May 1859, he wrote to George Sanders: "We mean to pay a long visit to London, after we have done with the consulate, of which (except as respects the emoluments), I am heartily tired." See *The Political Correspondence of the late Hon. George N. Sanders* (New York, 1914): the catalogue of a public sale by The American Art Association, 13 May 1914, item 73. Cf. *Our Old Home,* p. 55.

1. Hawthorne to Pike, 29 March 1853. This letter is printed by Randall Stewart, "Hawthorne and Politics," *loc. cit.,* pp. 252–53.

This is characteristic of Hawthorne's touchiness on the subject of the spoils. From this time on he proved exceedingly nervous whenever anything occurred that threatened, however slightly, a decrease in the profits of his office. And since several such threats were real enough, he was now and then reduced to conniving in a very utilitarian fashion simply for the sake of securing to himself a few pounds.

The first threat of encroachment upon the proceeds of the Liverpool office occurred within a few months of Hawthorne's succession to the consulate on 1 August, 1853. It came from Manchester, where there existed at that time a branch office in the charge of a consular agent. What little business there was at Manchester was transacted through the Liverpool office, and the income from it—amounting to about two hundred pounds [2]—came to Hawthorne. For his benefit, according to Hawthorne, "Pierce made a direct promise that the place should be kept open."[3] On the other hand, there was the possibility that representations would be made for the appointment either of a consul or a vice-consul there, in which case Hawthorne's income would immediately fall off two hundred pounds a year—as he put it, "a damnable slice out of my business."[4]

Admitting the likelihood of such an appointment, Hawthorne proposed first of all "to keep the place vacant and receive the proceeds as long as possible,"[5] and then, on being assured that he could continue in this way no longer, to appoint his friend Pike as vice-consul. In both instances, it is clear, he contemplated quite frankly making the best use he could of the spoils policy.

At the beginning of the year he again wrote to Pike, informing him that the conditions at Manchester remained unchanged, and sounding him out about the projected vice-consulship. By the end of the following April he felt constrained to write once more, this time to let Pike know that should he refuse the position it would shortly become necessary to appoint an American residing at Manchester in his stead.[6] Pike, of course, was employed at the Salem Custom House as weigher and gauger with a salary of $1,500 a year. In all probability (since he seems not to have shared Hawthorne's extreme distaste for the situation at Salem), he saw no advantage in going to England for a limited number of years in order to draw a stipend

2. Hawthorne to Pike, 15 September 1853 (printed by G. P. Lathrop, *Biographical Sketch of Nathaniel Hawthorne* [*Works*, XII], 520–23).

3. *Ibid.*

4. Hawthorne to Pike, 6 January 1854 (printed by Randall Stewart, "Hawthorne and Politics," *loc. cit.*, pp. 255–57).

5. Hawthorne to Pike, 15 September 1853. See Lathrop, *Biographical Sketch*, pp. 520–23.

6. These two letters, sent from Liverpool and dated 6 January 1854, and 29 April 1854, respectively, are printed by Randall Stewart, "Hawthorne and Politics," *loc. cit.*, pp. 255–58.

which was but two-thirds as large as the one he was already getting. At any rate, Hawthorne's intriguing, regardless of the outcome, was not without a materialistic shrewdness; and if the stake was not worth a whole career to Pike, it was at least too large to be relinquished by Hawthorne without a struggle to retain it.

The Manchester business is not the only instance of an attempt by Hawthorne to maneuver the law to his own use. A bill was passed by Congress, which took effect in January of the last year of his incumbency, authorizing the President to appoint "Consular Pupils" to be sent to the various consulates at salaries of $1,000 a year. In a letter written the previous November Hawthorne called this bill to Ticknor's attention, with the following suggestion regarding it:

If your son Howard is at leisure for a few months, I should consider it a good opportunity for him—not, of course, as a permanent situation—but merely as a visit to England. I should require no duty whatever of him; . . . and I think he might live, and see England pretty thoroughly, within the limits of his salary. The appointment, however, is not in my gift; but the President would probably have regard to my recommendation; and by next steamer I will send a letter for him, to be forwarded or not as you see fit.[7]

In this letter Hawthorne frankly stated his opinion that the measure was ridiculous. He was afraid that some wanton youth would be appointed to Liverpool who might harass him during the remainder of his term. He hoped to nullify this possibility by getting Howard Ticknor the appointment, and the inducement he offered was complete freedom from any duty at the consulate and entire liberty for travel and enjoyment on a tidy little appropriation which Congress would find itself rendering up exclusively for Howard's personal benefit.

In making this offer it did not occur to Hawthorne that there was any moral discrepancy in thus subverting the purposes of legislation. In fact, he had become so accustomed to the petty wiles of the local office-holders in Salem and so contemptuous of their more successful brothers in Washington, that he doubtless considered what public money a decent man could get away from the tribe of rascally politicians a more legitimate expenditure than the government usually made.

The principal reason for Hawthorne's acceptance of the Liverpool appointment was, of course, financial. It is not possible to know precisely the extent to which he expected to benefit by the office when he accepted it. He had told Bridge, before Pierce had even been

---

7. *Ticknor Letters*, II, 34. This letter is dated 6 November 1856. Compare his letter to Pike, dated 29 March 1853. "I want you at Liverpool for your own sake and mine, and I want it understood beforehand that you are to have the first situation that it may be in my power to give . . ." Stewart, "Hawthorne and Politics," *loc. cit.*, p. 253.

elected, that he could not afford to take a foreign mission. But he made a tentative exception of the post at Liverpool.[8] It is probable that during his conversations with Pierce in Washington, in the spring of 1853, some estimate was made of the proceeds which this office might reasonably be expected to yield, on the basis of the records of previous consuls. But Hawthorne may well have been misled at these conferences without discovering it until he had reached England and was actually engaged upon his duties. For instance, according to Ticknor the branch office at Manchester was supposed to have been worth $3,000 annually;[9] whereas it actually yielded but one-third that amount.[1] Soon after her arrival at Liverpool Mrs. Hawthorne wrote to disillusion her father:

. . . though so many persons at home, who might be supposed to know, account the consular income here to be so great, and the arrival of ships so abundant, they are sadly mistaken. . . . Ten and twelve thousand dollars has been hitherto the amount of the *whole* yearly income from whatever source,—about a quarter part of the estimate made of it.[2]

Of the discrepancy here between fancy and fact Hawthorne himself apparently took no notice. Mrs. Hawthorne further stated, "It is hoped that the business may increase; but perhaps it will be too late for us."[3]

Whatever his calculations and hopes at the outset, Hawthorne soon formed his own estimate as to how much he would profit from his position by dint of personal economy and official shrewdness over a period of four years. He had not been in office a day or two more than seven months when he wrote Ticknor in a manner worthy of the most frantic materialist:

Invest—invest—invest! I am in a hurry to be rich enough to get away from this dismal and forlorn hole. If I can once see $20,000 in a pile, I shan't care much for being turned out of office; and yet I ought to be a little richer than that. It won't be quite so easy for us to live on a thousand dollars, or less, as it used to be. I am getting spoilt, you see.[4]

Hawthorne professed himself pleased enough with his situation. He anticipated a net profit from it of close to $20,000, and if business should increase, as had been prophesied, he might even do somewhat better.

8. This letter, dated Concord, 13 October 1852, is printed in part in *Personal Recollections*, pp. 130–34; and also in George P. Lathrop, *Biographical Sketch*, pp. 509–11. The original is in the collection of Miss Maurice.

9. Caroline Ticknor, *Hawthorne and His Publisher*, p. 46. See also, *American Notebooks*, p. 337, n. 679.

1. See Hawthorne's letter to Pike, from Liverpool, 6 January 1854. Printed by Stewart, "Hawthorne and Politics," *loc. cit.*, pp. 255–57.

2. Part of this letter is printed in *Hawthorne and His Wife*, II, 30–32.   3. *Ibid.*

4. For this letter, dated 3 March 1854, see *Ticknor Letters*, I, 31–32.

But his computation and his hopes were doomed to be revised almost as soon as made. And he wrote again to Ticknor not quite two months later, on the thirtieth of April, 1854, in reference to the plan for a bill which would regulate the incomes of the various offices in the diplomatic and consular service by putting them on a salary basis.

I shall still get rather more than my $20,000 out of it. The truth is, it is a devilish good office;—if those jackasses at Washington (of course, I do not include the President under this polite phrase) will but let it alone. They are now tinkering at a bill involving the whole subject of diplomatic and consular emoluments; and if they touch the Liverpool consulate at all, it will be to limit it by a salary. Now, with the inevitable expenses of a residence here, a salary of ten thousand dollars would hardly make it worth my while to keep the office—and they would never think of giving more than six. But I trust in God, Pierce will not let them meddle with me.[5]

As a matter of fact Hawthorne had already written to Bridge requesting him to seek an interview with the President regarding his affairs.[6] In this letter he had outlined the expenses of associating with English dignitaries, and emphasized the cost of living which, he said, had "nearly doubled" within the year.[7] Crittenden, his predecessor, he added, assured him that he went home "with an aggregate of only $25,000 derived from his official savings." Is this, one wonders, such meager remuneration? Apparently Hawthorne thought it adequate as a minimum only, for he continued his letter in this vein:

Neither do I believe that we have a single consulship, in any part of the world, the net emoluments of which overpay the trouble and responsibility of the office . . . I beg and pray, therefore, that Pierce will look at the reason and common sense of this business; and not let Mr. Dudley Mann [8] shave off so much as a half-penny from my official emoluments.[9]

Hawthorne seems to have arrived at the figure of $20,000, at which he originally aimed, by accepting Crittenden's statement that he

5. This letter is dated 30 April 1854. See *ibid.*, I, 39–40.
6. An unpublished letter dated 17 April 1854. The original is in the collection of Miss Maurice.
7. Compare Mrs. Hawthorne's housewifely account in a letter to her father. "Living is much more expensive here than at home: meat never below fourteen cents, and some kinds twenty cents; potatoes thirty cents a peck; no tea below a dollar a pound; grapes are a penny apiece, and the fruit here is not good." *Hawthorne and His Wife*, II, 31.
8. Ambrose Dudley Mann (1801–89) at this time held the office of Assistant Secretary of State. With Perkins of the House foreign relations committee he was instrumental in reorganizing the diplomatic and consular service, with which he had had personal acquaintance as consul to Bremen, Germany, and as special agent of the United States to Kossuth's government in Hungary, and later to Switzerland. It is interesting, in view of Hawthorne's subsequent disparagement of the wisdom and efficiency of the bill, to find Mann described as "credulous and lacking in penetration" [*Dictionary of American Biography*].
9. Unpublished letter to Bridge, dated 30 April 1854, in the collection of Miss Maurice.

had saved $25,000 in four years through frugality and thrift, and then by deducting from this sum the extra expense of supporting a larger family than Crittenden had had. Though he might reasonably have consoled himself with $20,000 as a maximum if worse came to worse, Hawthorne grew less and less satisfied with it as a minimum. There was the prospect that several months might intervene before he should be affected by the new bill. Meanwhile the business of the office, in accordance with the earlier prognosis, increased so rapidly that the consul could not resist the temptation to revalue his position once more.

It must have been after some calculation that he wrote to Ticknor early in June: "If I can have the full swing of the emoluments for one more year, I shall not grumble much; though (to tell you the truth) I do not see how it will be possible for me to live, hereafter, on less than the interest of $40,000."[1]

Obviously, Hawthorne had just begun to realize how "devilish good" his office actually was. Instead of contemplating earnings that would be "bread and butter and clothes and means of educating the children,"[2] as Mrs. Hawthorne had once put it, he now appears to have toyed with the idea of accumulating enough wealth so that he might live upon the interest from the principal and feel relieved, as he wrote to Pike almost three years later, "that my wife and children will be left in comfortable circumstances, in case of my death."[3] For the moment, however, his actual working policy seems to have been to trust in the President's power and willingness to keep Congress from tampering with his emoluments, to gather gold as rapidly as possible, and to resign his office when and if the proceeds should be cut down so low as no longer to be a recompense for his troublesome duties.

In the meantime Hawthorne conducted a private investigation of the matter in one or two of its ramifications, and the letter to Bridge which he wrote on 28 November 1854, as a result of this research,[4] shows a keenness and sobriety that rarely characterizes his pronouncements on the subject. He began by calling attention first of all to the condition of British consuls, whose salaries "are not the whole emolument of the various officers, but are in addition to their official fees—which," he added, "so far as I am aware, are similar in nature and amount to our own." He insisted that the framer of the proposed consular bill who arranged the salaries, that of the Liver-

1. For this letter, dated 7 June 1854, see *Ticknor Letters*, i, 46–47.
2. See *Hawthorne and His Wife*, ii, 31. This remark is from a letter written by Mrs. Hawthorne to her father in the autumn of 1853.
3. This letter, dated 27 March 1857, is printed by Randall Stewart, "Hawthorne and Politics," *loc. cit.*, pp. 262–63. The profits within the first year of his incumbency were about $10,000. See *Ticknor Letters*, i, 46, 49.
4. This letter is published in part by G. P. Lathrop, *Biographical Sketch*, pp. 523–24.

pool consul being set at $7,500 "for all expenses, including . . . clerk-hire, rent, and all other charges whatever . . . ," could have known nothing of the expenses of that office.

In this judgment he was doubtless perfectly sound, as he was, to a greater or less degree, in his suggestion of how the whole affair should have been handled—if indeed it had to be brought up at all.

The proper way of arranging a bill of this kind would be, to make previous investigations into the economy and management of the various consulates, and then for the government to assign the number and assume the payment of the clerks, together with the other official expenses, and give the Consul a proper salary outright, instead of leaving him to drive a hard bargain with his clerks. I desire no such arrangement as this,[5] but it is obviously the proper mode, if any change is to be made.[6]

The purpose of the bill, as Hawthorne observed to Bridge, was to create "from the over-plus emoluments of large consulates, a considerable fund towards paying the salaries of the smaller ones."[7] But at the same time he foresaw rightly enough that this expectation would not be realized, inasmuch as a great part of the income from large consulates derived from business which a Notary Public might do as well, and which a Consul—not consequently bound to do it—would cease to transact once the proceeds went into the public treasury instead of his own pocket. For this reason, then, Hawthorne predicted a notable diminution in the income of consular offices at large.[8]

Practically speaking, this was the coolest and most penetrating judgment which Hawthorne made upon the proposed consular legislation. In it he appears most characteristically and at his best—observant, clinical. It represented a deliberate and business-like effort on his part to grasp the facts and the principles of the case, and to appreciate the various motives, aside from his own, which were involved. Furthermore, in his criticism of the method by which the bill was drawn up and in his estimate of its probable efficiency as a measure for reform, he showed himself capable of exercising a sagacity and common-sense not ordinarily credited to him. He had a talent for analysis which, when he chose so to apply it, proved as authentic in practical issues as in those ideal ones having to do with art.

But this almost legalistic attitude was of brief duration. As it grew increasingly evident that the bill would at one time or another become law, Hawthorne turned once more to his personal accounting.

5. It would have been less profitable to the consul by far.
6. Lathrop, *Biographical Sketch*, pp. 523–24.   7. Cf. *ibid.*
8. However, in accordance with the construction put upon the bill by the Attorney General, the government did not assume the notarial fees. Compare Hawthorne's letter to his publisher, 1 August 1855, *Ticknor Letters*, I, 101. See also letter to the same, 6 July 1855.

By the middle of March, 1855, he had abandoned his more grandiose hope of having, as he wrote to Bridge, "a sufficient income to live comfortably upon for the rest of my life, without the necessity of labor."[9] It was, to be sure, rather a sanguinary ambition, that of acquiring from a government office in four years enough wealth to render his family comfortable and himself independent for life. Yet he considered the action of Congress "most unjust and absurd." And he made the following resolution: "However, I shall be glad to get what advantage I can out of the office, and therefore I hope Pierce will give me as long a line as his conscience will let him."[1] A week later he wrote to Ticknor, noting that the new law was not to be operative until 1 January 1856, and making known his intention of declining re-appointment at that time, and of keeping the emoluments as receivable under the old law until his successor should appear.[2]

The idea behind this policy is quite clear. Hawthorne had decided to remain in office till the first of the following January and the few months thereafter while he waited for his successor to be appointed and to arrive—approximately a year, according to his reckoning, from the time he was writing. "Ten thousand dollars will pay well enough for a year's servitude; but I doubt whether I could be induced to stay here for any less consideration."[3] Should he have continued in office after January he would have been accountable to the State Department for the receipts of the six months preceding, on which, he feared, the government could establish a claim under the recent statute.[4] But by declining reappointment on the first of the year, he would not, as he figured, be obliged to make a report on those sums at all. And he related gleefully: "I have Uncle Sam on the hip, you see;—and good enough for him, the infernal old villain! If I could only make up my mind to be as much of a rogue as he is, I might remain in office and thrive by it."[5]

As a matter of fact, the expedients which Hawthorne contemplated at this juncture in order to circumvent Uncle Sam's attempt to cut down his emoluments had in them more deliberate roguery than those of the government he had chosen to regard as an interloper in his private affairs. What he proposed to do, in short, was to hold office as long as he could receive his emoluments under the old sys-

9. This letter, dated 23 March 1855, is printed in part by G. P. Lathrop, *Biographical Sketch*, pp. 524–25.

1. *Ibid.*   2. This letter was dated 30 March 1855. *Ticknor Letters*, I, 82–84.

3. In a letter to Ticknor, Liverpool, 18 April 1855, *ibid.*, I, 85. Compare the following statement from a letter to the same written eight days later, 26 April 1855: ". . . if the President adheres to his purpose of keeping the old system in force, the subsequent six months can hardly fail to give me five or six thousand more. If so I shall be well enough satisfied." *Ibid.*, I, 89–90.

4. See *ibid.*, I, 86–90.   5. *Ibid.*, I, 89.

tem. Then, when the new law became operative he planned to resign for the sake of avoiding any claims which the government might
make upon his receipts of the previous six months. But this was not
all! In addition he had carefully counted on about four months extra
between his resignation and the time it would take to have a new
consul appointed, confirmed, and installed. During that period he
hoped to go on drawing his fees in the old way, in spite of the laws
that would then be in effect. In plain language, he intended to appropriate four months' fees—to which the government might at that
point be legally entitled—on the grounds that he had formally resigned a commission under the new act, and was therefore responsible only to the old law while obliged to hold office pending the
arrival of a successor.

There arose only the question of what Uncle Sam might do at
finding himself thus hoodwinked, and upon wishing, not unnaturally,
to recover his loss. Hawthorne was inclined to the belief that he
could pursue his legal advantage with impunity, for he forwarded
to Ticknor the explanation that not even his bonds could be attached.

The only part of my receipts for which my bonds could possibly be held
responsible, would be the sums I receive from masters of vessels for wages
of seamen left behind; and these always fall far short of the advances made
by me for the support of seamen. Moreover, even those sums could not be
ascertained by the Department, unless I choose to make a return.[6]

Certainly Hawthorne had something of a right to the materialistic
glee which he vented over his skill in thwarting the purposes of Congress. He had undertaken a close intrigue in his own behalf for a
matter of a few thousand dollars perhaps. And he had acquitted himself, it must be admitted, pretty well for a man who, in earlier years,
had been rather oppressed by the grossness of materialism.

But the fact must not be forgotten that Hawthorne had become
increasingly aware of what it meant to have dependents. Hitherto,
except for his Custom House positions he had considered the pen his
"legitimate instrument"[7] for support. He had accepted the appointment to Liverpool with the frank expectation of improving his economic condition. His practical reasons for declining reappointment
were logical enough. Under the new law he simply could not afford
to devote his energies to a task which would supply him and his
family no more adequately than the alternative pursuit of writing—
a pursuit for which he was originally meant and qualified by nature.
With this in the back of his mind he sent a personal communication
on 7 June 1855, to the President himself.

6. *Ibid.*, I, 88–89.
7. See Hawthorne's letter to Bridge, 23 March 1855, in Lathrop, *Biographical Sketch*,
p. 525.

A Consul cannot possibly live here, with a family (unless he secludes himself from society, and foregoes all the social advantages of a residence in England) at a less expense than $5000 per annum. His personal salary should not be less than the whole sum allowed by the new law ($7500) for the entire emoluments and expenses of this office; whereas, allowing $3500 for clerk-hire, and $1500 for office-rent and other expenses (very moderate allowances, too), there will remain but $2500 to live upon. A man might be comfortable with this sum in a New England village, but not, I assure you, as the representative of America in the greatest commercial city in England. For Heaven's sake, do not let the next session pass without having this matter amended.[8]

Hawthorne's ideal and theoretical reasons for opposing the bill derived from his practical considerations, and appear on the surface to be equally sound. His letter to Pierce makes both lines of argument plain.

In my opinion it will be for the public advantage to retain Mr. Davy,[9] who is a highly respectable man, with some private fortune, and I assure you that this latter qualification will hereafter be found essential in all appointments to Consulates here in England. It is very singular that our people do not see that the salaries, as arranged by the new bill, must throw these offices into the hands of a moneyed aristocracy, and that therefore it is anything but a democratic measure. To my office, when I quit it, you must appoint either a rich man or a rogue—no poor, honest, and capable man will think of holding it.[1]

Hawthorne's practical objection, then, was the economic insufficiency of the office under the new act as it stood in June, 1855. It was not remunerative enough to make it attractive to the average American, capable of supporting himself equally well if not better elsewhere. He would be obliged to relinquish what he already had for a mission that might prove to be not only unprofitable, but expensive.

His ideal objection to the act was just as succinct. By restricting the office to those who were not obliged by their financial situation to view it from an economic standpoint, it was undemocratic—it tended to be plutocratic. Democratic conditions were, of course, those for which Hawthorne kept a lifelong sympathy and hope. And there can be no doubt that he was sincere in attacking the new law on the grounds that it failed to insure their maintenance. As a matter of fact, his theoretical argument here was an honest republican criticism.

Not long after Hawthorne had sent the above communication to

8. This letter to Pierce was printed by John Ball Osborne, "Nathaniel Hawthorne as American Consul," *The Bookman*, XVI (January, 1903), 162–63.

9. Albert Davy, American consul at Leeds.

1. J. B. Osborne, "Hawthorne as American Consul," *loc. cit.*, 162–63.

the White House, there began a series of incidents which obviated the necessity for carrying out the financial intrigue he had projected, and which led ultimately to his holding office throughout the full term of four years—the last few months of which fell under Buchanan's administration.

In the first place, Cushing, the Attorney-General, returned a decision on the bill which permitted the consuls to retain their notarial fees and caused Hawthorne to waver somewhat in his original intention of resigning on the first of the following year. It was a circumstance that acted, as he wrote to Ticknor, "more for my pecuniary benefit than the first construction put upon the bill, supposing I were to continue in office two years longer."[2] On this basis he now commenced to reckon what his profits would be in the event that he stayed at his post for a whole term. With things in their present state he calculated to "clear" about $8,000 per annum. And confining himself drastically to $3,000 of this for living expenses, he counted on salting away approximately $5,000 a year.[3]

Notwithstanding, the period continued to be one of indecision. Bridge had sought an interview with the President in reference to Hawthorne's circumstances and had then written to Liverpool broaching the subject of a change of office. He suggested the Lisbon mission to Hawthorne, partly no doubt because Mrs. Hawthorne needed the climate of the Continent, and Lisbon seemed as good a place as any for her to go.[4] But Hawthorne felt it wiser to retain the Liverpool office both because he was acquainted there and because he would receive little benefit financially by an exchange.[5] With this in mind he wrote to Ticknor in September informing him of Bridge's interview with Pierce and his own intention of remaining at Liverpool for another year provided matters grew no more intolerable.

I have every reason to suppose that Frank wishes to do all he can for my benefit; but he has not much in his power. For instance, if he wishes to give me another office in exchange for this, he could not do it, because there is no other that I would accept. I should like well enough to keep the consulate till next September, and will do so unless the next Congress makes it worse than it now is; but I want nothing else.[6]

But the actual payment of money to the Treasury Department proved too much for Hawthorne's temper, and a month later he was

2. See Hawthorne's letter to his publisher, dated 6 July 1855, in the Morgan Library.
3. *Ibid.*
4. Several months later Mrs. Hawthorne actually did go to Lisbon on an extended visit to her friends, the O'Sullivans, while O'Sullivan held his commission there. For Hawthorne's letters to her during that period, see *Love Letters*, II, 232–57.
5. See his letter to Bridge, dated 31 August 1855, in the collection of Miss Maurice.
6. This letter was written at London, 27 September 1855. The original is in the Berg Collection.

determined to give up his duties at least by the next spring. He wrote to Ticknor:

According to the last quarter's accounts, I am to pay over to Government, nearly £800, which, if that damnable law had not gone into effect, I should have transmitted to you. This is sheer robbery. I am disgusted with the business, and can hardly bear to think of continuing at the present miserably reduced rate of compensation. I *must* and *will* resign, next spring at farthest.[7]

In this resolution he was quite serious at the moment, for he requested Ticknor to ascertain how sound legally was his title to the New York property of O'Sullivan's father-in-law, sold to him by O'Sullivan. "If it is safe," he concluded, "I can afford to resign."[8] But by the middle of November he had once more changed his mind, this time because he had decided that he wanted to spend another summer travelling in England and would, for that reason, like the salary from the consulate.[9] Nevertheless, he still desired to be free from his duties and the necessity of handing over to the government what he might once have kept himself.

My official responsibilities are much heavier than under the old law,—for instance, I have many thousand dollars of public money (which should have been my own) now in my keeping; . . . I cannot express, nor can you conceive, the irksomeness of my position, and how I long to get free from it.[1]

In addition, he had Mrs. Hawthorne's health to consider. He had made up his mind that rather than keep her in England to her peril during another winter, he would relinquish the profits of a fourth year and be satisfied with what he had already accumulated.[2] Still he was not incapable of looking somewhat longingly at the reward of those last twelve months. He admitted to Ticknor:

If I could remain in the consulate till the four years are quite expired, I should not fall very far short of $30,000; but there is very little prospect of my holding on through next winter. Unless Mrs. Hawthorne's health shall be more improved than I venture to hope, I shall quit England for the Continent in November next.[3]

Mrs. Hawthorne returned to England in the early part of June, her health much improved. On June twentieth Hawthorne wrote Ticknor: "She has little or no cough left, and earnestly wishes to spend

7. *Ticknor Letters*, I, 111. This letter is dated 26 October 1855.
8. *Ibid.*, I, 112.   9. See his letter to Ticknor, 23 November 1855, *ibid.*, I, 118.
1. *Ticknor Letters*, I, 123. This letter bears the date, 17 January 1856.
2. See Hawthorne to Ticknor, 11 April 1856: "If it becomes necessary to give up the consulate, before another winter, I shall do so without much apprehension as to my pecuniary prospects . . ." *Ticknor Letters*, II, 7–8.
3. *Ibid.*, II, 11. This letter is dated 24 April 1856.

another winter in England."[4] And in a little less than a month afterward he wrote again, expressing at last his own inclination "to stay the four years out."[5] His reasons were made clear in a letter to Ticknor written in September.

I begin to feel as if it were not worth while to grow much richer; but (Mrs. Hawthorne's health permitting) I shall hold on to the end of my term. The office (but this is a secret for yourself alone), is not worth less than $10,000 clear of expenses, in spite of the reduction.[6]

However, the fees were again curtailed, and he was prompted once more to quibble over his right to larger emoluments than the government allowed him. He wrote to Ticknor scarcely three months before giving up his office:

. . . the law that took effect from the first of January last . . . cuts deeper than the former one into the fees that rightfully belong to the consul. I shall assert my right to these fees, and hold on to them, if possible; and perhaps the Auditor may allow them, either from a sense of justice, or more probably from ignorance or negligence. If I lose them, it will make a difference of some hundreds of pounds.[7]

What with the general irksomeness of his duties and the steadily diminishing returns of the business it is easy to understand why, as early as the previous November, Hawthorne expressed complete indifference to his chances of remaining in office under Buchanan.[8] "Poor Devil!" he said of his successor. "I pity him, whoever he may be; especially as he will never get so much solid sweet out of the office as I have."[9]

The "solid sweet" which Hawthorne managed to extract from the Liverpool Consulate amounted in the end to considerably more than thirty thousand dollars.[1] This fact explains adequately enough why he had not quit his position long before. Owing to a tremendous increase in business, the office proved to be far more lucrative than he had anticipated, notwithstanding all that the con-

4. *Ibid.*, II, 18.   5. *Ibid.*, II, 21. This letter is dated 17 July 1856.
6. *Ibid.*, II, 26. This letter is dated 26 September 1856.
7. *Ibid.*, II, 57. This letter is dated 5 June 1857.
8. See his letter to Ticknor, dated 6 November 1856. "You speak of my chances under Buchanan. Nothing earthly would induce me to stay in office another winter after the coming one." *Ibid.*, II, 34–35.
9. *Ibid.*, II, 40. This letter is dated 31 January 1857.
1. In a letter to Ticknor, dated 13 March 1857, Hawthorne made a rough estimate of the money which he had actually saved during his incumbency. ". . . I should suppose I might count on the interest of nearly or quite $30,000" [*ibid.*, II, 45]. Meanwhile, though they had not lived in the "grand style," the Hawthornes had travelled in England and Scotland, and resided for a season at the resort town of Southport. Mrs. Hawthorne with her two daughters had spent some time on the Continent, and Hawthorne himself had purchased the doubtful luxury of financing Delia Bacon's Shakespeare fiasco. He had also kept $200 a year in an account for his sister Elizabeth (*ibid.*, I, 11).

sular bill had done to it. In four years' time he had amassed a little fortune, the income from which was enough to provide the necessities of life for him and his family thereafter, and to insure the comfort of his wife and children in the event of his demise. "I may say," he wrote to Pike, "in this respect, 'the bitterness of death is past.' "[2]

So also was his bitterness toward the office which had stood him in such good stead throughout his brief incumbency. He had been obliged to struggle not only with a task that was not congenial to his nature, but with the attempts of Congress to restrict the spoils which alone had made that task tolerable. He had admitted to Ticknor, ". . . money cannot pay me for the irksomeness of this office, at least, only a very large amount can do it."[3]

Hawthorne's attitude carries implicit criticism of governments that try to be too paternalistic. In this respect he belonged with those who, like Jefferson and like Jackson after him, believed in restricting the government to the preservation of order and in leaving the rest to individual initiative. One of Septimius Felton's immortal projects, one recalls, was "to fit the people to govern itself, to do with little government, to do with none."[4] With this belief in *laissez faire* Hawthorne never quite overcame his resentment at Uncle Sam's interference in what at times he almost mistook to be his personal business. This failure to distinguish between public service and private enterprise was an easy error to fall into three thousand miles from Washington. The government had not endeared itself to Hawthorne, and he afterward lost few occasions to refer to it irascibly, or to profess pleasure whenever he saw a chance that it might be victimized with a little of its own lack of scruple. "There is a pleasure," he wrote, "in getting around such a mean old scoundrel as Uncle Sam."[5] Regarding the new Consul, Mr. Beverly Tucker, he said, ". . . he will immediately find himself in possession of funds (not his own, to be sure) that will put him beyond the necessity of fleecing anybody but Uncle Sam. To that I have no objection, provided his own conscience will permit him."[6]

And here it must be observed to Hawthorne's credit that his own conscience never sanctioned the outright appropriation of government funds. In spite of the fact that he was entirely willing to get all the spoils he could by taking full advantage of the slightest loophole or laxness which the law allowed, he was scrupulously honest when it came to dealing with funds definitely not his own. Four years after resigning his consulship he wrote to Charles Sumner in regard to a

2. This letter, dated 27 March 1857, is printed by Randall Stewart, "Hawthorne and Politics," *loc. cit.*, pp. 262–63.
3. *Ticknor Letters*, I, 108. This letter bears the date 12 October 1855.
4. *Septimius Felton*, p. 408. 5. *Ticknor Letters*, II, 3. Cf. *ibid.*, I, 101; II, 52, 61.
6. *Ibid.*, II, 62–63. This letter is dated 26 September 1857.

matter of $205.86 which had accrued from sums deposited with him by masters of vessels, as wages of seamen discharged from ships of those masters in Liverpool. These wages had never been called for by the seamen. And in the meantime, owing to the illness of his clerk,[7] Hawthorne had neglected to turn over the money either to the new consul or to the Treasury Department. In his explanation to Sumner he said: ". . . I discovered the enclosed paper only a few days since. It is a great pity I found it at all; for it makes me two hundred dollars the poorer."[8] He then asked Sumner to inform the Secretary of the Treasury that the amount was held payable to the Treasury Department by Messrs. Ticknor & Fields, Boston.

But an alteration in his former attitude is noticeable at this time, for before concluding he mentioned the fact that nothing prevented a consul from appropriating funds like those which he was returning, and he suggested that to preclude defalcation the Department should make its Consuls accountable for such funds hereafter.[9] This attitude, formed in the sobriety of several years' removal from the irritation of holding office, presents a fair contrast to the cavalier nonchalance with which he had treated all thought of fleecing Uncle Sam earlier. Though Hawthorne lacked a conscience as nice as George P. Bradford's, which was somehow faintly distasteful to him,[1] he was an honest man, as far as honest men go. But as far as honest men go, he went. Yet it must be remembered that all this transpired in the days when the system of spoils was in vogue and no one thought seriously of the golden mean.

It was Hawthorne's good fortune, in one sense, and in another sense his misfortune to come under such a system at such a period in American political history. So drastic an application of the patronage as that which prevailed at the mid-century all but prohibited, as he himself intimated, the democratic possibility of an average, respectable, and intelligent citizen's making a career of politics. In the face of a virtually complete periodical turnover, an ordinary office-holder could count with reliability on no more than a four-year tenure. The result of this uncertainty was twofold. In the first place, it had the effect of forcing the abler citizens into other and more secure occupations. And in the case of the office-holder, far from being an incentive to him to make something out of his office, it developed

7. Wilding, the clerk, was stricken with a nervous fever and delirium just at the time when Hawthorne was closing his official affairs. See his letter to Ticknor, dated Leamington, 5 November 1857. ". . . the continued illness of Mr. Wilding has thus far prevented me from understanding precisely how the balance stands between myself and the Treasury Department." *Ibid.*, II, 66.

8. This letter, dated Concord, 11 April 1861, is in the Sumner Collection of the Widener Library at Harvard.

9. *Ibid.*

1. See *English Notebooks*, pp. 75, 77; also, *Hawthorne and His Wife*, II, 43.

to an appalling extent the policy of exploit or be exploited, of making all the hay possible while the sun shone.

Of such political brigandism Hawthorne is a fairly sober example. He himself was not interested in politics as a career, but merely as a supplement to his pen, an additional means of supporting himself and his family when the pinch became tight. The spoils system, though he disparaged it, was wholly to his personal advantage. So that he was again caught between the pragmatic and the ideal, and placed in the awkward position of having to enjoy in fact a policy he had not been ready to endorse in theory.

After all the ink Hawthorne had spilled in priggishly denouncing the materialists of American society, no greater inconsistency could be found than this change, almost overnight, to that very materialistic attitude which had once been such a bogey to him. But it is perhaps a fortunate inconsistency, for it marks the partial disappearance of that earlier maladjustment which had caused him to approach society with such rigid principles and often in so sanguinary a frame of mind. "I am a good deal changed since those times," he told Fields in reference to the days when he had written the sketches included in *Mosses*, "and to tell you the truth, my past self is not very much to my taste as I see myself in this book."[2]

The chapter in Hawthorne's life which has to do with his consulship is indicative of a conviction of the America in which he lived —the conviction that the individual must shift for himself. Hawthorne's materialism as consul was typical of the philosophy of his times in the notion that the common good was best served when the enlightened individual was left free to pursue his self-interest.

Because he had partaken of the prevailing spirit of his age, joined his fellow Americans in the hard business of making a fortune, and because he had proved to himself that he could be a success as well as anyone, he experienced the spiritual comfort which so frequently depends upon material things. "I think I have been happier, this Christmas, than ever before,"[3] he wrote in 1854. Once he had joined in, the hue and cry seemed less obnoxious than hitherto, when he had stood aloof from the indecorous antics and tumult of the pack of materialists.

Though the chase seemed frenzied to him while he did not participate, once he had thrown himself into the spirit of the thing his own excitement, in company with that of his countrymen, put a wholly different aspect on the matter. The materialism of democratic America became something more than the mere selfish accumulation

2. Hawthorne to J. T. Fields, Liverpool, 13 April 1854. The original is in the Huntington Library.
3. *English Notebooks*, p. 98.

of worldly goods. It came to be, for Hawthorne, evidence of a new power and resourcefulness.

By contrast the same thing in the old world appeared to be infinitely more sordid. In a letter to Ticknor after he had been in England only a few months, he wrote: "I have been quite surprised to find that our respectable merchants have a higher moral standard than the same class of men here. We Americans are the best people in the world,—but it is a poor world at that."[4] Surprisingly enough, he objected to the English intolerance of "men who attain wealth by any other than the ordinary and regular methods," accusing them of dishonesty when they had been "only dexterous and shifty."[5] Of downtown London he said, "It is human life; it is this material world;" and he added that he had never, in America for example, had "the same sense of being surrounded by materialisms."[6]

The materialism which in the old society seemed "gross even in ghostliness"[7] was, in America, a sign of prodigious national energy, of youthfulness, of democratic progress. Without the perspective acquired from his hard-headed pursuit of business in another land, Hawthorne would never have put so whole-heartedly his trust in America, nor identified himself for better or worse with the workings of her utilitarian society. He could never have cast his ballot, as he later did, in favor of the progressivism of democracy.

Meanwhile, before he could unconstrainedly approve the ethic of efficiency Hawthorne had to be certain that the progress which it facilitated was preferable, as a state of society, to the tradition it tended to displace. The reasoning by which he came to favor whatever contributed to progress is perfectly revealed through his reflections upon the ancient English churches. These churches, as they stood in the heart of metropolitan business districts, were a superb symbol of the way England's traditional past provided a kind of spiritual sanity and restraint in the midst of her industrial present. Hawthorne found the sanitary effect of dim St. Paul's more than once refreshing in the center of London's commercial heat and hubbub.[8] However, regarding venerable St. Nicholas' Church in Liverpool, around which was "the very busiest bustle of commerce, rumbling wheels, hurrying men, porter-shops—everything that pertains to the grossest and most practical life,"[9] he speculated:

If this spacious church-yard stood in a similar position in one of our American cities, I rather suspect that, long ere now, it would have run the risk of being laid out in building lots and covered with warehouses; and if the

4. *Ticknor Letters*, I, 42–43. This letter is dated 12 May 1854.
5. *English Notebooks*, p. 424.   6. *Ibid.*, p. 607.
7. *Ibid.*   8. *Ibid.*, p. 204; see also *Our Old Home*, p. 255.
9. *Ibid.*, p. 10.

church itself escaped—but it would not escape, longer than till its disrepair afforded excuse for tearing it down. And why should it?—when its purposes might be better served in another spot.[1]

He eventually believed that traditions like those of English society should not be permitted to clutter the utilitarian path of a strong, progressive society like that of democratic America. But in his clinical fashion he first pondered long and deeply the traditionalism that through many centuries had apparently stood England in good stead.

1. *Ibid.*

IV

"Our Old Home"

*'. . . in America, the solemn decrees and resolutions of millions melt away
like vapor, and everything shifts like the pomp of sunset clouds . . .
Heaven intended the past as a foundation for the present, to keep it from
vibrating and being blown away with every breeze.'*
Colcord to Redclyffe: *Doctor Grimshawe's Secret*

WRITING in retrospect Hawthorne was more disposed to
dwell on the duty and function of consulship than he had
been at any time during his actual incumbency. In *Our
Old Home*, though it is true he still flatly confessed that he had
found "nothing pleasant about the whole affair, except the emoluments,"[1] he discoursed at some length in an idealistic vein.

One great part of a consul's duty, for example, should consist in building
up for himself a recognized position in the society where he resides, so
that his local influence might be felt in behalf of his own country, and, so
far as they are compatible (as they generally are to the utmost extent),
for the interests of both nations. The foreign city should know that it has
a permanent inhabitant and a hearty well-wisher in him. . . . He might
throw his weight into the balance against mischief-makers; he might have
set his foot on the first little spark of malignant purpose, which the next
wind may blow into a national war. But we wilfully give up all advantages
of this kind. The position is totally beyond the attainments of an American; there to-day, bristling all over with the porcupine quills of our Republic, and gone to-morrow, just as he is becoming sensible of the broader
and more generous patriotism which might almost amalgamate with that
of England, without losing an atom of its native force and flavor. In the
changes that appear to await us, . . . let us hope for a reform in this
matter.[2]

To what extent these sentiments are a part of Hawthorne's atti-
tudinizing will appear in the more unofficial aspects of his consulship.
Doubtless he himself did not go to the lengths which he outlined
several years later in interpreting his consular duty.[3] But that he had
some such outline in mind while he was still consul, and that he
made a special effort on frequent occasions to abide by his subsequent prescriptions is almost inevitable. For no man's behavior can
quite escape the influence of his own ideals.

1. *Our Old Home*, p. 55.   2. *Ibid.*, p. 54.   3. *Ibid.*, pp. 54–55.

The reform that Hawthorne expressed a desire to see would have done away with the unpredictability which characterized all the social and political institutions of America. He wished, for example, that a representative of the United States government in England might endure in office long enough to establish a bond between the societies of both nations. His own brief sojourn in England had done two things. It had made him uneasily aware of the uncertain and neurotic nature of the democratic society in the United States, and by contrast it had roused his curiosity and admiration over the measured, dependable society of old England, where no novelty was accepted unless some sort of precedent could be found for it, and no precedent was discarded until some novelty had been discovered which was old and tried enough to be a reliable substitute.

Hawthorne was well aware that the United States had nothing to compare with the genial and beautiful existence of the English upper classes; American institutions altogether lacked the seasoning which seemed to give strength and sanction to the social and political deportment of the British. To him the American way of life stood for progress, with all its vagaries and its nerve-racking experimentation, while England represented the established regularities and decorums of tradition.

Never in too complete accord with what he had once called "brawling and boisterous America,"[4] and frequently impatient over the lack of initiative in England's ritualistic mode of living, Hawthorne came somehow to believe that each society was precisely what the other needed, each was the other's complement. The history of his social thought during the years he spent in England, as it is written in the journals, in *Our Old Home,* and especially in the unfinished English romance, is the story of his theoretical attempt to amalgamate on the basis of blood relationship the best elements to be found in these two widely separate societies. That story ends with his failure to envision satisfactorily any nexus between the patriarchal order of the old world and the democratic system of the new, and with his final reception of the latter as alone containing the hope of man's social future. And in deference to Hawthorne, it must be said that his conclusion was influenced by a pretty honest appraisal of the merits and deficiencies of the traditional society and the progressive one, and not by shallow patriotic excitement.

Hawthorne was qualified by nature for reasonably impartial comparison of English and American society, since he never contracted the malignant type of patriotism which now and then during the century reached epidemic proportions among his countrymen. He was not patriotic in the usual sense of the term. Of this he was him-

4. *English Notebooks,* p. 280.

self quite conscious during his residence in a nationally minded country like England. Temperamentally averse to most enthusiasms, he remained clinical even in respect to patriotism. The sight of a whole company of Englishmen, rising as one man at the "tootings and thrummings"[5] of *God Save the Queen* and joining in the chorus, "their ample faces glowing with wine, enthusiasm, perspiration, and loyalty,"[6] struck him off-hand as being a trifle ludicrous. Certainly Americans were incapable of such a demonstration of loyalty, not, however, because the motive was non-existent in them. But the loyalty of an Englishman, according to Hawthorne's diagnosis,[7] came from his heart, owing to the fact that it was inspired by a monarch who was a venerable tradition in herself. Whereas the loyalty of an American was seated in his convictions; and in the vast machinery of democracy, where a President counted as no more than "a stuffed scarecrow straddling in a cornfield"[8] for a season, it remained a purely functional matter—or, in its more emotional stages, a luxury which most republicans were willing to forego.[9]

At the same time, if patriotism was a pleasant sentiment to contemplate in others, Hawthorne himself was not insensible of "some very agreeable titillations of the heart."[1] Upon leaving an American Circus company which was in Liverpool in the spring of 1857, he observed:

I . . . had been happy to perceive that the fact of its being an American establishment, really induced some slight swelling of the heart within me. It is ridiculous enough, to be sure; but I like to find myself not wholly destitute of this noble weakness, patriotism.[2]

Yet these are scarcely the words of a man who was accustomed to being carried away by patriotic excitement, or even desirous of such transportation. They are, in fact, patronizing to a fine degree.

Hawthorne was entranced mainly with the rare spectacle of his susceptibility to the heroic nostalgia of patriotism,[3] the causes of

5. *Our Old Home*, p. 379.   6. *English Notebooks*, p. 12.
7. Cf. *Our Old Home*, pp. 379–80, and *Doctor Grimshawe's Secret*, pp. 252–53.
8. *Our Old Home*, p. 380.
9. Compare the Englishman's criticism of America in *Doctor Grimshawe's Secret*, pp. 198–99. "It is a great fault of the country that its sons find it impossible to feel any patriotism for it. . . How can you feel a heart's love for a mere political arrangement, like your Union?"
1. *Our Old Home*, p. 380. Cf. *Doctor Grimshawe's Secret*, pp. 252–53.
2. *English Notebooks*, p. 462.
3. In a letter to Fields, written in a somewhat playful and facetious vein, Hawthorne had remarked within two months of his arrival in England, "Unlike yourself (traitor that you are) I have grown to be a staunch patriot on this side of the water." This letter, dated Liverpool, 16 September 1853, is printed in part in *Yesterdays With Authors* (Boston, 1879), pp. 73–74. Fields' sympathies were so strongly pro-British that he threatened to fight for England if war developed over the enlistment controversy and the Nicaraguan dispute. See *English Notebooks*, p. 282.

which might vary from a few "tootings and thrummings" to a circus. He lacked, and he admitted it, an intense nationalism like the Englishman's; and he once wrote to Longfellow in an attempt to explain the fact.

I am not particularly patriotic, myself;—indeed, I never considered myself at all so, at home; . . . The English are intensely patriotic; their island being not too big to be taken bodily into each of their hearts; whereas, *we* must dilute and attenuate our patriotism till it becomes little better than none. We have so much country that we have really no country at all; and I feel the want of one, every day of my life. This is a sad thing.[4]

The United States was too large almost to be taken into the mind at this time, when its earlier frontiers were being augmented by wholesale annexation of vast territories like that of Texas. About all this enormous land which Hawthorne was able to receive into his heart was a State or a group of States like New England.[5] "You cannot love anything beyond the soil of your own estate," the Englishman in *Doctor Grimshawe's Secret* tells his friend from America, "or in your case, if your heart is very large, you may possibly take in, in a quiet sort of way, the whole of New England. What more is possible?"[6] With this the American hero of an earlier draft of the English novel concurs.

'Our space is so vast that we shall never come to know and love it, inch by inch, . . . for where land changes its ownership every few years, it does not become imbued with the personalities of the people who live on it. It is but so much grass; so much dirt, where a succession of people have dwelt too little to make it really their own.'[7]

Previously, Hawthorne had spoken of the American's limited kinship with the soil from which he had sprung, and of "the mere sensuous sympathy of dust for dust," which few of his countrymen knew, "nor, as frequent transplantation is perhaps better for the stock, need they consider it desirable to know."[8] He had speculated on these matters before ever going abroad.

But he must have upset the gentle Longfellow, who seems oddly enough to have been the recipient of his bluntest criticism not only of England but of America, when he wrote: "our country looks very disagreeable and uncomfortable, morally, socially, and climatically, from this side of the water; . . . I *love* America, but do not *like* it."

4. Hawthorne to Longfellow, 24 October 1854. The original of this letter is in the Craigie House.
5. See Hawthorne to Ticknor, 2 March 1855: "I do love old Massachusetts, in spite of its ten thousand varieties of nonsense." *Ticknor Letters*, I, 81.
6. *Doctor Grimshawe's Secret*, p. 198.
7. *The Ancestral Footstep* (Works, XI), 470.
8. *The Scarlet Letter*, pp. 23–24. See also *ibid.*, pp. 26–27.

And he added, as if somewhat unsettled himself by his feelings, "Pray don't tell anybody this."[9] On another occasion, he had already elaborated on the same theme.

America is a good land for young people, but not for those who are past their prime. It is impossible to grow old comfortably there; for nothing keeps one in countenance. For my part, I have no love for England nor Englishmen, and I do love my own country; but, for all that, the honest truth is, I care little whether I ever set eyes on it again. Everything is so delightfully sluggish here! It is so pleasant to find people holding on to old ideas, and hardly now beginning to dream of matters that are already old with us! I have had enough of progress;—now I want to stand stock still; or rather, to go back twenty years or so;—and that is just what I seem to have done, in coming to England.[1]

Hawthorne's affection for America was primarily intellectual and moral, rather than sentimental. His failure to "like" it, on the other hand, was due to the fact that it looked, from his position in England, like an uncomfortable place in which to try to settle down. Hawthorne's sense of its instability was aggravated at this time by the slavery agitation, which had become involved with America's territorial problems of expansion. Free-soilers, anti-slavery men and pro-slavery men—all had raised public hue and cry against "Frank" Pierce and his administration, after the political *débâcle* which had been touched off by the Kansas-Nebraska dispute. By such indecorous demonstrations of fanaticism as those to which the parties and the press had given themselves over, Hawthorne, as Pierce's loyal friend, could not have been otherwise than painfully distressed.

It was only through a peculiar condition of heart and intellect that Hawthorne was able to achieve personally to a considerable degree that "broader and more generous patriotism which might," as he had put it, "almost amalgamate with that of England, without losing an atom of its native force and flavor."[2] His own frame of mind was too critical for him not to see the folly of the nationalistic attitude, which must by its very nature conflict with every other nationalistic attitude. It promoted war, with which, as "A Peaceable Man,"[3] he was not in sympathy;[4] it prohibited *a priori* the admiration of one society for

9. Hawthorne to Longfellow, 22 November 1855; the original is in the Craigie House.
1. Hawthorne to Longfellow, 30 August 1854; the original is in the Craigie House.
2. See above, p. 68.
3. This *nom de plume* of Hawthorne's was attached notably, and with appropriate significance, to the satirical little piece, "Chiefly About War Matters."
4. Regarding the American flags, which hung in the chapel of Chelsea Hospital for infirm soldiers as trophies of battles won by the British, Hawthorne remarked:
"It is a good method of teaching a man how imperfectly cosmopolitan he is, to show him his country's flag occupying a position of dishonor in a foreign land. But, in truth, the whole system of a people crowing over its military triumphs had far better be dispensed with, both on account of the ill-blood that it helps to keep fermenting among the nations, and because it operates as an accumulative inducement to future generations to

the peculiar excellences of another, and thereby lamentably narrowed the vision and culture of any given country.[5] In this respect, Hawthorne observed that the English were "beset by a curious and inevitable infelicity, which compels them, as it were, to keep up what they seem to consider a wholesome bitterness of feeling between themselves and all other nationalities, especially that of America. They will never confess it; nevertheless, it is as essential a tonic to them as their bitter ale."[6] He expressed regret over this state of mind in the words of his character Middleton, who remarked in speaking of the British and Americans to an old Englishman; "they are at all events two noble breeds of men, and ought to appreciate one another. And America has the breadth of idea to do this for England, whether reciprocated or not."[7] A "broader and more generous patriotism" Hawthorne was actually capable of through his very incapacity for the ordinary kind.

But his reactions were equivocal and often undecided. The existence of an almost uninterrupted substratum of Americanism has already been detected underlying his commentary upon England.[8] And it will become increasingly apparent hereafter that he maintained for his own country an unwavering intellectual devotion, and that he looked to her to be the leader in the hierarchy of nations in the civilization to come. But this bias of his may easily be overemphasized by the critic who fails to take into account that sheer petulance and self-consciousness in the face of English smugness are responsible for no small part of his noisiest Americanism. As a matter of fact, he was not unaware himself of the feeling of defiance on the part of Americans.[9] He once protested to Longfellow, "You ask why I do not take the more heartily to England. It is only as an American that I am hostile to England, and because she hates us."[1] Much of his patriotism, in other words, was defensive rather than intensive. The somewhat ungracious and tactless behavior of Englishmen at large never permitted him to forget while he was in their midst the distinction between English and American.[2] Yet, even while he

aim at a kind of glory, the gain of which has generally proved more ruinous than its loss." (*Our Old Home*, pp. 303–04.)

5. Compare Hawthorne's reference to "a similar narrowness" in the American character, *ibid.*, p. 84.

6. *Ibid.* Cf. *Doctor Grimshawe's Secret*, p. 210.

7. *The Ancestral Footstep*, p. 466.

8. Randall Stewart, "Hawthorne in England: The Patriotic Motive in the Note-Books," *The New England Quarterly*, VIII (March, 1935), 3–13.

9. See *Doctor Grimshawe's Secret*, pp. 209–10; also p. 198. In reply to Redclyffe's asseveration of patriotism, the Englishman says, ". . . it is only the feeling of self-assertion that rises against the self-complacency of the English, . . ."

1. Hawthorne to Longfellow, 16 February 1855; the original is in the Craigie House. Compare his letter to the same, dated 24 October 1854.

2. *English Notebooks*, p. 270.

brandished his Americanism rather militantly on the one hand, he
explored English society ceaselessly for those things which, in the
society of his own nation, he had missed and craved.

His attitude toward America was on many occasions as peevish
as it was toward England. "Well—I am sick of America, and feel it
a relief to escape all knowledge of its affairs," he complained to Ticknor, "for I have been more bothered with my own countrymen and
their troublesome peculiarities, since coming to England, than ever
before in my life."[3] He followed this with a caustic comment upon
his consular experiences. "I have gained a better acquaintance with
my own countrymen, since taking this office, than in all my previous
life . . ." he told his publisher, "and, to say the truth, I wish to get
farther off, in the hope of liking them better."[4]

America had her faults, so far as Hawthorne was concerned. And
his strictures upon her are by no means superficially attributable to
annoyance over the slavery agitation,[5] nor to disparity between the
obstreperous youthfulness of her spirit and his own middle-aged
temper. Age had no doubt increased his temperamental aversion
to the boisterousness of immature democracy. But after all, these were
but signs and symptoms of something more basic that had caused
him to view the new world as taxing, and hard to live in. As early
as 1838 James Fenimore Cooper had described America as a nation
of changes. "The whole country," he wrote, "is in such a constant state
of mutation that I can only liken it to the game of children, in which,
as one quits his corner, another runs into it."[6] Hawthorne likewise
sensed, unmistakably though vaguely, a certain moral confusion at
the center of what he had called "the Republican whirlpool."[7] And
wholeheartedly he wished it cured.

The Englishman in *Doctor Grimshawe's Secret* who charged that
the face of America changed like one of its own sheets of water
"under the influence of sun, cloud, and wind"[8] was not an idle or a
shallow critic. Hawthorne himself had seen close at hand the fantastic ideas of Fourier preoccupy his gullible countrymen, only to
disappear and be replaced by more dangerous enthusiasms like abolitionism. On the still more kaleidoscopic political scene, he had heard
Pierce first acclaimed and then reviled, had himself held office one
moment and lost it in the midst of ignominious motives the next.

Thus it is that a sense of something hectic, of a lack of ethical clear-

---

3. *Ticknor Letters*, I, 99.   4. *Ibid.*, I, 105.
5. See Stewart, "Hawthorne in England," *loc. cit.*, p. 12.
6. James Fenimore Cooper, *Home As Found* (New York, 1902), p. 131.
7. Hawthorne to George Hillard, Redcar, Yorkshire, 23 July 1859, in the Berg Collection.
8. *Doctor Grimshawe's Secret*, p. 198.

sightedness and co-ordination in the democratic society overshadows young Redclyffe's meditations at frequent intervals.

He thought within himself, that his prospects in his own galvanized country, that seemed to him, a few years since, to offer such a career for an adventurous young man, conscious of motive power, had nothing so enticing as such a nook as this,—a quiet recess of unchangeable old time, around which the turbulent tide now eddied and rushed, but could not disturb it. Here, to be sure, hope, love, ambition, came not, progress came not; but here was what, just now, the early wearied American could appreciate better than aught else,—here was rest.[9]

"Once in a long while," interpolated Hawthorne, "the weary actors in the headlong drama of life must have such repose or else go mad or die."[1] What menaced Redclyffe menaced in a larger sense his fellow Americans. In the constant onrush of their existence Hawthorne foresaw that they might either be carried wide of the true mark or burnt out before they reached it. Like Phoebe Pyncheon it made him a little dizzy "to think of such a shifting world."[2] And in sharp contrast to this scene upon which there were forebodings that progress might someday run wild, was the society of England, bonded in the traditions of her exacting past.

There was a fragrance of old learning in this ancient library; a soothing influence, as the American felt, of time-honored ideas, where the strife, novelties, uneasy agitating conflict, attrition of unsettled theories, fresh-springing thought, did not attain a foothold; . . . How unlike what he had hitherto known, and was destined to know,—the quick, violent struggle of his mother country, which had traced lines in his young brow already. How much would be saved by taking his former existence, not as dealing with things yet malleable, but with fossils, things that had had their life, and now were unchangeable, and revered, here![3]

Doubtless there is an undercurrent of hesitancy throughout these reveries which suggests that Redclyffe and Hawthorne felt the splendor of British society to be decadent, and its stability to be petrific. But all this longing for quietude, for order, signified not merely a lassitude of the nerves or of the spirit, forcing the American mind to affect English definiteness. It is more than that; it is the result of an ethical sensitiveness which Hawthorne possessed to an acute degree—an ethical sensitiveness which quite naturally recoiled from the increasingly bedlamite aspect of American society. Although this ethical-mindedness may have been flattered at recurrent intervals by the superb prospect of the social destiny in store for a great de-

9. *Ibid.*, pp. 176–77.
2. *Seven Gables*, p. 220.
1. *Ibid.*, p. 162.
3. *Doctor Grimshawe's Secret*, p. 174.

mocracy, it still retained the primary object of all moralistic out-
looks—the contemplation of man conducting himself, individually
and collectively, according to some categorical standard. Hawthorne,
consequently, was lured into accepting the comfortable rubric under
which social England had persisted so long, because it seemed to
fill temporarily at least the void left in his moral consciousness by the
absence of anything resembling concerted social and political behavior on the part of his countrymen. "It is good for the moral nature
of an American," he once said, "to live in England, among a more
simple and natural people than ourselves. Ale is an excellent moral
nutriment; so is English mutton; and perhaps the effect of both will
be visible in my next romance."[4]

The autobiographical record of Hawthorne's English years reveals
how deep a satisfaction he derived from the antique customs and
precedents that seemed to render English society so vertebrate, so
authoritative and reliable in the nervous view of an American. "What
an excellent thing it is," he confided to his journal, "to have . . .
landmarks and timemarks, that they serve to affix historical incidents to, and thus, as it were, nail down the Past for the benefit of
all future ages!"[5] As an American he acknowledged growth and
change to be the law of his national and private existence while maintaining simultaneously, as a native of the only section of his country
where the past was an active force upon the everyday present, a
singular sympathy for the age-encrusted institutions of what he called
the mother-country.[6]

Hawthorne's veneration of antiquity has become a critical commonplace that needs no reiteration. He was in a mood particularly
favorable to the indulgence of it just prior to his departure from the
United States. The over-dramatized, apathetic Miles Coverdale, had
remarked of social progress, ". . . let them believe in it who can,
and aid in it who choose."[7] And though the indifference of Coverdale
is a little too studied to be a faithful reproduction of Hawthorne's
temper, it approximated his state of mind closely enough at the
time. There could be no better mental preparation for appreciating
the salient aspects of English culture and civilization.

English society became for Hawthorne the national incarnation
of tradition. In whatever observable guise, antiquity delighted him
even against his critical instinct, which told him that many of the
oldest customs were part of British exhibitionism and had never
risen above the level of vanity and parade. The gaudy uniforms of
coachmen, the heraldic finery of footmen and other richly liveried

---

4. Hawthorne to Longfellow, 11 May 1855; printed in part by Samuel Longfellow
(ed.), *Life of Henry Wadsworth Longfellow* . . . (Boston, 1886), II, 258–59.
5. *English Notebooks*, p. 537.   6. *Our Old Home*, p. 79.
7. *The Blithedale Romance*, p. 598.

servants impressed him as being in bad taste. He cynically assumed that there was little distinction between the people who dressed themselves thus by means of their *entourages,* and those who actually wore the stuff on their persons. "Meanwhile," he confessed, "I am glad the fashion has endured till my day; for I love to see it."[8] He displayed the same combination of disapproval and pleasure over a little village nook near Leamington where "forefathers, and fore-fore-fathers and mothers had grown up together, . . . the same family names, the same family features, repeated from generation to generation."[9] And while an American found it tiresome to think of any social group persisting so unaltered for centuries, he also found a pleasant sense of sanctuary in the knowledge that such things did really exist. The king, too, Hawthorne felt, was "but the liveried and bedizened footman of his people, and the toy of their delight." Yet he parenthetically added, "I am very glad that I came to this country, while the English are still playing with such a toy."[1]

It was, he thought, impossible even for the citizen of a democracy not to feel something like awe, "at least a profound respect," for the stately institutions represented by Hampton Court, for the sovereigns whose "moral magnificence" required such a residence, and for the permanence pervading it all. "By no possibility," he exclaimed reluctantly, "can we ever have such a place in America."[2]

Much of this pomp and circumstance had had its origin in the frankest utilitarian motives and purposes. But now, being no longer useful it was retained for reasons of tradition, like the guard which Hawthorne one day noticed before the doorway of a public building. Yet he shrewdly remarked of this figure who was, from one point of view, only fronting for a bygone age:

Still, if he and his horse were to be withdrawn from their post, . . . it seems [as] if the monarchy would be subverted, and the British Constitution crumble into rubbish; and, in honest fact, it will signify something like that, when guard is relieved there for the last time.[3]

It was quite possible that even the most outmoded of these relics served a more than decorative function—were in fact more useful than ever before, though less directly so, in their stabilizing effect upon the social morale of England.

From the same New England heritage that had given him a sense of the sacrosanctity of tradition, Hawthorne had derived a knowledge of its power and value as a spiritual influence upon the social nature of men. Yankee that he was, for example, he maintained a scrupulous regard for Thanksgiving Day, as being a time-honored festival both in fancy and in fact. "We kept the New England Thanks-

8. *English Notebooks,* p. 249.
1. *Ibid.,* p. 424.   2. *Ibid.,* p. 286.

9. *Ibid.,* p. 126.
3. *Ibid.,* p. 205.

giving," he wrote to Ticknor from England in 1854, "as descendants of the old Puritans should."[4] Twelve years earlier (only a few months after his marriage) he had written in his journal:

Novr 24th, *Thursday*. This is Thanksgiving Day—a good old festival; and my wife and I have kept it with our hearts, . . . There was a new and livelier sense, I think, that we have at last found a home, and that a new family has been gathered since the last Thanksgiving Day.[5]

On that day, too, out of all others in the year, the dissolute daughter in the story *John Englefield's Thanksgiving* returns home.[6] Sin itself was not more firmly intrenched in her guilty soul than this single tradition, the last stray remnant of her childhood innocence.

"An old thing is no better than a new thing, unless it [be] a symbol of something, or have some value in itself," wrote Hawthorne in his English journal.[7] As symbols, traditions are spiritually valuable, for they are the only way a race has of knowing in the history of civilization where and to what it belongs. It was precisely this sense of belonging that Hawthorne felt the restless society of mid-century America lacked. The hero of *Doctor Grimshawe's Secret* passionately relates his longing "to be connected with somebody," yet in the Heraclitean flux and rootlessness of his life never feeling himself so.[8]

I have tried to keep down this yearning, to stifle it, annihilate it, by making a position for myself, by being my own fact; but I cannot overcome the natural horror of being a creature floating in the air, attached to nothing; ever this feeling that there is no reality in the life and fortunes, good or bad, of a being so unconnected.[9]

This American is the representative of his race, and his moral need of definite social origins is symbolical of the similar larger necessity of his whole country. He voices what Hawthorne took to be the deficiency of the new democratic world, and what he once hoped might be its restorative, when he cries: "There is not even a grave, not a heap of dry bones, not a pinch of dust, with which I can claim kindred, unless I find it here!"[1]

The entire culture of English society was built upon the foundation which America's untried democracy did not have. For an American, Hawthorne said of St. Botolph's Church—in the township that joined Boston, Massachusetts, to the English past—"it is good to think of such an age-long giant, connecting the present epoch with a long past, and getting quite imbued with human nature by being so long connected with men's knowledge and interests."[2] It was equally pleasant for an American to imagine the "good life" which the master

---

4. *Ticknor Letters*, I, 71.   5. *American Notebooks*, p. 172.
6. This story first appeared in 1840, in the *Democratic Review*.
7. *English Notebooks*, p. 127.   8. *Doctor Grimshawe's Secret*, pp. 275–76.
9. *Ibid.*, p. 276.   1. *Ibid.*   2. *English Notebooks*, p. 475.

of Leicester's Hospital might lead, "linked to old customs, welded in with an ancient system, never dreaming of change, and bringing all the mellowness and richness of the past down into the midst of these railway-times."[3]

Hawthorne saw a social asset in the fact that an antiquity had its source in human need and owed its longevity to human nature, with which, as a token of men's aspirations and beliefs, it had been impregnated for so long that divorce was impossible; it had in it a succession of past lives equally with those to come, "so that there was a rare and successful contrivance for giving length, fullness, body, substance, to this thin and frail matter of human life."[4] Traditions, he thought, were the guy-wires of society and served to keep it in line.

Democratic society was almost entirely modern, so that it had as yet no settled foundation upon which to rest and no fixed dimensions within which it could develop symmetrically. Of an ancient English castle which seemed to be used in the nineteenth century for coal depots and perhaps small dwellings, Hawthorne observed: "The English characteristically patch new things into old things, in this manner, materially and physically, legally, constitutionally, and morally."[5] Similarly the houses in Southampton displayed modern fronts upon their antique structures.[6] But it was in the village of Coventry that he discovered what seemed the best emblem of what England itself really was, "—with a great deal of antiquity in it, and what is new chiefly a modification of the old."[7] Yet the new things were so dependent upon the old and incorporated into them, that for all the limitations and impediment represented by such massive antiquity it was impossible to get rid of it without bringing the entire structure of English society down in ruin.

A few years later, when the pendulum had swung away from England to America, Hawthorne was to rewrite this idea, patronizing the English traditions and designating England's past as a "mouldy accretion, . . . by no means without its charm for a disinterested and unencumbered observer."[8] Meanwhile, however, he had been ready enough to find in this past the stabilizing force almost entirely lacking in the social scene in the United States, where political conditions were aleatory, and where one fad after another from occultism to the "quick lunch" swept across the democratic stage in tumultuous succession.

In the domestic and patriarchal society of England, Hawthorne found what was to him the most inclusive form of traditionalism, embracing all the ethical sense of "belongingness" and the spiritual association of the past with the present which sooner or later mark the

3. *Ibid.*, p. 586.   4. *Doctor Grimshawe's Secret*, p. 229.
5. *English Notebooks*, p. 257.   6. *Ibid.*
7. *Ibid.*, p. 141.   8. Cf. *English Notebooks*, p. 257, and *Our Old Home*, p. 90.

best cultures. To Americans like him, whose restlessness and curiosity urged them to spend their resources in aesthetic peregrinations over Europe,[9] the English home was an incredible wonder and delight. It was an institution not to be had in the migratory society of America.[1] It led Hawthorne to comment discontentedly in his journal; "The moral effect of being without a settled abode is very wearisome."[2] In a land where a mere farm house was comparable to the very handsome residences which America reserved for its Senators, Judges, and similar state dignitaries,[3] Hawthorne could not avoid speculating as to whether the gypsy life of his own family, for example, would spoil them for any other, or whether it would be possible to "enjoy our quiet Wayside as we never did before."[4] So smitten was he with the residential virtues of England that he wrote to Ticknor morosely complaining of his own home in Concord.

I wish I had a better house to live in, when I come home. It will be necessary to repair and enlarge it; and I sometimes think it would be well to sell the place, and look out for a more inhabitable one. . . . What do you think of this matter? The fact is, I do not take root anywhere, and never shall, unless I could establish myself in some old manor-house like those I see in England.[5]

This blandishing comfort, which was a property even of the humbler English dwellings, by sheer contrast heightened the unpleasantness of the glimpses Hawthorne was constantly catching and recording of social misfortune. A procession of charity-schoolboys looked especially unjoyous in England without home or parents' love.[6]

Of all the hereditary institutions of England the home was most grounded on social necessity and rich in social values. It was a place where "wedded pairs have spent their honeymoons," where children have been born and "grown old and died."[7] This, Hawthorne had realized long before seeing England, was what made a home. Any such establishment, associated as it had been for generation after generation with men's sufficiencies and insufficiencies, could only be compared unfavorably with those that the occupant does not build for himself but which "speculators build to let."[8] Of the modern commercial houses in Warwickshire which had been contrived

9. See *Our Old Home*, pp. 25–26.   1. *English Notebooks*, p. 104.
2. *Ibid.*, p. 186.   3. See *ibid.*, p. 120.   4. *Ibid.*, p. 424.
5. *Ticknor Letters*, II, 39. This letter bears the date 31 January 1857. See also another letter to Ticknor in a similar vein, 24 April 1857. "I shall leave the Consulate joyfully, but England with some regret; for it is a good country to live in, and if I were rich enough, I doubt whether I should ever leave it for a permanent residence elsewhere." (*Ibid.*, II, 51.) This half-fanciful desire for an English estate recurs frequently in Hawthorne's letters and journals. See, for example, *English Notebooks*, pp. 564–65, and a letter to Ticknor from Leamington, dated 21 June 1855 (*Ticknor Letters*, I, 96–98, *passim*).
6. See *English Notebooks*, p. 452.
7. *American Notebooks*, p. 150.   8. *English Notebooks*, p. 565.

mainly for the convenience and economy of an industrial society not unlike many American communities, Hawthorne wrote disconsolately: ". . . nobody seems to be building a house in real earnest, to live and die in, but rather as a sort of plaything. We are likely to leave no fashions for another age to copy, when we shall have become an antiquity."[9] He deplored even Sir Walter Scott's Abbotsford, because it impressed him as being unreal and lacking seriousness; instead of a sanctuary for human beings to die or to be born in, it was a toy.[10] "It is very strange," he mused, "how nothing but a genuine home can ever look homelike."[2] Houses that were built to let, to sell, or to amuse were "like a ready-made garment,—a tolerable fit, but only tolerable,"[3] the productions of a make-shift society. They lacked "some nameless property,"[4] some "subtle element"[5] that belonged at once to the unpretentious officers' dwellings at Salisbury Cathedral, "so cozy, so indicative of domestic comfort for whole centuries together—houses so fit to live in, or to die in."[6] It was of little consequence that in a community of this sort social progress was negligible, that the onrushing urgency of life subsided, "with perhaps a gentle circular eddy, but no onward movement."[7] For Hawthorne asserted: "In my opinion, the very tediousness of home and friends makes a part of what we love them for."[8] And here it cannot pass unnoticed that in another mood he was to controvert this opinion unabashedly.[9]

As the chief means a modern society had of appreciating its pedigree and its identity in the midst of so much that was transient and distracted in the nineteenth century, the true English homes could sometimes be evaluated according to the length and intimacy of their association with the families that occupied them. Only through a long process could the amplitude of domestic comfort which was the basis of a real home be achieved. It required "the thoughts of many successive generations, intent upon adding all possible household charm to the house which they loved," to produce anything like Charlecote Hall, the Sir Thomas Lucy estate—"one man's life is not enough for it; especially when he feels that he is probably making his house warm and delightful for a miscellaneous race of successors none of whom are likely to be of his blood."[1] The English trust in an infallible perpetuity of one generation's spiritual and physical heritage to its heirs gave Hawthorne the delusion of "a sort of permanence to the intangible present,"[2] as if society, and even time itself, were as cumulative an affair as an English family.

In view of this element of permanence—so indispensable in the

9. *Ibid.*, p. 127. 10. *Ibid.*, p. 341. 2. *Ibid.*, p. 546.
3. *Our Old Home*, p. 65. 4. *Ibid.* 5. *English Notebooks*, p. 546.
6. *Ibid.*, p. 128. 7. *Ibid.* 8. *Our Old Home*, p. 58.
9. See *ibid.*, p. 79. 1. *English Notebooks*, pp. 135–36.
2. *Our Old Home*, p. 146.

long run to the solidity of any culture—Hawthorne drew from the patriarchal system a sort of domestic or household ethic. In his report of Charlecote Hall he wrote:

Looking at this estate, it seemed very possible for those who inherit [it], and the many in England similar to it, to lead noble and beautiful lives, quietly doing good and lovely things, and deeds of simple greatness, should circumstances require such. Why should not the ideal of humanity grow up, like ideal trees, amid such soil and culture?[3]

Or again, he said, speaking of the great Duke of Marlborough's estate at Blenheim, "Republican as I am, I should still love to think that noblemen lead noble lives, and that all this stately and beautiful environment may serve to elevate them a little above the rest of us."[4] But equalitarian that he was, too, he could not confine the moral salubrity of home to the upper classes merely. The humbler life about the grounds of Peterborough Cathedral—"that of the family, that of the affections"—seemed to him to be the natural existence "which, one deludes oneself with imagining, may be made into something sweeter and purer in this beautiful spot than anywhere else."[5] Conversely, he was struck by the unmoral quality of unlovely dwellings like Mossgiel Farm, where Burns lived as a youth, and where there was no evidence that several generations had cherished their surroundings and tried to make them habitable. The atmosphere of meanness and frowziness which permeated the place led him to reflect that it could be no better morally than it was physically. "No virgin can keep a holy awe about her, stowed higgledy-piggledy into this narrowness and filth," he wrote deprecatingly; "it must make beasts of men and women."[6]

The contrast between such poverty as that which he found in Scotland and the almost unreal grace of the English Lake Region left Hawthorne with nothing but unreserved admiration for the latter.

It makes one think the more cheerfully of human life to see . . . such sweet, rural, peaceful, flower-bordered cottages; not cottages of gentility, but real dwellings of the laboring poor . . . . adorned, more and more, year after year, with the care and after-thought of people who mean to live there a great while, and feel as if their children might live there after them—and so they plant trees to overshadow their walks, . . . and so live for the future in another sense than we Americans do. And the climate helps them out, and makes everything so moist and green, . . . instead of being dry and arid; as human life and vegetable life is so apt to be with us. Certainly, England can present a more attractive face than we can; even in its humbler modes of life; to say nothing of the beautiful lives that might, . . . be led by the higher classes. . . .[7]

3. *English Notebooks*, p. 136.   4. *English Notebooks*, p. 410.
5. *Ibid.*, p. 484.   6. *Ibid.*, p. 504.   7. *Ibid.*, p. 172.

Here Hawthorne nearly stumbled upon a natural Utopia, embodying those elements of life for which he had long sought a congenial place where they might flourish all together. Yet he was troubled at the very height of his excitement by the realization that the society before his eyes was on its way out.

All this is passing away; and society must assume new relations; but there is no harm in believing that there has been something very good in English life—good for all classes—while the world was in a state out of which these forms naturally grew.[8]

Disturbed by this sense of transience, at least, if not of progress, Hawthorne gazed into the future to see if perhaps it did not hold a promise of something which would be equally congenial to the same ideal elements, and include them all.

The home and the family were the very nucleus of English society and provided it with the great centrality which social America wanted. Politics described an orbit about them, as did naval, diplomatic, and even clerical careers. Quite the opposite of this was the meteoric aspect of identical vocations in the democratic order of the new world. Yet there was a huge compensation in the mere economic fact that the opportunism of the modern system, which made men's well-being more precarious, also rendered it, by the same logic, less irretrievable if once lost.[9] Hawthorne had personally benefitted from this opportunism to such a degree that he never lost sight of it as one of the prime credentials of America's civil and political philosophy, even while he glibly paid tribute to the institutions of England.

At Nuneham Courtenay, the seat of the Harcourt family, he had found what seemed to him to be "as perfect as anything earthly can be; utterly and entirely finished; as if the years and generations had done all for it, that the heart and mind of the possessors could think of, for a place they loved."[1] Similarly, to Redclyffe, the American hero of *Doctor Grimshawe's Secret,* Braithwaite Hall supplied the ideal of home. Coming as he did from a society whose homes were but the "poor tents of a day, inns of a night, where nothing was certain, save that the family of him who built it would not dwell here,"[2] the American became enchanted with the notion that his own old home was on English soil, amid English traditions. "He spread out his arms in a kind of rapture, and exclaimed:—'O home, my home, my forefathers' home! I have come back to thee! The wanderer has come back!' "[3] England offered its inhabitants something an American could not find on the other side of the Atlantic.

---

8. *Ibid.*   9. *Ibid.,* p. 95.   1. *Ibid.* pp. 421–22.
2. *Doctor Grimshawe's Secret,* p. 230.   3. *Ibid.,* p. 278.

Such homes as Nuneham Courtney are among the splendid results of long hereditary possession; and we Republicans, whose households melt away like new-fallen snow in a spring morning, must content ourselves with our many counterbalancing advantages,—for this one, so apparently desirable to the far-projecting selfishness of our nature, we are certain never to attain.[4]

"Posterity!" Hawthorne expostulated. "An American can have none."[5]

Still, with an American's instinctive appreciation of the future as well as the past, Hawthorne also understood that on her part America held out to Americans something which Englishmen could not cultivate successfully on their island. Referring to Mr. Ireland, editor of the Manchester *Examiner,* one of the few Englishmen who had read Thoreau and who professed to be acquainted with the writings of Margaret Fuller and *The Dial,* Hawthorne wrote:

Somehow or other, this vein of literary taste does not augur very great things, in Englishmen or Scotchmen; and, on the whole, I think the illiberals, the conservatives, the men who despise and hate new things and new thoughts, are the best worth knowing. The others, with all their zeal for novelty, do not seem to originate anything; and one feels, as it were, a little disgusted to find them setting forth their poor little views of progress, especially if one happens to have been a Brook Farmer. The best thing a man, born in this island, can do, is to . . . take things as they are, . . . In this way, he is natural, wholesome, and good; a being fit for the present time and circumstances, and entitled to let the future alone.[6]

On one side of the Atlantic was a society with little or no stability, but with plenty of progressive energy; and on the other side was the older society from which it had originally derived, whose traditional solidarity was great but whose gestures toward novelty seemed a trifle senile.

British society assuredly represented a wholesomeness which democratic America did not. Doctor Grimshawe had this in mind when he conversed with the Yankee schoolmaster. "You do not clothe yourself in substance. Your souls are not coated sufficiently. Beef and brandy would have saved you. You have exhaled for lack of them."[7] Hawthorne reiterated the same sentiment often, and perhaps most notably in the passage from *Our Old Home* in which he discourses at some length upon the American's frank appreciation of the island belonging to his English cousins.

For my part, I used to wish that we could annex it, transferring their thirty millions of inhabitants to some convenient wilderness in the great West, and putting half or a quarter as many of ourselves in their places.

4. *Our Old Home,* p. 228.   5. *Doctor Grimshawe's Secret,* p. 230.
6. *English Notebooks,* p. 351.
7. *Doctor Grimshawe's Secret,* p. 68. Cf. *ibid.,* pp. 177–78.

The change would be beneficial to both parties. We, in our dry atmosphere, are getting too nervous, haggard, dyspeptic, extenuated, unsubstantial, theoretic, and need to be made grosser. John Bull, on the other hand, has grown bulbous, long-bodied, short-legged, heavy-witted, material, and, in a word, too intensely English. In a few more centuries he will be the earthliest creature that ever the earth saw. Heretofore Providence has obviated such a result by timely intermixtures of alien races with the old English stock; . . .[8] Cannot America and England hit upon some scheme to secure even greater advantages to both nations?[9]

Before he left England Hawthorne had partially worked out in his mind a complementary relationship between these two societies which appeared beneficial to both and feasible enough at first. At a banquet which celebrated the dedication of a Free Library in Liverpool, Lord Stanley—whom Hawthorne supposed to occupy "the foremost position among the young men of England"[1]—was called upon to respond to a toast to "The House of Stanley." This is the American Consul's criticism of what he said:

It was a noble subject, giving scope for as much eloquence as any man could have brought to bear upon it; . . . there could not be a richer opportunity for reconciling and making friends betwixt the old system of society and the new; but Lord Stanley did not seem to make anything of it. . . . I wish I could have responded to the 'House of Stanley,' and his lordship could have spoken in my behalf.[2]

Hawthorne persevered in his attempt to hit upon some such reconciliation, despite certain premonitions which crop up in fiction in the old pensioner's earnest warning to Redclyffe to abandon all hope of a transatlantic social alignment.[3]

The result of all this was simple but significant—a rather internationalistic cast of thought which enabled Hawthorne to view Great Britain and the United States not as two separate nations, but as individual stages of a single social growth. On the one hand there was England, standing for the security of traditions; and on the other, facing into the future toward an ideal state of society, was young America. Unlike Henry James, Hawthorne could not set his seal upon the former, and lacking the glandular mysticism of the irrepressible Whitman he was unable to rejoice unreservedly in the latter. Furthermore, he had disavowed the utopian panaceas of the Fourierites and Brook Farmers. His stand in the matter was more democratic than James's, broader and more critical than Whitman's, and more political than that of the experimentalists. On the basis of a heredi-

8. Cf. *ibid.*, pp. 260–61.
9. *Our Old Home*, p. 84. This passage also occurs virtually unaltered in *Doctor Grimshawe's Secret*, pp. 238–39.
1. *English Notebooks*, p. 457.
2. *Ibid.*, p. 459.   3. *Doctor Grimshawe's Secret*, p. 276.

tary attachment and historical divergence, he was tempted to visual-
ize, through a grafting of the traditionalism of England to the progressiveness of America, something like a better social arrangement
for mankind in so far as it was practicable on earth.

Edward Mather, in his recent book on Hawthorne, recognizes the
personal side of Hawthorne's feeling of relationship with England.[4]
And it is true that he made an effort to personalize this relationship
somewhat by attempting to trace his own ancestry back into the
British past.[5] But it is likewise true that there was a more intellectual
motive behind the entire matter of an Anglo-American connection
than the "long-lost cousin"[6] complex which he had found so laughable
in many of his compatriots.[7] "I hope," he enunciated, "that I do not
compromise my American patriotism by acknowledging that I was
often conscious of a fervent hereditary attachment to the native soil
of our forefathers, and felt it to be our own Old Home."[8]

This sense of "hereditary attachment" was certainly "fervent";
moreover, it was enhanced by a genuinely cosmopolitan instinct. "It
is singular," Hawthorne wrote of London, which he adored, "that I
feel more at home and familiar there than even in Boston, or in old
Salem itself. Being the great metropolis of the world, it is every
man's home."[9] But to Americans, lineal descendants of the English, London, its landmarks and venerable monuments, its ancient
cathedrals and its guildhalls had a still more intimate significance.
Hawthorne believed that as an American he had a special right to
be proud of Westminster Abbey, for example, inasmuch as most of
the men who slept in it were, to his way of thinking, America's great
men as well as England's.[1] On at least one important occasion—the
Lord Mayor's dinner at the Mansion-house—he had publicly voiced
this feeling and had been cheered by the assembled guests when he
spoke of the boldness of his compatriots which caused them to regard
London "in the high and comprehensive sense" as being "their metropolis too."[2] The same idea underlies his painstaking letter to the
Provincial Assembly of Lancashire and Cheshire, in which he re-
grets that he must refuse an invitation to be present at one of their
convocations.

4. Edward Mather, *Nathaniel Hawthorne: A Modest Man* (New York, 1940), pp.
281–83.
5. *Ibid.* Compare Hawthorne's letter to James T. Fields, Liverpool, 16 September
1853 (partially printed in *Yesterdays*, pp. 73–74); also, *English Notebooks*, pp. 40, 61–
62, 92, 383, 395.
6. Mather, *Nathaniel Hawthorne*, p. 282.
7. See *Our Old Home*, pp. 30–35; *The Ancestral Footstep* (Works XI), 519; *Doctor Grimshawe's Secret*, p. 170; *English Notebooks*, p. 93.
8. *Our Old Home*, p. 57.   9. *Ticknor Letters*, I, 118.
1. See *English Notebooks*, p. 213.
2. See the report of this speech in *The Illustrated London News*, No. 793, XXVIII
(12 April 1856), 382.

And it seems to me a noble and beautiful testimony to the truth of our religious convictions, that after so long a period, coming down from the past with an ocean between us, the liberal churches of England and America should nevertheless have arrived at the same results; that an American, an offspring of Puritan sires, still finds himself in brotherly relations with the posterity of those free-minded men who exchanged a parting pressure of the hand with his forefathers more than two centuries ago; . . .[3]

Back of these expressions of kinship, however, lay a determination to appropriate the traditional society of England to take the place of the past which America lacked—a past she badly needed to keep her from being top-heavy with too much future and grotesque with too much novelty. And it must be admitted that this determination was partly caused by the natural acquisitiveness of the American, and the accompanying desire to assimilate into his own adolescent worthiness whatever he deemed worthy in others. "What a wonderful land!" exclaimed Hawthorne, in one of his rare moments of exuberance. "It is our forefathers' land; our land; for I will not give up such a precious inheritance."[4] Again and again he tried to find reasons which would authenticate the affiliation which he felt to be his with the land from which his ancestors had emigrated.

My ancestor left England in 1635. I return in 1853. I sometimes feel as if I myself had been absent these two hundred and eighteen years—leaving England just emerging from the feudal system, and finding it on the verge of Republicanism. It brings the two far-separated points of time very closely together, to view the matter thus.[5]

In almost the same phrases, disguised only by the thinnest pretexts of fiction, Hawthorne describes the state of mind of the young American in *The Ancestral Footstep*.[6]

The story of this state of mind is eloquently told in two tragically fragmentary novels. Both Middleton, the hero of *The Ancestral Footstep*, and Redclyffe, as he later became in *Doctor Grimshawe's Secret*, upon reaching England see "indistinctly a thread, to which the thread that he had so long held in his hand—the hereditary thread that an-

3. This letter is printed in *Hawthorne and His Wife*, ii, 61.
4. *English Notebooks*, p. 495.
5. *Ibid.*, p. 92. Cf. *Our Old Home*, p. 83, and *The Ancestral Footstep*, p. 447.
6. *Ibid.*, p. 493. As Hawthorne's letter to Ticknor, 19 January 1855 (*Ticknor Letters*, i, 75), proves, he had been contemplating a novel based upon his experience in England for some little time previous to the first allusion to it in his journals on 12 April 1855, which is the *terminus a quo* given by George P. Lathrop (see his "Introductory Note," *The Ancestral Footstep* [Works xi], 434). Other references to this romance in the English journals for 21 August 1856, and 21 December 1856, show that Hawthorne's mind kept returning to the matter between 1855 and 1858 when *The Ancestral Footstep* was actually commenced in Italy. For a detailed discussion of the composition of this fragment and *Doctor Grimshawe's Secret*, see Edward H. Davidson, *The Last Phase of Nathaniel Hawthorne, 1858–1864*, unpublished dissertation (Yale, 1940), pp. 61–188.

cestor after ancestor had handed down—might seem ready to join on."[7]

It could be only the old, very deepest, inherent nature, which the Englishman, his progenitor, carried over the sea with him, nearly two hundred years before, and which had lain buried all that time under heaps of new things, new customs, new institutions, . . . but, now, his return had seemed to dissolve or dig away all this incrustation, . . . so that he saw the green grass, the hedgerows, . . . with a recognition, and yet a newness. . . . He had, as it were, the quietude of the old man about him, and the freshness of his own still youthful years.[8]

The American felt as if the two threads, one of which he found waiting his arrival in England, "were the two points of an electric chain, which being joined, an instantaneous effect must follow."[9] In all probability had Hawthorne ever been willing to determine the precise nature of that "effect," or the proper means of bringing it about, the plan by which—as he said in the foreword to *Our Old Home*— "I ambitiously proposed to convey more of various modes of truth than I could have grasped by a direct effort"[1] would have been worked through to a finish. Yet, in its existing state it perhaps allows a closer inspection of the allegorical superstructure on which were to be hung these various truths respecting two noble and divergent societies than it would have permitted as a complete product.

The Ancestral Footstep—with its unadorned unity of atmosphere and allegory, and *Doctor Grimshawe's Secret*—with its obliquity of plot and indistinctness of purpose, express through the fictional interrelations of human beings what Hawthorne had elsewhere set forth in exposition. "The general tenor of the book," he wrote in one of the sketches of the English romance which does not appear in his published work, "must illustrate the sympathy and difference between Americans and Englishmen."[2] In another of these unpublished drafts he made the following memorandum: "Here will be ample opportunity of giving all the good and picturesque points of English ancestral homes, English rank, and high society; with the American point of view of them."[3] Again, showing the minuteness and discrimination with which he worked to create the proper symbolical means of conveying these matters, he wrote distractedly:

. . . the feelings of the Democrat and Aristocrat will be brought out in all the stronger contrast, . . . But then, the family secret, partially lost, but

7. *The Ancestral Footstep*, p. 442.
8. *Dr. Grimshawe's Secret*, pp. 205–06.   9. *The Ancestral Footstep*, p. 442.
1. *Our Old Home*, p. 16.
2. Quoted by Davidson, *Last Phase*, Appendix, xix. The original is in the possession of the Massachusetts Historical Society (The Washburn Papers, xix).
3. Quoted, *ibid.*, vii. The original of this draft is in the Huntington Library.

to which the American brings the lost part;—what can that be? . . .
How? how? how? I don't know, really. How in heaven?[4]

The social theory expressed through the allegory of the truncated
English romance occupies a distinct phase of Hawthorne's criticism.
He so openly admired the beautiful existence of the English aristocracy that even in the more material accessories of it he thought he
saw the means whereby people were facilitated in their desire to
lead the right and good life. The absence of the elements of domes-
ticity, heredity, tradition, from his own society made him feel somehow impoverished, for it was obvious that they graced exceedingly
the culture where they were to be found. The assets of democracy
did not quite compensate for this lack, though they might counter-
balance or offset it. It was a romantic reluctance to do without these
last mellowed and felicitous survivals of feudalism that drove Hawthorne to seek out, in fact and in fiction, a scheme whereby the most
enviable contribution of an already moribund social order might be
legitimately appropriated to the uses of a newer one.

Hawthorne's case was built upon the moment of English history
when feudalism had been made to bleed in the name of religious,
political, and civil liberty. Between the social ideals of the men who
subscribed to the beheading of Charles I and those of the republicans
in the New World he was quick to perceive a rough resemblance.
Thereafter, according to his version of it, the revolutionary principles of the regicides became exiled to America, where the reactionary
branch of English society ripened into Jacksonian Democracy after
some two hundred years of independent existence apart from its
kindred branch, whose freedom had slowly broadened down, meantime, among the ancient and traditional modes of life in the old
country. By reasserting its kinship with this conservative branch,
then, Western civilization might reasonably press a claim to those
institutions which its ancestors, by their denunciation of the old
society, had had to leave behind for the delectation of their illiberal
brothers.

Such is the elaborate juridical argument which the fiction was intended to present in allegorical form. The legendary footprint which
Hawthorne had examined at Smithell's Hall in the summer of 1855
developed into the symbol of this estrangement between Englishmen,
resulting in a division of the line, one part of which became American.[5]

4. Quoted, *ibid.*, v.
5. Though Hawthorne thought the actual legend surrounding the bloody print a
good one (see *English Notebooks*, pp. 194–95), it is of some negative significance that
he made no use of it in the proposed English romance, only listing it in the variorum
account of the legend which Redclyffe perused in the Warden's library. *Doctor Grimshawe's Secret*, p. 186.

The tradition had lost, if it ever had, some of its connecting links; but it referred to a murder, to the expulsion of a brother from the hereditary house, in some strange way, and to a Bloody Footstep which he had left impressed into the threshold, as he turned about to make a last remonstrance.[6]

So far a simple expatriation is implicit in the symbol of the bloody step. The precise evil from which it resulted Hawthorne has not yet settled upon in his mind. In *The Ancestral Footstep* he got no further than the suggestion that the matter took place "on account, probably, of a love affair,"[7] in which two brothers had become attached to the same lady. But he did append this modification:

It was rumored, however, or vaguely understood, that the expelled brother was not altogether an innocent man; but that there had been wrong done, as well as crime committed, insomuch that his reasons were strong that led him, subsequently, to imbibe the most gloomy religious views, and to bury himself in the Western wilderness.[8]

This pointed likeness to the American's Calvinistic refugee ancestor is at once made explicit by Doctor Grimshawe's tale of the Puritan regicide on the side of Parliament, the renegade son of a royalist family whose rebellious tread had extended even to the scaffold, where it had become daubed with the king's blood.[9] The complicity of plot and the entangled motivation of *Doctor Grimshawe's Secret* do not allow a casuist much opportunity for evolving a consistent interpretation of the allegory. The fact that no such consistency existed in the first place may be taken as a symptom of the growing creative derangement which Hawthorne was undergoing at the time. But the general direction of his thought is perceptible enough if one ignores the diffuseness in detail and concentrates only upon the broad outlines that are visible throughout. It is not without meaning that the American's ancestor was a revolutionist against the social, political, and religious traditions of which monarchy was the crest. Nor is it to be presumed that he did not bear along with him, in his migration to America, the attributes of his protestation.[1]

6. *The Ancestral Footstep*, p. 444.   7. *Ibid.*, p. 482. Cf. *ibid.*, p. 449.
8. *Ibid.*, p. 444.   9. *Doctor Grimshawe's Secret*, pp. 29–31.
  1. Davidson contends that since the bloody footprint was simply intended "to be the emblem of ancestral forces working for good or evil" (*Last Phase*, p. 764), and since Hawthorne had a "larger purpose" in *Doctor Grimshawe's Secret* than "that of illustrating the ancestral connections between English and American . . ." (*ibid.*, p. 177) which had been his theme in *The Ancestral Footstep*, the bloody print fails to occupy "any sensible or even symbolic place" in the former. (*Ibid.*, p. 764.) This analysis of the symbolical meaning of the footprint is confused to say the least. Moreover, such an over-simplified version of the theme of *The Ancestral Footstep* is hardly adequate to any careful interpretation of this fragment. *The Ancestral Footstep* is as freighted, in proportion to its narrower capacity, as is *Doctor Grimshawe's Secret* with Hawthorne's attempt "to demonstrate the racial, social, and political relations which created such

The estranged line descended in America independently, therefore, and according to social conditions as different and novel as those which its progenitor had once attempted to impose by violence upon his well established world. However, this line might yet retain a subtle hereditary connection with the line which had descended in the old country. In fact, Redclyffe had little more than set foot on English soil when he suffered immediate titillations of this fancy.

. . . he began to feel the deep yearning which a sensitive American—his mind full of English thoughts, . . . his heart of English character and sentiment—cannot fail to be influenced by,—the yearning of the blood within his veins for that from which it has been estranged; . . . from the men who are still so like himself, from these habits of life and thought which (though he may not have known them for two centuries) he still perceives to have remained in some mysterious way latent in the depths of his character, and soon to be reassumed, not as a foreigner would do it, but like habits native to him, and only suspended for a season.[2]

These are the social fetishes to which are tied the threads, in whatever symbolical form, that the American of the nineteenth century—only faintly aware of the innate relationship of the two great lines—sought to join. One thread reaches into the past where it connects with a society based upon a nation's ingrained precedents—the distinctions of class with all their material and moral appurtenances. The other is attached—if such an attachment is not wholly beyond probability—to the future, and to whatever aligns itself with progress. The American has a barely perceptible lien on the first by virtue of hereditary ties. The second is his birthright.

For a while Hawthorne clung tenaciously to the theory that an amalgamation of the old and new societies would have a salutary effect on both, and be of particular benefit to the old. What America lacked was the very stability from which England surfeited. By assuming the best of the British institutions, she would not only consolidate her own way of life, but she would interfuse some of her own excessive vitality into the gradually aging arteries of the patriarchal system. Thus Hawthorne wrote speculatively in *Our Old Home:*

. . . if England had been wise enough to twine our new vigor round about her ancient strength, her power would have been too firmly established ever to yield, in its due season, to the otherwise immutable law of imperial

differences in the national point of view" (Davidson, *op. cit.*, p. 177) of England and America. Middleton's conversation and meditation alone render this fact evident. The symbolism of the print is also clearly emblematic of more specific matters than the vague "crime which could not be expiated for many generations" (*ibid.*). It is equally clear from the very definiteness with which it appears in *Doctor Grimshawe's Secret*, in contrast to Hawthorne's early indecision regarding its details, that the print itself is as "sensible," "symbolic," and organic a part of the later work as it was of the earlier.

2. *Doctor Grimshawe's Secret*, pp. 180–81.

vicissitude. The earth might then have beheld the intolerable spectacle of a sovereignty and institutions, imperfect, but indestructible.[3]

But Hawthorne and his heroes, keenly aware of this power of democracy to act as a social restorative, are a bit dashed by the Englishman's unwillingness to have himself and his institutions thus rejuvenated.

Middleton arrived in England "bringing half of a story, being the only part known in America, to join it on to the other half, which is the only part known in England."[4] It is his belief, as it was Hawthorne's, that his part of the story constitutes, in the words of the Master of the Hospital, "the something that the lost son of the family carried away with him, and by which through these centuries he has impeded the progress of the race,"[5] the race, that is, from which he had departed in exile two centuries ago. Strong within his descendant was "the sentiment that impelled him to connect himself with the old life of England, to join on the broken thread of ancestry and descent, and feel every link well established."[6] Equally strong within him was the prevailing and somewhat flatulent assurance, voiced by the American, "that many English secrets might find their solution in America, if the two threads of a story could be brought together, disjoined as they have been by time and the ocean."[7]

He was fond of talking about the unsuspected relationship that must now be existing between many families in England and unknown consanguinity in the new world, where, perhaps, really the main stock of the family tree was now existing, and with a new spirit and life, which the representative growth here in England had lost by too long continuance in one air and one mode of life.[8]

The ultimate confutation of each of these persuasions in turn is foreshadowed by an Englishman in both *The Ancestral Footstep* and *Doctor Grimshawe's Secret.*

England will never understand America; . . . and whatever you may say about kindred, America is as much a foreign country as France itself. These two hundred years of a different climate and circumstances . . . of the endless intermixture of nationalities in every part of the United States, . . . have created a new and decidedly original type of national character. It is as well for both parties that they should not aim at any very intimate connection. It will never do.[9]

In the face of similar pleas urgently pressed upon him by his feminine counterpart, Hawthorne's American hero remained obdurate, though

3. *Our Old Home*, p. 34.   4. *The Ancestral Footstep*, p. 484.
5. *Ibid.*, p. 450.   6. *Ibid.*, p. 472.
7. *Ibid.*, p. 449.   8. *Doctor Grimshawe's Secret*, p. 238.
9. *The Ancestral Footstep*, pp. 466, 471. See also *Doctor Grimshawe's Secret*, p. 200.

in the long run he was compelled to countenance the wisdom of all who had attempted to dissuade him from seeking fulfillment of his cherished anticipation of a reunion. The British doubtless did not feel incumbent upon them that "breadth of idea" which would have made them as anxious as their descendants to splice threads with America. And unquestionably their intransigence was one reason why the idea of a reconciliation gradually assumed the aspect of impossibility in Hawthorne's mind. But there was another reason for his abandoning all thought of an Anglo-American connection, a more basic reason which had lurked behind his thoughts from the beginning.

The fragmentary romance is a pre-eminent allegorist's account of his effort—and his singular failure—to ascertain some collateral relationship between the society of the Old World and that of the New. He came eventually to the point where he could not sustain his idea without running counter to the lessons of history, and to his own nature as the citizen of a thriving democracy. In the last analysis Hawthorne held to the realization of something irreconcilable, after two hundred years of bifurcated existence, in the societies of England and America. He wrote in one of the unfinished drafts of his English novel: "It must be shown, I think, throughout, that there is an essential difference between English and American character, and that the former must assimilate itself to the latter, if there is to be any union."[1]

There was a threat contained in the institutions of the new society against those of the old. The rudimentary enmity of the rebel ancestor toward the traditional social forms of England was doubtless passed on to his posterity, magnified and intensified by long separation from the older ways. It is the possibility of the former violence being duplicated anew by the perpetrator's unwitting descendant that rouses the aged pensioner to dire imprecations against Redclyffe's plans for entering the ancestral home. " 'Step not across it; there is blood on that threshold! . . . A bloody footstep emerging. Take heed that there be not as bloody a one entering in!' "[2] The Englishmen of the two unfinished sketches are just enough aware of this aberrant quality in the American to sense trouble. They are made vaguely uneasy beneath their hospitable manners by the presence of the hero. The heroine of *The Ancestral Footstep* is fully and intuitively conscious, throughout her admonitions of Middleton to return to his native land where he belongs, of the deep discrepancy between his nature and his temporary aspirations. And Elsie is equally

1. Quoted by Davidson, *Last Phase*, Appendix, xii. The original of this draft is in the Huntington Library.
2. *Doctor Grimshawe's Secret*, p. 276.

concerned over the discrepancy between Redclyffe's hopes and the undisclosed fact.[3]

Hawthorne fancied that the democratic mode of life had developed a vital incompatibility to the traditional institutions which had so long rendered the society of England vertebrate. The patriarchal system, upon which in one way or another the whole structure of English society rested, was menaced by something in the American way of living. This premonition is plainly evinced in the sketches of the unfinished romance.

Hawthorne had first imagined his hero descending upon England with a talisman that spelled destruction for the ancient family.

In my Romance, the original emigrant to America may have carried away with him a family secret, whereby it was in his power (had he so chosen) to have brought about the ruin of the family. This secret he transmits to his American progeny, by whom it is inherited throughout all the intervening generations. At last, the hero of the Romance comes to England, and finds that, by means of this secret, he still has it in his power to procure the downfal[l] of the family.[4]

Symbolic of the essential antagonism between American life and the patriarchal society of England is the fact that Middleton unintentionally causes the family name to become tragically extinguished, by establishing in his own right a claim to it that he promptly resigns.[5] Redclyffe, on the other hand, following part way the career of his predecessor, discovers that he has no hold or effect whatever upon the patrimonial estate. Instead, that hold belongs to an ineffectual, childless old man, an erstwhile inept schoolmaster of New England.

Musing upon the social arrangement that confronted him in England, Redclyffe was moved to nostalgia by his simultaneous recognition of its singular appeal and its imminent doom.

'All this sort of thing is beautiful; the family institution was beautiful in its day. . . . but it is a thing of the past. It is dying out in England; and as for ourselves, we never had it. Something better will come up; but as for this, it is past.'[6]

Despite the fact that there was much in the new social movements from which Hawthorne could draw little confidence and no delight, he nevertheless imputed a higher value to them than to all that which they were daily outdistancing. If he was aesthetically unattuned to modern developments like "the mean and new brick lodging-

3. *Ibid.*, p. 365. In a note Hawthorne wrote: "Elsie must know the baselessness of Redclyffe's claims [i. e., to the family], and be loath to tell him, because she sees that he is so much interested in them."

4. *English Notebooks*, p. 107.   5. *The Ancestral Footstep*, p. 490.

6. *Doctor Grimshawe's Secret*, p. 230.

houses"[7] on the outskirts of Birmingham, he excused his distress with the explanation that what was most worthy and poetic in the new order had not yet been demonstrated by its sages nor celebrated by its bards.

A lodging in a wigwam or under a tent has really as many advantages, when we come to know them, as a home beneath the roof-tree of Charlecote Hall. But, alas! our philosophers have not yet taught us what is best, nor have our poets sung us what is beautifullest, in the kind of life that we must lead; and therefore we still read the old English wisdom, and harp upon the ancient strings. And thence it happens, that, when we look at a time-honored hall, it seems more possible for men who inherit such a home, than for ourselves, to lead noble and graceful lives, . . .[8]

It had once been Emerson's complaint, too, that Americans had not yet chanted "our own times and social circumstance."[9]

We have yet had no genius in America, with tyrannous eye, which knew the value of our incomparable materials, and saw, in the barbarism and materialism of the times, another carnival of the same gods whose picture he so much admires in Homer; then in the Middle Age; then in Calvinism.[1]

But in 1855 Emerson sent Whitman that panegyric upon *Leaves of Grass* which he one day regretted,[2] whereas Hawthorne, in the next decade, still had found no cause for retracting his accusation of remissness in the poets and philosophers of his country.

Hawthorne remained sensible of the delinquencies of the traditional English way of life. In the ivy which literally supported the ruined walls of Kenilworth Castle, he saw an analogue of English social conditions; the plant that clung to the stones "at first only for its own convenience," now bore them up "lest it should be ruined by their fall."[3] He added: "Thus an abuse has strongly grown into a use; and I think we may sometimes see the same fact, morally, in English matters."[4]

In the end he suffered a resurgence of the discontent formerly aroused by the past as it had appeared to him in New England. However, the past of the old country shed a more benign influence over the present than that of Calvinistic New England, so that his vilifications of it were less harsh. He had found, after all, much wisdom in the antiquity of England. It was not quite the same thing, therefore, as

7. *English Notebooks*, p. 120.   8. *Our Old Home*, pp. 146–47.
9. *Emerson's Complete Works* (Riverside Edition; Cambridge, 1883), III, "The Poet," 40.
1. *Ibid.*
2. According to Professor Rusk, Emerson's subsequent silence on the subject of *Leaves of Grass* was due to "the astonishment and dismay of a number of his personal friends." See Ralph L. Rusk (ed.), *The Letters of Ralph Waldo Emerson* (New York, 1939), IV, 520–21.
3. *English Notebooks*, p. 569.   4. *Ibid.*

"that odious and abominable Past"[5] which Holgrave, in *The House of the Seven Gables,* had thought so execrable. But though Holgrave's malice toward everything old is so immitigable that it verges at times upon nihilism,[6] he nevertheless strikes the note to which Hawthorne subsequently returned. Once during a visit to the British Museum Hawthorne impiously wished the Parthenon frieze and the Elgin Marbles "burnt into lime," the ancient mummies "turned to dust," and the Egyptian statues hewn into building-blocks.[7] "The present," he explained, "is burthened too much with the past. . . . I do not see how future ages are to stagger onward under all this dead weight, with the additions that will be continually made to it."[8]

Hawthorne's enjoyment of noble reliquaries like Westminster Hall became overshadowed by ominous prefigurations of their place in the world's future.

I cannot help imagining that this rich and noble edifice has more to do with the past than with the future; . . . the perfect bloom of this great stone flower, growing out of the institutions of England, forebodes that they have nearly lived out their life. It sums up all. Its beauty and magnificence are made out of ideas that are gone by.[9]

And his former elation at the sight of placid English hamlets like Whitnash, which had once seemed to him such necessary places of refuge from the ruptures of modern society,[1] palled on him.

But methinks it must be weary, weary, weary, this rusty, unchangeable village-life, . . . Such a village must, in former times, have been a stagnant pool, and may be little better even now, when the rush of the main current of life has probably created a little movement.[2]

Side by side with his conviction that "a man with a full mind, and objects to employ his affection, might be very happy here,"[3] Hawthorne experienced the contrary mood. "Tedious beyond imagination!" he exclaimed. "Such I think is the final impression on the mind of an American visitor, when his delight at finding something permanent begins to yield to his Western love of change."[4] From a Yankee's point of view there was something sad in all this meaningless round which never brought anything to pass. Redclyffe's ejaculation, "I should go mad of it!" contains Hawthorne's reaction as well. "The stirring blood of the new land,—where no man dwells in his father's house,—where no man thinks of dying in his birthplace," had finally risen in him; and though in another state of mind "the village might have seemed a picture of rural peace, which it would have

5. *Seven Gables,* p. 221.　　6. *Ibid.,* p. 220.　　7. *English Notebooks,* p. 294.
8. *Ibid.*　　　　　　　　9. *Ibid.,* p. 246.　　1. See above, pp. 79–81.
3. *Ibid.,* p. 484.　　　　　4. *Our Old Home,* p. 78.
2. *English Notebooks,* p. 589. Cf. *ibid.,* pp. 483–84.

been worth while to give up ambition to enjoy," now he revolted against all the hereditary pretensions that he had so strongly fancied heretofore.[5] "Better than this," he finally wrote, "is the lot of our restless countrymen, whose modern instinct bids them tend always towards 'fresh woods and pastures new.'"[6]

Hawthorne had acquired at last a passion for "thronged streets and the intensest bustle of human life."[7] He had become bored with the thought of these English people traversing their monotonous cycle generation after generation; so he discarded their unprogressive way of life because it was scheduled shortly to become defunct.

Rather than such monotony of sluggish ages, . . . let us welcome whatever change may come,—change of place, social customs, political institutions, modes of worship,—trusting that, if all present things shall vanish, they will but make room for better systems, and for a higher type of man to clothe his life in them, and to fling them off in turn.[8]

Unfortunately, Hawthorne did not live to determine what the better circumstance might be toward which America was heading. The civil struggle into which the Union was plunged throughout his declining years rendered him creatively impotent to round out this equalitarian ideal. But in *Doctor Grimshawe's Secret* he had reached a decision that left the way open for it. He had decided, after what previous starts we have seen, that the old society was waning of its own accord—was in fact becoming devitalized within itself.[9] It would die its own death without pressure from republican contingencies.

Earlier, it is possible that Hawthorne may have been as undecided upon this point as Middleton, who, "half bewildered, can scarcely tell how much . . . is due to his own agency; how much is independent of him and would have happened had he stayed on his own side of the water."[1] But in time the certainty grew that the great patrimonial system was held together more and more by a comfortable fiction.[2] Generations had vegetated, "rusting out and dying" inertly within its sanctuary.[3] Colcord, as the innocuous and lonely old pensioner, is the living symbol of its inherent frailty. Hawthorne had taken more pains to get the true cast of this symbol than he had taken with any other.[4] No accident made him end the book in a sort

5. *Doctor Grimshawe's Secret*, pp. 220–21.   6. *Our Old Home*, p. 79.
7. *English Notebooks*, p. 591.   8. *Our Old Home*, p. 79.
9. *The Ancestral Footstep*, p. 441. " 'This decay of old families . . . is much greater than would appear on the surface of things.' "
1. *Ibid.*, p. 490.   2. *Ibid.*, p. 441.   3. *Ibid.*, pp. 450–51.
4. Davidson, *Last Phase*, pp. 171–74. Hawthorne discovered that his initial concept of this character, as a "man endowed with great practical ability," hampered the progress of the plot. For his subsequent model of young Colcord in young Bronson Alcott, see *ibid.*, pp. 142–44, and of the old man in George P. Bradford, *ibid.*, pp. 173–74.

of dissipated radiance, shedding on the heir to the ancient mode of living a mere afterglow of dignity.[5]

Having in one attempt experimented with the correlation of the antique system of society with the modern and found it to be unsatisfactory to the second and disastrous to the first, Hawthorne ended by dissociating entirely the old and new. Redclyffe, whose presence at the final discovery in Braithwaite Hall is that of a complete outsider and a foreigner, is Hawthorne's final repudiation of that very social consanguinity with respect to which he and his heroes had entertained so many elaborate fantasies.

Sociologically, it could not have made too much difference whether America's position was analogous to Redclyffe's or Middleton's. For the one had no real connection at all with the parent country; while the other abjured his, though not until he had inadvertently ruined a gentleman who had been bred, and who therefore belonged, in the tradition where he had once catastrophically sought to install himself. The moral which Hawthorne intended Americans to gather from these "petty and wretched circumstances" is the crux of the allegorical pattern.

'Let the past alone: do not seek to renew it; press on to higher and better things,—at all events, to other things; and be assured that the right way can never be that which leads you back to the identical shapes that you long ago left behind. Onward, onward, onward!'[6]

Hawthorne saw—or thought he saw—the will of Providence in a decree that the American must stick to his own last and prevent the old prescriptions and formulas from impeding the business of progress enjoined upon him. This bit of higher social jurisdiction had been made explicitly clear in *Our Old Home*.

After all these bloody wars and vindictive animosities, we have still an unspeakable yearning towards England. When our forefathers left the old home, they pulled up many of their roots, but trailed along with them others, which were never snapt asunder . . . It has required nothing less than the boorishness, the stolidity, the self-sufficiency, the contemptuous jealousy, ...that characterize this strange people, to compel us to be a great nation in our own right, instead of continuing virtually, if not in name, a province of their small island. It might seem their folly, but was really their fate, or, rather, the Providence of God, who has doubtless a work for us to do, in which the massive materiality of the English character would have been too ponderous a dead-weight upon our progress.[7]

There is at least as much to be said for the judgment of Morse, who adds Clifford Pyncheon to the list of Colcord's prototypes. See "Nathaniel Hawthorne Again," *loc. cit.*, p. 310.

5. See *Doctor Grimshawe's Secret*, p. 343.
6. *The Ancestral Footstep*, pp. 488–89.
7. *Our Old Home*, pp. 33–34.

The same Providential motive appears in the fiction as well. Among Middleton's several realizations the one most conspicuous is that which leaves him conscious of "a higher and a deeper law than any connected with ancestral claims," a law that "bade him keep to the country which his ancestor had chosen and to its institutions, and not meddle nor make with England."[8] Before such a law any American who sought hereditary attachment with England stood condemned. Middleton and Redclyffe, not to mention the author himself, were obliged to conclude that the roots of their family tree could not extend beneath an ocean; at most they were but "seedlings" from that tree.[9]

Above all else there had triumphed in Hawthorne an inevitable sense that the American race was "destined to higher purposes" than any other.[1] Using his heroine as spokesman he reasserted his opinion that the bastions of tradition, however striking and secure, should not be allowed to obfuscate the progress of this race.

The American who comes hither and persuades himself that he is one with Englishmen, . . . makes a great mistake; at least, if he is correct in such an idea he is not worthy of his own country, and the high development that awaits it . . . I should think ill of the Americans who, . . . even for the sake of any of those old, delightful ideas of the past, the associations of ancestry, the loveliness of an age-long home, . . . would give up the chance of acting upon the unmolded future of America.[2]

Tradition, the permanence of idea and custom, in England made the individual less outstanding than in America, where a man's family had no ancestral acres and where a whole metropolis might dissolve, like Silver City in the Sierras, and become a ghost town within a single decade. In America the individual was not overshadowed by his family or his society because they were often more ephemeral and of less economic or political importance than he.

It was Hawthorne's ultimate conclusion that an American has a true sympathy only "with what is strong and vivacious to-day; none with what was so yesterday."[3] Tradition was an Englishman's birthright; to an American it was merely a luxury.[4] "Do what he could, Redclyffe still was not conscious of that deep home-feeling which he had imagined he should experience when, if ever, he should come back to the old ancestral place."[5] A more useful and salubrious life awaited him in his own country.[6] And he argued for it in his musing.

8. *The Ancestral Footstep*, p. 475. 9. *Ibid.* 1. *Ibid.*, pp. 503–04.
2. *Ibid.*, pp. 504–05. Compare Elsie's advice to Redclyffe to lead his own life, *Doctor Grimshawe's Secret*, p. 280.
3. *The Ancestral Footstep*, p. 500.
4. *Doctor Grimshawe's Secret*, p. 182. Cf. *Our Old Home*, p. 69: "Old associations are sure to be fragrant herbs in English nostrils, we [Americans] pull them up as weeds."
5. *Doctor Grimshawe's Secret*, p. 284. 6. *Ibid.*, p. 320.

'I am not fit to be here,—I, so strongly susceptible of a newer, more stirring life . . . I, who feel that, whatever the thought and cultivation of
England may be, my own countrymen have gone forward a long, long
march beyond them, not intellectually, but in a way that gives them a
further start. If I come back hither, . . . then for me America has been
discovered in vain. . .[7]

Similarly, Hawthorne himself had protested against the alluring
social scene of England. Seductive as it was in many respects, he
forced himself to believe and to keep in mind that its appeal was to a
less lofty human impulse and a less worthy human need.[8] There were
times when this conviction had been difficult to maintain. The man
who vowed in the event America should "sink" that he would return
"and sink with her"[9] had also told Longfellow that she looked "very
disagreeable and uncomfortable, morally, socially, and climatically"[1]
from the other side of the Atlantic. "I wish we could annex this island
to the Union," he confessed another time, "and that I could have
an estate here in Warwickshire."[2] He did not relinquish these daydreams "without having to repress a deep yearning for that sense of
long, long rest in an age-consecrated home, which he had felt so
deeply to be the happy lot of Englishmen." Nor did he do so without having to remind himself that it was his moral obligation to
abandon these things "as not belonging to his country, nor to the age,
nor any longer possible."[3]

Like his heroes Middleton and Redclyffe, he vacillated between
fascination and contempt for the English patriarchy, and love and
distaste for the uncertain, shifting scene in the extemporized society
of America. But like his heroes, too, he knew his place to be with the
latter, though he might have been the victim of an occasional wish
to find it elsewhere. "The new American was stronger in him than
the hereditary Englishman."[4] The American's lot was in his own land,
and Hawthorne reaffirmed his prediction that it was such a lot as
the world had not yet seen.[5] In the face of the social destiny which
was in store for the United States, he confidently expected that the
faults, the weaknesses, and the errors of his countrymen—cumulative
though they had been—would yet "vanish away like morning mists
before the rising sun."[6] So it was that he dispatched his hero and his
heroine to become "the Adam and Eve of a new epoch, and the fitting
missionaries of a new social faith."[10]

7. *Ibid.*, pp. 297–98.   8. *The Ancestral Footstep*, p. 505.
9. Hawthorne to Ticknor, 15 February 1856, in the Huntington Library.
1. Hawthorne to Longfellow, 22 November 1855.
2. *Ticknor Letters*, I, 98.   3. *The Ancestral Footstep*, p. 518.
4. *Doctor Grimshawe's Secret*, p. 221.   5. *The Ancestral Footstep*, p. 489.
6. *Ibid.*   10. *Ibid.*, p. 490.

V

"Young America"

'But,' said Redclyffe, 'I would not see in my country what I see elsewhere, —the Past hanging like a mill-stone round a country's neck, or encrusted in stony layers over the living form; so that, to all intents and purposes, it is dead.'

Redclyffe to Colcord: *Doctor Grimshawe's Secret*

THE new social faith of which Hawthorne's hero and heroine were to be the high priest and priestess was, of course, equalitarianism. Democratic standards were the prime requisite for a higher type of social culture and civilization than that which still existed in the Old World. The rivalry of the old and new orders was for Hawthorne, as for many of his fellows, a national issue. America stood for democracy. Democracy, in fact, *was* America. With this belief, and with a truly evangelical desire to spread abroad the gospel of equalitarianism, there arose at the mid-century a movement known as Young America.

Alice and Middleton, in *The Ancestral Footstep,* are young Americans.[1] In the crudest terms, the object of those belonging to or in any way associated with this movement was the world-wide improvement of society through the pervasive influence for democracy of the United States. At a moment when the young republic was still seeking *lebensraum,* and one kind of pioneer was pushing westward, another kind, the civic pioneer, with even greater illusions of American grandeur, looked forward to seeing his country rise to an international position where she could impress the virtues of her way of life upon the benighted rest of the world.

This ambition served as an *esprit de corps* not only for a relatively small number of social and political adventurers who constituted the actual organization of Young America, but it managed also to unite a peripheral group of disciples, like Hawthorne, who partook of its sentiments without actively engaging in their dissemination. Hawthorne's position abroad proved especially favorable for observing those historical events of Pierce's administration which seemed to conspire in strengthening democracy's international prestige. It was in England that he came to uphold Young America, and it is through his endorsement of the movement that one sees best how far-reaching

1. The term Young America is used by Hawthorne in a letter to Ticknor, 9 November 1855. (*Ticknor Letters,* I, 115.) The name lingered in his mind; see *Sketches,* p. 312, n. 1.

he and so many of his more ebullient countrymen intended the doctrine of equalitarianism to be.

Almost never has a great people come so unanimously into a consciousness of its collective social mission as did the citizens of the United States during the course of the nineteenth century. Throughout the middle of this century in particular, there was an exaggerated confidence that the munificent civilization of Europe was dwindling away and that sooner or later the societies of that continent must either be taken in tow by the United States or left to founder irrecoverably in the wake of democracy.

Even James Fenimore Cooper, before his Tory prejudices became jarred by Jacksonian Democracy, had written to the United States from England in the early part of the century: "Rely on it, in all the essentials of true civilization, you are a century in advance of every other country."[2] Much later the "yawp" of Walt Whitman was sounded on the subject. "Thirty years from this date," he cried in 1846, "America will be confessed the *first nation* on the earth."

For the time will surely come—that holy millennium of liberty—when the 'Victory of endurance born' shall lift the masses of the down-trodden of Europe, and make them achieve something of that destiny which we may suppose God intends eligible for mankind. And this problem is to be worked out through the people, territory, and government of the United States.[3]

"Let the Old World wag on under its cumbrous load of form and conservatism," Whitman vouchsafed benignantly, "we are of a newer, fresher race and land. And all we have to say is, to point to fifty years hence and say, Let those laugh who win!"[4] The Democratic convention meeting at Baltimore in May, 1852, adopted this resolution:

. . . that with the recent development of this grand political truth,—of the sovereignty of the people and their capacity and power for self-government, which is prostrating thrones and erecting republics on the ruins of despotism in the Old World,—we feel that a high and sacred duty is devolved, with increasing responsibility, upon the Democratic party of this country . . . to sustain and advance among us constitutional liberty, . . . and uphold the Union as it was, the Union as it is, and the Union as it shall be.[5]

Later, in New England, Ralph Waldo Emerson wrote in Miltonic prose the following testament:

The office of America is to liberate, to abolish kingcraft, priestcraft, caste, monopoly, to pull down the gallows, to burn up the bloody statute-book,

2. J. F. Cooper, ed., *Correspondence of James Fenimore-Cooper* (New Haven, Yale University Press; 1922), I, 274.

3. Walt Whitman, *The Gathering of the Forces*, C. Rodgers and John Black, eds. (New York, 1920), I, 27–28. An editorial in the *Brooklyn Daily Eagle*, 24 November 1846.   4. Editorial for the *Brooklyn Daily Eagle*, 8 February 1847, *ibid.*, I, 33.

5. Edward Stanwood, *A History of the Presidency* (Boston, 1898), p. 235.

to take in the immigrant, to open the doors of the sea and the fields of the earth,—to extemporize government in Texas, in California, in Oregon,—to make provisional law where statute law is not ready.[6]

For, as he confided in his *Journal* at this time, "It is not a question whether we shall be a nation, or only a multitude of people; but whether we shall be the new nation, the leading Guide and Lawgiver of the world, as having clearly chosen and firmly held the simplest and best rule of political society."[7]

It was a period in which a primal faith flourished that American institutions were destined to supplant the effete institutions of monarchical Europe. And where did Hawthorne stand upon such a scene? He had suspected strength in certain of the ancient modes of English living. Like Whitman he had considered Americans the "descendants" of the British.[8] He had found in the exhausting pace of American life something antipathetic to his temperament and to his moral sense. In a word, he had been tempted to give the Old World its due in more than one instance and would no doubt have met someone like Henry James half-way, had he been less equalitarian in his social theory. Had it not been for the "democratic strain in his composition"[9] to which James himself has called attention, he might one day, perhaps, have seen through to a finish that irresolute idea of an Anglo-American attachment which assumed partial shape in two projected novels. But behind such quiet comments as the one he made to Ticknor, prognosticating the eventual doom of an older civilization, lay an affiliation with the new American impulse that was just as real and politically more alert than Whitman's or Emerson's.

After all the slander against Americans, there is no people worthy even to take the second place behind us, for liberality of idea and practice. The more I see of the rest of the world, the better I think of my own country . . . and, thank God, England's day is past forever.[1]

Thus Hawthorne had written in 1855, and he added more strongly, "I have such a conviction of the decline and fall of England, that I am about as well satisfied as if it had already taken place."[2]

6. *Journals of Ralph Waldo Emerson*, x, 195.

7. *Ibid.* See also *The Young American* (1844). Emerson's by no means uncritical patriotism reached its highest level of optimism after the successful close of the Civil War, in such essays as *Resources, Civilization, Progress of Culture*, and *The Fortune of the Republic*. For a discussion of his attitude to progress in general, see Mildred Silver, "Emerson and the Idea of Progress," *American Literature*, xii (March, 1940), 1–19.

8. Whitman wrote, in an editorial for the *Brooklyn Daily Eagle*, 13 December 1847, *loc. cit.*, 1, 47): "Why should they [the English] not record with pride, the great courage and dauntless bravery, and unequalled perseverance, of *their descendants?*"

9. Henry James, *Hawthorne* (New York, 1887), p. 47.

1. Hawthorne to Ticknor, 12 October 1855. *Ticknor Letters*, I, 109.

2. *Ibid.* This curious belief that England neared the brink of revolution had been prevalent for some time. Prince Metternich told the American historian George Ticknor,

The young republic upon which the future of the world depended certainly held the fate of Great Britain in her hands.[3] In fact, so eager was Hawthorne to be an eye-witness of the millennium that he hailed with righteous approbation any aggressive action which the United States took, as bringing the world one step nearer the true social circumstances of democracy. "I should like well," he confessed, "to be superseded in my consular duties by the arrival of a Yankee Commodore or General."[4] The root of such sentiments as these was a resolute Americanism, not the least stimulus for which was Hawthorne's relationship to the most progressive wing of the Democratic party, the very political translation into action of all those ideals that pertained to self-assertive America.

Hawthorne's connections with the movement called "Young America," slight though they were, had a marked influence on his thinking. While he was never an actual participant in the movement itself, his references to it and his relations with one or two of its more notorious participants suffice to show that in spirit he condoned the purposes, the ambitions, the set of ideals for which it stood. This, indeed, is the important thing; for the movement as such was of short duration, while as a slogan and as an attitude of mind it remained for some time stamped upon the self-consciousness of American society.[5]

Superficial though it may have been, Hawthorne's association with the personnel of "Young America" is indicative of his political sympathies. John L. O'Sullivan, one time editor of the *Democratic Review*—a magazine which was recognized as the organ of the progressive wing of the Democratic party even before Young America took it over[6]—belonged to an Eastern group closely related to the movement. Hawthorne had contributed frequently to the *Democratic Review*,[7] and largely through the initiative of Mrs. Hawthorne O'Sullivan himself later became an associate of the family.[8]

On one occasion during his consulship Hawthorne met Stephen A.

---

in 1836, that such was his profoundest expectation. See George Ticknor, *Life, Letters and Journals*, edited by G. S. Hillard (Boston, 1876), II, 15.

3. Hawthorne to Ticknor, 9 November 1855. *Ticknor Letters*, I, 113.

4. Hawthorne to Ticknor, 26 October 1855. *Ibid.*, I, 111.

5. Merle E. Curti, "'Young America,'" *The American Historical Review*, XXXII (October, 1926), 54–55.

6. In 1852, George N. Sanders, chief source of energy for Young America, bought and edited the magazine, using it as a political medium through which to champion the nomination of Stephen A. Douglas as Young America's candidate for the Presidency.

7. Among the pieces which appeared in this magazine were *Howe's Masquerade* (May, 1838), *Lady Eleanore's Mantle* (December, 1838), *The Procession of Life* (April, 1843), *The Artist of the Beautiful* (June, 1844), *Rappaccini's Daughter* (December, 1844).

8. For Hawthorne's rather hypercritical estimate of O'Sullivan, see *Love Letters*, II, 240–43.

Douglas, whom he described as "the chosen man of young America" and a person who struck him as being of "uncommon dignity of manner, without seeming to aim at it, being free and simple in manners. I judge him to be a very able man," he added, "with the Western sociability and free-fellowship."[9] But by far the most noteworthy acquaintance was with George N. Sanders himself, the impulse and genius of the movement.

Sanders was acting consul in London during the early part of Hawthorne's consulship at Liverpool. He was appointed to the office by Pierce in June, 1853, and took over his station on the following November. Immediately he set about establishing intimate relations with the social nonconformists of Europe who had fled for refuge to the English capital. Before long the London consulate had become the virtual headquarters of radical social reformers like Kossuth, Mazzini, and Garibaldi, whose activities Sanders facilitated by the clandestine practice of using the official dispatch bag of the American legation for sending personal communications. These revolutionaries in the cause of social and political freedom had on one occasion been graced at a dinner party by no less a dignitary than the American minister, Buchanan, who justified his presence there with the statement that he should have felt himself "degraded as an American citizen to have refused the invitation of a friend, simply because men who have suffered in the cause of liberty were to be present."[1] Similar invitations to Hawthorne and his wife to stay with the Sanders family in London were never accepted;[2] though Hawthorne later reciprocated (with motives that were perhaps similar to Buchanan's) by urging the Sanders family to make use of his home before leaving England. "I deeply regret that your wife and children should have returned without becoming acquainted with mine . . . come and stay at my house in the interim, the longer the better. I live at Rock Park, Rock Ferry, and Mrs. Hawthorne will do her best to make you comfortable. Do come."[3]

In the short space of a few months Sanders exerted himself strenuously in behalf of democracy in Europe, and achieved widespread

9. *English Notebooks,* p. 35; cf. *Passages From The English Note-Books,* p. 464.

1. Dispatch to Secretary of State Marcy, 24 February 1854. See *Marcy Papers,* p. 48, in the Library of Congress.

2. See Hawthorne's letters to Sanders, dated 1 February, 11 May, 1 July 1854. *The Political Correspondence of . . . George N. Sanders,* catalogue of public sale, 13 May 1914, by American Art Galleries, New York, pp. 70, 73, 75.

3. *Ibid.,* p. 76. This letter is dated 23 November 1854. Hawthorne's correspondence with Sanders during the brief interval from November, 1853, to November, 1854, consists of eight letters of which there is record. (See *ibid.,* pp. 69–76.) The subject matter is varied: some of the letters have to do with private affairs such as Hawthorne's projected visit to London; still others relate to official business. One of the most important is the letter which Hawthorne wrote concerning Kossuth and the question of American slavery (quoted below, chapter VII), which is in the Berg Collection.

notoriety by his letters to English and American newspapers, among which was an urgent message to the President of the Swiss Confederation charging Switzerland with "certain solemn responsibilities" like those incumbent upon the great republic in the western hemisphere, "our own America."[4] But these manifestos of republicanism in Europe and proclamations for the political program of men like Louis Kossuth, so open and so lacking the curb of discretion appropriate to an American official abroad, were not long in working to Sanders' discredit. In February, 1854, the Senate, some of whose members were living evidence of Sanders' faculty for making enemies, refused to confirm his nomination as consul in London.

The disillusionment of the best known radicals at this "untoward occurrence" which, as Garibaldi wrote, had put a cruel mortification upon "the model of generous men (sympathizing in soul with my unhappy land)," was heartfelt. Sanders' removal was deemed a "hard and mischievous blow" at democracy's prospects in Europe. It looked as though the cause of the down-trodden European societies had been ignominiously deserted by the country which was the mightiest exponent of political liberty.

To the commiseration of famous exiles like Kossuth, Mazzini, Garibaldi, was added that of Hawthorne. "I will not try to express to you," he wrote, "my regret and mortification at the action of the Senate on your case."[5] A little less than two months later he made an even stronger commitment. "I hope to Heaven Pierce will do the right and honorable thing in your case," he told Sanders. "If he follows his own nature, he will do it."[6] But Pierce himself had been upset by Sanders' epistolary excesses, not the least of which was the anarchistic letter in which, without turning a hair, he had advocated in all seriousness the outright assassination of Louis Napoleon.[7]

No doubt Hawthorne had reason to suppose that Pierce condoned Sanders and the main principles which he exemplified. For it is improbable that he was fully cognizant of the aberrations—or of their seriousness—in Sanders' conduct as a responsible agent of the United States government. Had he been so, he would doubtless have written more circumspectly. So far as he was aware, however, Sanders had been the President's own choice for the London post, and the American legislature had again interfered with the policy of the administration.

For his own part Hawthorne was aligned with Sanders on a double score, not only through personal sympathy for many of his principles,

4. The London *Times*, 21 August 1854.
5. Hawthorne to Sanders, 11 May 1854. *The Political Correspondence of . . . George N. Sanders*, p. 73.
6. *Ibid.*, p. 75. This letter is dated 1 July 1854.
7. See M. E. Curti, " 'Young America,' " *loc. cit.*, p. 52, n. 107.

but also through their mutual accord with the administration, which Hawthorne believed to be amenable in its turn to the aspirations of the whole Young America movement. Nor was this notion wholly unfounded. When Douglas failed to receive the Democratic nomination, Pierce was seized upon as a "discreet representative of Young America."[8] Douglas himself campaigned for Pierce during the summer of 1852, using the ideals of Young America for his talking points.[9] Even the *Democratic Review,* organ of that body, had indicated Pierce's capacity for fulfilling its requirements on the grounds, first of all, that he was not an "Old Fogy."[1]

We believe that Franklin Pierce possesses all the attributes capable, when developed, of fulfilling the type of president we have indicated. . . . No man of ordinary shrewdness can be insensible to the fact that he is the candidate of progress, the nominee and the chosen son of young democracy . . . the creation and first palpable effect of young America.[2]

Moreover, the platform drafted by the Democratic party at its Baltimore convention corresponded so significantly with Young American projects that it too was extravagantly welcomed by the *Democratic Review* as "the sweeping and whole-souled declaration of the Democracy," containing "everything needful for a platform."[3]

Thus, in underwriting the Baltimore platform Hawthorne had automatically fallen in line with the declarations of Young America. And in respect to domestic policy, at least, he professed entire satisfaction not only with Pierce's position regarding the differences between North and South, but also with an equivocating letter in which Sanders exposed his willingness to side-step completely the moral issue of slavery in the United States, when it threatened the concentrated unity of a nation that was singled out to be the tutelary genius of oppressed peoples.[4]

At the same time Young America espoused an ambitious, not to say vivid, foreign policy. Its assertion by the Pierce administration received no more fervent approbation from anyone than it did from Hawthorne. He was moved even to discard his somewhat artful role of disinterested spectator and exert a certain amount of initiative in forwarding to his country occasional scraps of information which he had picked up in connection with his official adventures at Liverpool, and which contained not a little suggestive value in his eyes. For example, Young America had recognized for some time that without a powerful and efficient navy and merchant service the United States' foreign policy could be aggressive only on paper, and it had accordingly sponsored a naval building program in order to

8. See The New York *Herald,* 10 June 1852.
1. *Democratic Review,* xxx (June, 1852), 485.
3. *Ibid.,* p. 491.
9. *Ibid.,* 11 September 1852.
2. *Ibid.,* p. 492.
4. See below, chapter vii.

supply the gaping deficiencies which existed.[5] To this end Hawthorne contributed voluntarily a sample of the candles used by the
unequalled fleet of Great Britain, a set of plans of an invention for
keeping a sinking ship afloat,[6] and long and grave letters to Secretary of State Cass, Senator Charles Sumner, and others, lamenting
the deplorable and unworthy condition of the American merchant
marine, and urging that the steps which he indicated be taken under
immediate cognizance to insure some improvement in the personnel
manning American vessels.[7] In a letter to Secretary of State Marcy,
he compared assiduously the provisions of the new British Passenger
Act "which came into operation on the 1st of October instant," and
observed that "its provisions generally are of a more stringent character, than those of our own Passenger Act of 3 March 1855."

Hawthorne kept a diligent and disparaging eye on all matters
promising to bring discredit upon the American mercantile service
abroad. Repeatedly there occur in his official notes to shipmasters
phrases like these: "Such a practice is . . . calculated to bring so
much discredit & inquiry to our commerce, that I am sure it cannot
be sanctioned to you."[8] Or again, "As I said to you yesterday, this
kind of thing is driving the best men out of our vessels, and I must
request you to put a stop to it."[9] But at the same time that he represented American shipmasters as being "far superior to the same
class of Englishmen,"[1] he deplored, notwithstanding, the system
which brutalized them. A weak navy and merchant marine might
one day oblige aggressive American diplomats to eat their own foreign policy, word by word. No Young American realized this more
than Hawthorne, who wrote acidly to Sumner: "I should like to know
what is to become of us at sea, in case of war—but *that* you don't
care about."[2]

In addition to considering matters of pure utility, a habit of his
countrymen which he had once abhorred, he turned his attention to
means of fostering the cultural development and reputation of the
young democracy. Enclosing an advertisement of an international
competition for architects to design new government buildings in
London, Hawthorne wrote to Secretary of State Marcy:

5. See "Our Mission—Diplomacy and Navy," *Democratic Review,* xxxi (July,
1852), 33–43.

6. Hawthorne to Charles Sumner, 1 March, 1855. The original is in the Sumner
Collection of the Widener Library at Harvard.

7. For a full discussion of Hawthorne's efforts in behalf of naval reform see above,
chapter ii.

8. Hawthorne to Captain Berry, Ship *Courser,* 26 June 1855. *Official Correspondence.*

9. Hawthorne to Captain Blake, Ship *Pelicanstate,* 6 July 1855. *Ibid.*

1. Hawthorne to Charles Sumner, 23 May 1855. (Sumner Collection). Compare his
letter to Monckton Milnes, 30 July 1859.

2. Hawthorne to Charles Sumner, *ibid.*

I have the honor to forward herewith copy of an advertisement appearing in the London Globe & submit whether it would not be well to give it publicity in America.

The premiums will no doubt be handsome enough to be worth competing for, & competition for a building of such magnitude, cannot fail to have a highly improving effect on the competitors, & tend to advance the art of Architecture in America.[3]

As an organization for the world-wide promulgation of the principles and the superiority of democratic society Young America died a gradual death not long after Sanders' recall from the London Consulate. At this time, too, Hawthorne's contact with the movement and its participants ceased for good. But though the organization became dissipated, the ideas, and above all the self-confidence and spirit upon which they had risen to prominence had been too instinct with much of the ideology of the new democracy not to remain in force. Young Americanism was not a cliché, nor a conclave of the socially or politically elect who had ostracized themselves for the sake of keeping their opinions immaculate in the midst of all others. It grew out of a popular tendency, and it became, at its best, the representative ideology of many Americans who had never read its literature, nor known its chief professors, nor even dreamed of its existence.

If Cushing, the Attorney General, could be accused by his contemporaries of Young Americanism,[4] and if Young America itself could consider Pierce its president, Hawthorne's alignment with the movement is equally obvious. In somewhat less oriflamme colors he had painted the same picture of the function of democratic society under Pierce's guidance. The "sacred Union," he wrote, was "the immovable basis from which the destinies, not of America alone, but of mankind at large, may be carried upward and consummated." It was thus, he finally concluded, that "men stand together, . . . awaiting the new movement in advance which all these tokens indicate."[5] Scarcely more oracular in accent was the pronouncement made by Young America:

America springs to her position among the nations, and the oppressed of the earth . . . will derive new strength, and higher and more certain hopes, from him whom a great nation has sought out in the valleys of the

3. *Official Correspondence,* 3 October 1856. The advertisement alluded to was made by Alfred Austin, Secretary Office of Works &c., Whitehall. It was dated 20 September 1856, and announced that commissioners of her Majesty's Works and Public Buildings were "prepared to receive Designs from Architects of all countries" for new government buildings to be erected on a site between Whitehall and the New Palace at Westminster.

4. M. E. Curti, "Young America," *loc cit.*, p. 50.

5. *Life of Franklin Pierce* (Works, xii), 436.

White Mountains, to lead its youngest and its greatest generation to the battle for the world's liberty, and to the fulfilment of its magnificent destiny.[6]

With the inflammable ambitions of these extremists, these youthful and highly imaginative members of his party, Hawthorne was in direct contact. He was far from conservative. In fact he was no more conservative in his faith respecting the social righteousness of democracy than Walt Whitman, or even the most ardent and passionate supporters of Young Americanism: only less mystical than the first, a little less evangelical than the last, and more inhibited than either. Above all, he shared their conviction that the future was about to disclose over the entire globe the manifest, magnificent destiny of the United States as the chosen nation of a new and surpassing social order.

On the European side of the Atlantic this conviction was held more stubbornly by Hawthorne during the middle of the decade of the fifties than by many of his contemporaries at home. It is true that he suffered minor distresses over the calumnious attacks upon Pierce, the hysterical propaganda into which the Kansas-Nebraska Bill had plunged all parties, and the general internal discord of which he was kept remotely conscious by American newspapers. But his optimism and his confidence in the virility of America's democratic society withstood those slight disturbances. He sent his publisher a perverse refusal to consider such upsets of major political or social importance.

Pray do not be so hopeless about our political concerns. We shall grow and flourish, in spite of the devil. Affairs do not look so very bad, at this distance, whatever they may seem to you who are in the midst of the confusion. For my part, I keep a steadfast faith in the destinies of my own country, and will not be staggered, whatever happens.[7]

Fortunately for Hawthorne's peace of mind the future was hidden, and he himself was blinded where domestic ruptures were concerned by America's diplomatic maneuvering on the international scene. Democracy's world-wide reputation, he thought, had so far never quite measured up to its actual worth. He had stipulated that it was a part of the duty of a foreign official like the consul to advertise, by the example both of his private and official conduct, the virtues of the society from which he was accredited.

But he was gratified most of all during his consulship by a historical incident which, according to his interpretation of it, gave unexpected international publicity to the efficacy of democracy. That incident was the culmination of the long simmering trouble between Great

6. *Democratic Review*, xxx (June, 1852), 492.
7. *Ticknor Letters*, ii, 19. This letter is dated 20 June 1856.

Britain and the United States over the Central American settlement represented in the Clayton-Bulwer Treaty. The Anglo-American bickerings over this affair were no mere diplomatic wrangle to Hawthorne. He seized upon them as the physical manifestation of a rivalry between two systems of society. The fresh and vigorous democratic order was jostling for its rightful place in the sun, while a crotchety aristocratic society, with unfounded and blundering conceit, attempted superciliously to brush aside the upstart. The whole matter thus bears upon Hawthorne's social criticism because it contains what he took to be democracy's bid for international recognition, and because the successful prosecution of the American case symbolized democracy's power to supplant social prejudice or political injustice throughout the world.

Nowhere is the coincidence of Hawthorne's social theory and that of Young America more apparent than in the matter of American foreign policy. Here Hawthorne was in whole-hearted agreement both with the Pierce administration and the Young Americans— whose views concurred though their methods and the irresponsible grandiosity of their aims did not. During the controversy between his own and the English government, arising from what the *Democratic Review* had acclaimed as "the re-assertion, vigorously and practically, of the Monroe doctrine in Central America and on the Isthmus,"[8] it was to Young America that Hawthorne looked for the proper response to the whole dispute; and it was on Pierce as Young America's president that he bestowed the credit for it when it came.

The attention of the United States and Great Britain had for some time been directed intermittently toward Central America. The imperfect settlement of Central American problems by the Clayton-Bulwer Treaty had failed to harmonize the conflicting interests of the two governments. Each was inclined, therefore, to view with suspicion any move which the other might make in respect to this territory, where the concern of both countries in business and transportation was implicated. The anti-British sentiments of the Pierce government were consequently roused by the high-handed occupation of the Bay Islands, in the summer of 1852, by crown officials. This maneuver was an outright violation of the terms of the Clayton-Bulwer treaty, and in direct opposition to the principles laid down by the Monroe Doctrine, which Pierce's inaugural address had reaffirmed.[9] A sense of outrage—enhanced by the spirit that had fanned Young America into flames—quickly spread over the country; and with the advent of the new administration a stern diplomatic stand against England was anticipated. However, the subsequent earnest

8. *Democratic Review*, xxx (June, 1852), 492.
9. Roy Franklin Nichols, "The Democratic Machine: 1850–1854," *loc. cit.*, p. 183.

efforts of Buchanan, as American ambassador in London, to arbitrate the matter with Lord Clarendon in a reciprocally satisfactory manner failed. At the base of the American attitude lay the principles of the Monroe Doctrine and an unwillingness to brook British intolerance of American foreign policy. Lord Clarendon, for his part, declined to continue negotiations on the ground that England could not consider the Monroe Doctrine a statute of international law.[1]

The Pierce administration, with its expansive plans, might have remained thus deadlocked with the government of the belligerent Palmerston had it not been for the moral advantage given the Secretary of State, William Marcy, by the irregular conduct of John Crampton, the British minister. Great Britain in direct violation of American neutrality laws had authorized Crampton to proceed with a project for recruiting men in the large cities of the United States to be used by the British army in the Crimean War.[2] This flagrant disregard for American neutrality rights immediately caused another flurry in the relations of the two nations.

The situation became further strained by the rumor that Great Britain was sending into American waters a large naval detachment. According to Lord Clarendon the fleet had been intended for several reasons, one of which was to prepare for the mythical expedition planned by Celtic sympathizers in the United States to invade Ireland. Of this fabulous adventure Hawthorne wrote to Ticknor:

There is a strange idea, on this side of the water, that we are going to send a filibustering expedition against Ireland!! If we have any design of the kind, I go in for attacking England at once; and there is very little (in the way of fortifications) to hinder an American fleet from sailing up the Mersey. . . . The truth is, I love England so much that I want to annex it, and it is by no means beyond the scope of possibility that we may do so, though hardly in my time.[3]

Of all the conceptions of "manifest destiny" and American expansion which ever prevailed, Hawthorne's, semi-serious though it is, is hard to equal for extravagance. It leaves no doubt of his stand in the foregoing controversy.

As a matter of fact Hawthorne received gleefully the first rumors of a war between England and the United States. He wrote to Mrs. Hawthorne in November, 1855, telling her of a letter said to have been written with Buchanan's cognizance, which informed Americans in England of "the breach of treaties, and a determination on the part of the British Government to force us into war." He goes on

1. See John B. Henderson, Jr., *American Diplomatic Questions* (New York, 1901), pp. 127–29.
2. For a full account of the enlistment controversy, see Samuel Flagg Bemis (ed.), *The American Secretaries of State . . .* (New York, 1928), VI, 237–62.
3. *Ticknor Letters*, II, 110–11.

with incredible assurance: "We hold the fate of England in our hands, and it is time we crushed her . . . not," he adds cautiously, "but what she has still vitality enough to do us a good deal of mischief, before we quite annihilate her."[4]

But he wrote to Ticknor a few days later in a less magniloquent fashion. His more deliberate judgments, when distinguished from those which are brought out of hand by a high pitch of excitement not characteristic of him, reveal a cool and reasonably accurate appraisal of the situation. He did not look forward to war, but he heartily hoped that his government would not "bate an inch of honor for the sake of avoiding it;"[5] particularly when England lay conveniently at the mercy of her youthful rival. Here at last was the moment for Young Americanism to be resplendent. Hawthorne wrote to Ticknor:

I shall wait with much interest for the response of Young America to the hostile demonstrations on the part of England. . . . John Bull is now heartily afraid of the consequences of what he has done, and will gladly seize any decent method of getting out of the scrape. If we do not fight him now, I doubt whether he will ever give us another chance. He has partly learned what he himself is, and begins to have some idea of what we are. There has been a great change, on both these points, since I first came to England.[6]

Actually, what Hawthorne expected was to see Crampton handed his passports. "I am mistaken in Franklin Pierce," he had written his wife on the third of November, "if Mr. Crampton has not already been ejected from Washington."[7] It was plainly enough, he felt, the function of any government in a country with America's immodest propensity for expansion—a physical manifestation of the vitality of the democratic mode of living—to confirm its strength to the world. By February, 1856, he was writing Ticknor,

What do you think of the prospects of war? . . . I will disown Frank Pierce if he backs out one inch, (but I am sure he never will,) and I would rather see America sink (in which case I will come back and sink with her) than have her give up her just rights.[8]

And with Young America's precocious poise he added, "There is no danger of our sinking."[9]

At the same time he was inclined to believe in the wisdom of getting along with John Bull as peaceably as possible, confident that

4. *Love Letters*, II, 234–35.   5. *Ticknor Letters*, I, 113.

6. *Ibid.*, I, 115–16. This letter is dated 9 November 1855. Compare his letter to the same a fortnight later (23 November 1855). "The English people will not let their Government go to war with us . . ." *Ibid.*, I, 116.

7. *Love Letters*, II, 237.

8. This letter dated 15 February 1856 is in the Huntington Library.

9. *Ibid.*

the capitulation of England's outmoded institutions to the robust democratic society of America would be only a matter of time.[1] To this end he actively devoted himself in his speeches at public dinners. Early in 1856 he told his publisher, ". . . my soul is in peril already with the lies I have told at the mayor's dinner-table, in regard to the good feeling of America towards England."[2] Nevertheless, at the risk of damnation he continued to express pacific sentiments. In his journal for 4 April 1856, he gives a report of a dinner at the Milton Club, which was attended by several prominent newspaper men of the day, among whom he mentions the proprietor and editor of *The Illustrated London News,* Dr. Charles Mackay. Sitting next Mackay Hawthorne became acquainted with him during the dinner.

I made another little bit of a speech, too, in response to something that was said in reference to the present difficulties between England and America, and ended with (as a proof that I deemed war impossible) drinking success to the British Army, . . . the applause was vociferous, and I could hear them whispering about the table, 'Good! Good.'[3]

Four days later at a banquet given by the Lord Mayor of London, he made another speech of a similar nature, though in more momentous circumstances. Mackay's paper carried the following account of it on Saturday.

In regard to the sentiments entertained in that assembly respecting his country, he should say that it was now some time since he left his native land, and it must be greatly changed in its pervading sentiments if it was not ready to respond, as it ever had done, to every friendly demonstration regarding England (Cheers). He believed there was never yet a kind word spoken or a kind action performed by an Englishman towards an American that the American was not ready to respond to by an action or a word at least as kind, if not more so.[4]

Notwithstanding Hawthorne's comments to the contrary,[5] this seems to have been a reasonably truthful representation of his attitude. Doubtless he was a trifle chagrined the next day to discover how exuberant he had been in expressing an international good will of which England had been systematically taking advantage.

1. See *Ticknor Letters,* I, 80. This letter is dated 16 February 1855.
2. *Ibid.,* I, 123.   3. *English Notebooks,* p. 312.
4. *The Illustrated London News,* No. 793, XXVIII (12 April 1856), 382.
5. See *English Notebooks,* p. 323: "This speech was sent down to Liverpool by electric telegraph, posted in the exchange, and has since been printed all over the kingdom; and, in the shape in which it appears before the public, it is nothing short of ridiculous." Cf. *Ticknor Letters,* II, 14. But Hawthorne was nearly always dissatisfied with the newspaper accounts of his speeches. He complains similarly of the reports of a speech which he gave in response to a toast by Richard Monckton Milnes, at a banquet in Liverpool celebrating the dedication of a Free Library, 15 April 1857. See *English Notebooks,* p. 460.

I have read various reports of what I said, none of them correct, all ob-
literating the best points, and all exaggerating the sentiment of international kindness, which I myself had too strongly expressed.[6]

He would, of course, have been unwilling to see his kindness exaggerated to the point where it could be construed as timidity in the
face of English superiority. Such superiority, he believed, existed
only in the English mind, and he welcomed the growing signs of its
diminution.[7] Consequently, the deliberate attempt to leave American
friendliness dependent upon the British attitude can only be regarded
as his own method of fostering amicable relations at the same time
that he subtly inserted his conscientious objection to England's past
failure to reciprocate in kind.

Meanwhile, events had been moving with great rapidity. On
28 December 1855, Marcy had made a request to the British Secretary of State for Crampton's recall. The Earl of Clarendon, in a reply
on 30 April to Mr. Dallas, virtually refused to recognize any grounds
for the request.[8] In the interval, however, the matter had been called
out in Parliament and a demand was made for publication of the official correspondence regarding the controversy in question.[9] Finally,
on 28 May the actual dismissal of Crampton took place. Simultaneously, as an added retaliation for the indignities of the British ministry, President Pierce recognized the government which Walker had
set up in Nicaragua, despite Marcy's objection that Walker was no
more than a disreputable free-lancer commanding a filibustering campaign in utter disregard of the laws of the United States.[1]

Hawthorne's reaction to these decisive moves on the part of his
government was distinctly sympathetic. Like Pierce, he did not
share Marcy's scruples, and he was quite prepared to ignore Walker's
legal status in favor of his political position. On the sixth of June, nine
days after Crampton's dismissal, he wrote to Ticknor as follows:

Our relations with England seem to me to bear a more pacific aspect than
for many months past. Frank Pierce never did a better thing than in recognizing Walker's Government; it has brought John Bull to his bearings,
. . . Crampton ought to have been dismissed more promptly; but it is better late than never. Most people here think that Dallas will be sent home,
and, I believe, he is himself very uneasy. I hope he *will* be sent home, because it will be such a very foolish act on the part of the British Govern-

6. *English Notebooks*, p. 323.   7. *Ticknor Letters*, II, 16–17, 19–20.
8. *American Secretaries of State*, VI, 258. The Hon. George Mifflin Dallas had succeeded Buchanan as ambassador, chiefly to take up the business of "peacemaker," as the
British themselves were aware (see *The Illustrated London News*, No. 792, XXVIII
[5 April 1856], 348).
9. *Ibid.*, p. 259.
1. See Roy Franklin Nichols, *Franklin Pierce* (Philadelphia, 1931), p. 462.

ment—and, moreover, he will be no loss to anybody.—But I am of opinion that they will let him stay.[2]

In this he proved himself a more competent judge of national opinion and of government policy than many who, it is to be supposed, were better qualified for the job. As early as the previous November he had his eye upon popular sentiment.

The English people will not let their Government go to war with us; not from any liking for America, but from a wholesome apprehension of the consequences. This feeling is very manifest, all over the country.[3]

On the following April he wrote of his visit to the regiment at Aldershot Camp: "I fraternized very strongly with them all, from the Colonel downwards; and I don't think there will be any war between England and America."[4] Hawthorne had further evidence for these convictions in the enthusiastic way in which his own conciliatory expressions were received in public.

There was a pervading spirit of pacifism, at least on the part of more liberal social thinkers, friends of democracy like Hawthorne's acquaintance Dr. Mackay, and the hope that all questions could be amicably settled to the full satisfaction of both nations. Dr. Mackay's paper, *The Illustrated London News*, made the following comment on the subject in an editorial for 5 April 1856:

We trust that . . . the good sense and good feeling existent on both sides of the Atlantic will preserve the world from so fratricidal a catastrophe as war.[5]

In a letter to Ticknor more than a month before, Hawthorne had shrewdly recognized an ancillary reason for the decreasing belligerence of John Bull.

The war-talk has entirely died away; and I hope, on the American side of the water, we shall say nothing more about fighting, unless we really mean to come to the scratch. It is considered very doubtful here whether the conferences at Paris will result in peace with Russia; and this is probably one of the reasons why the English tone is less hostile with regard to us.[6]

Neither the people nor the English government itself, in fact, felt that the policy adopted with respect to enlistment in the United States was a defensible one. During one of the debates in Parliament over the tactics of the ministry, Disraeli had said, "I think, Sir, it

2. *Ticknor Letters*, II, 16–17.   3. *Ibid.*, I, 116.
4. *Ibid.*, II, 12–13. Cf. *English Notebooks*, p. 298. "I fraternized with these military gentlemen [members of the North Cork Rifles] in a way that augurs the very best things for the future peace of the two countries."
5. No. 792, XXVIII, 342.   6. *Ticknor Letters*, II, 4.

would be wise if England would at last recognize that the United States, like all the great countries of Europe, have a policy, and that they have a right to have a policy."[7] Dallas was retained. On June 20, Hawthorne wrote triumphantly to Ticknor:

You see, I was right in my opinion that Dallas would not be sent home. We have gained a great triumph over England, . . . for, I can assure you, Englishmen feel that they have given up forever the pretensions to superiority, and the haughty tone, which they have hitherto held towards us. We have gone through a crisis, and come out right side up. Give Frank Pierce credit for this, at least; for it was his spirit that did it.[8]

These are the emotions of one of Franklin Pierce's staunchest defenders at a time when he was much in need of support.

It is difficult to understand the importance which Hawthorne attached to this international fracas without observing it in the sociological light in which he himself viewed it. Not until several years later did he tend to minimize the significance of the dispute, and then only when the possibility of civil war outweighed almost any other social or political consideration of the century.[9]

There are cogent reasons for the fact that Hawthorne's Americanism was measurably strengthened by residence abroad.[1] This diplomatic squabble was one of them. In the monarchical societies of Europe which were so rapidly depreciating and yet so stubbornly persisting in the very face of their insufficiency, Hawthorne saw the obstacle to the advancement of American democracy. There was, as he had pointed out, still enough vigor in their bigotry to do America "a good deal of mischief" before she could gain the leading position for which she was destined. It was on this account as much as any other, that he felt obliged to maintain a properly democratic antagonism toward England, however fond he may have been of her. Thus, he told Ticknor, "I HATE England; though I love some Englishmen, and like them generally, in fact."[2] With Longfellow he was equally outspoken, at the same time offering something of an exegesis.

You ask why I do not take more heartily to England. It is only as an American that I am hostile to England, and because she hates us. Individually, I like almost every Englishman I know, and they certainly are kind to me—kinder, I imagine, than they would be to any American except yourself. So you can judge of the strength of my public virtue, when it counterbalances so much private feeling![3]

7. Hansard, *Parliamentary Debates*, Third Series, CXLII, 1511.
8. *Ticknor Letters*, II, 19–20. 9. See *Our Old Home*, p. 401.
1. See Stewart "Hawthorne in England," *loc. cit.*, p. 13.
2. *Ticknor Letters*, II, 113. This letter bears the date 9 November 1855.
3. Hawthorne to Longfellow, 16 February 1855. The original of this letter is deposited in the Craigie House.

Reactions of a similar kind dictated Hawthorne's views of the Crimean War as well, that imperialistic fiasco upon which England was tenaciously engaged during part of his consulship. He had personally upheld Russia's part in this war—an attitude which is singular in view of the Czar's motives. It is not at once apparent what he meant when he said: "Whatever the Czar may propose to himself, it is for the interest of Democracy that he should not be easily put down."[4] Nicholas I might have been surprised to learn that he was fighting in so good a cause. Offhand one would suppose that nothing could have seemed more remote from the interests of democracy than this shabby entanglement which had been poorly inspired by the imperialistic greed of one European nation and the imperialistic vanity of others. Yet, in a letter to Longfellow, Hawthorne had called it "our battle."

For my part, what few sympathies I have are with the Russians; for they are fighting our battle, and unless they win it, we may have to fight it over again. I must confess, I feel like a traitor and a spy among these Englishmen, who seem to look upon me almost as one of themselves, . . . and all the while, if I have any wish about the matter, it is that they may be thrashed.[5]

What, exactly, could the battle have been which Hawthorne expected democracy to inherit from Russia? Partly no doubt, it was another of those vague contests against the arrogance of an aristocratic British government, which far from being limited to Europe had galled and hindered democracy in her own hemisphere.

From a similar letter written to Emerson approximately two years later, this would seem to have been excuse enough for an American's sympathetic affiliation with Russia. Speaking of Englishmen Hawthorne said:

Individually, they suit me well; it is very comfortable to live among them. But yet I am not unconscious of a certain malevolence and hostility in my own breast, such as a man must necessarily feel, who lives in England without melting entirely into the mass of Englishmen. I must confess to have sympathized with Russia more than England, in the late war; and nothing has given me quite so much pleasure since I left home, as the stoop which I saw in every Englishman's shoulders, after the settlement of the Enlistment question.[6]

Actually more lay behind this hostility in Hawthorne's breast than British complaisance in the face of the not unnatural wish of the

4. *English Notebooks,* p. 47
5. Hawthorne to Longfellow, 24 October 1854. The original is in the Craigie House.
6. Hawthorne to Emerson, 10 September 1856. The original manuscript of this letter is in the possession of the Emerson Memorial Association in the Widener Library at Harvard.

American democracy to see itself respected, at any rate, if not raised
to a position of some worldly eminence in the eyes of other nations.

Correctly or incorrectly the Crimean War was laid at the doors of
the English aristocracy. It had been Cobden and Bright, men from
the middle classes, who vociferously denounced it, and Lord Palmerston who had mawkishly attempted to glorify it. Many people concurred in the belief that the upper classes had thrust the Russian
conflict upon the Empire. "The aristocracy were anxious to get the
people into a war,"[7] Edward Search wrote to William Lloyd Garrison
from London. Thus Hawthorne may have argued that the Czar, regardless of his own autocratic intentions, was unwittingly furthering
the cause of democracy by imperiling the cause of its enemies—a
position strangely parallel to that of Russia today. In any case, early
in 1855 Hawthorne communicated to his journal these gratifying
reflections:

This war has given the country a vast impulse towards democracy. The
nobility will never hereafter, I think, assume, or be permitted, to rule the
nation in peace, or command armies in war, on any ground except the
individual ability which may appertain to one of their number, as well as
to a commoner. . . . relatively to the rest of the world, they do not
maintain their old place. The pressure of the war has tested and proved
this fact, at home and abroad. . . . This one year has done the work of
fifty ordinary ones;—or more accurately, perhaps, it has made apparent
what has long been preparing itself.[8]

The fact is, like many of his countrymen Hawthorne thought the
gods of the old order had presided overlong, and he was perhaps inclined to hasten the *Götterdämmerung*. England in particular came
to represent in his mind a sort of arch foe of Equalitarianism, so that
her harassment at anyone's hands was indirectly a benefit to the new
democratic way of life. Always equalitarian in his views, and sometimes outrageously so, Hawthorne could not help giving the differences between England and the United States an ideological basis.
And so long as he held democracy to be the principle of all future
social progress, he must resent the hampering presence of the time-
honored aristocratic modes, and rejoice at each fresh sign that the
course of his century was wearing them away.

Throughout his sojourn in England Hawthorne remained constantly on the lookout for these signs, and his diligence seldom went
unrewarded. "The progress of the age," he once announced, "is trampling over the aristocratic institutions of England, and they crumble
beneath it."[9] The evidence supporting so heroic a statement came
from many phases of English life. In politics Hawthorne had felt

7. Search to Garrison, 28 April 1854. Printed in *The Liberator* for 26 May 1854.
8. *English Notebooks*, p. 99.   9. *Ibid.*

himself drawn to Disraeli as a man who had cut his own niche "among a hostile aristocracy,"[1] and who dominated instead of pampering them. Among the intellectuals with whom he rubbed elbows in London literary circles, he was attracted to people whose religious, social, and political ideas were "not precisely in train with the establishment in church and state."[2] These were non-conformists, dissenters from the hereditary social philosophies and modes of government, men with temperately equalitarian tendencies like Dr. Charles Mackay, whose investigation of the United States Hawthorne later facilitated by three disproportionately flattering letters to Duyckinck, Emerson, and Franklin Pierce.[3] There was also Douglas Jerrold, distinguished by his wit and his pungent contributions to *Punch*, who reminded Hawthorne of Ellery Channing "in the richer veins of the latter."[4] As the self-invited guest of these men[5] Hawthorne gained admittance to a society which, in true English fashion, had made provision for the physical convenience of its radical tendencies by organizing the so-called Reform Club and Milton Club. The latter was formed, in the words of Dr. Mackay, "in honour of the name and principles of the great John Milton." A political rather than a literary association, it took its name from the poet who became an "uncompromising advocate of civil and religious liberty."[6]

In society Hawthorne's personal avoidance of any pretense whatever was so ostentatious as to be itself a pretension. When they learned at the Clarendon Hotel in Leamington, for example, that he held the title of Honorable in his own country, they "greatly regretted," he said somewhat fatuously, "that I had entered myself as plain Mister in the book."[7] But no one ought to be deceived by this behavior; it was a time when the United States was advertising its unpretentiousness. On the pretext of equalitarian simplicity, and with the authority of his government, Buchanan was making himself the cynosure of all eyes by wearing ordinary street clothes at the English court.[8] In his smaller way, Hawthorne too, as an officer of the American government, endeavored to distinguish himself as much as possible by his democratic inconspicuousness.

It was excellent showmanship. But it was a pose that Hawthorne

---

1. *Ibid.*, p. 325. 2. *Ibid.*, p. 310.

3. These three letters are dated 24 September 1857. The one to E. A. Duyckinck is in the possession of the New York Public Library; the one to Emerson is deposited with the Emerson Memorial Association; that to Pierce is in the Library of Congress.

4. *English Notebooks*, p. 315.

5. See Charles Mackay, *Forty Years' Recollections of Life, Literature, and Public Affairs from 1830 to 1870* (London, 1877) II, 272.

6. *Ibid.*, II, 271. 7. *English Notebooks*, p. 120.

8. For a discussion of the question of American diplomatic uniform at this time, see *American Secretaries of State*, VI, 263–68.

was unable to rid himself of even in his private meditation. Just as he patronizingly observed that rank had been "the general passport to admission"[9] to the chapel of Henry VII in Westminster Abbey, so now he walked into the Reform Club with the same jaundiced eye. He painstakingly disapproved of the portraits of English reformers which adorned a colonnade in the Club.

I remarked that the larger part of the portraits already hung up are of men of high rank; the Duke of Sussex, for instance, Lord Durham, Lord Gray,—and, indeed, I remember no commoner.[1]

But he was in all probability dazzled by the sight of a facsimile of the Declaration of Independence hanging in an adjacent room, for Dr. Charles Mackay subsequently took inventory of what his American guest had either omitted or through ignorance failed to identify.

Mr. Hawthorne might have known, had he enquired, that the portraits of these men were placed where he saw them, not because of their high rank, but of their eminent services to the Liberal party and the cause of Reform. He might also have discovered, had he looked, the portraits of Daniel O'Connell, a commoner, and of Mr. J. W. Denison, M. P., another commoner, and an excellent bust of John Hampden, a third commoner, more illustrious than either, and whose name is almost as dear to the British people as that of George Washington is to the Americans.[2]

Hawthorne's deprecatory statement in reference to one gentleman's white silk stockings—"these English reformers do not seem to include Republican simplicity of manners in their system"—this time elicited a downright contradiction from Dr. Mackay. "The white silk stockings," wrote Mackay some time after they had had a chance to rankle in his memory, "were things of Mr. Hawthorne's imagination, but served to point an innuendo against English manners and in favour of those of his own country."[3]

There was an undeniable admixture of snobbery in Hawthorne's suspicious and often ungenerous equalitarianism. Of the conversation during the dinner with Mackay and Jerrold at the Reform Club, he wrote:

Jerrold spoke of the Duke of Devonshire with great warmth, as a true, honest, simple, most kind hearted man, . . . and I (Heaven forgive me!) queried within myself, whether this English reforming author would have been quite so sensible of the Duke's excellence, if he had not been a Duke. But, indeed, a nobleman, who is at the same time a true and whole-hearted man, feeling his brotherhood with men, does really deserve some credit for it.[4]

9. *English Notebooks*, p. 618.
2. *Forty Years' Recollections*, II, 274, n.
4. *English Notebooks*, p. 315.

1. *Ibid.*, p. 314.
3. *Ibid.*, II, 275, n.

His condescension occasionally overreached itself. He had an infelicitous notion that equalitarianism was at that time the copyright of Americans. "Nothing," he once said contemptuously of a young Frenchman who claimed to be a naturalized citizen of the United States, "is so absolutely abominable as the sense of freedom and equality, pertaining to an American, grafted on the mind of a native of any other country in the world. I do HATE a naturalized citizen; nobody has a right to our ideas, unless born to them."[5]

But much as he may seem to have made equalitarianism conditional upon birth, he never considered it the exclusive right of an elect body whose position would be that of a kind of democratic peerage. Any man on earth could lay claim to equalitarian ideals on the day that they became part of his own country's social consciousness. Meanwhile, Hawthorne observed, "All exiles for liberty come to me, as if the representative of America were their representative."[6] And from this fact he derived a deep and twofold satisfaction. He saw that most men who looked for it at all sought the hope of the world's future and the promise of social progress in America. And he read in their allegiance, more clearly even than in the ceremonious homage paid by the Reform Club to the Declaration of Independence, the fact that this future was already near at hand.

The longer Hawthorne travelled through England the more conclusive grew his evidence of the inroads which the new order was making on the old. He had had a forecast of it previously in his own country. Over fifteen years before at Gardiner, Maine, he had surveyed the mansion of Robert Hallowell Gardiner, unfinished for lack of funds, and that of General Knox near Thomaston, depreciated over a period of years from a like cause, and had felt that both offered food for reflection "in reference to the indulgence of aristocratic pomp among democratic institutions."[7] Even in these outlandish places he saw that "the cursed shadow of Europe" had been cast.[8]

But during the decades of the thirties and forties there had developed in him a marked sensibility to the shortening of this shadow, to the dwindling of hereditary possessions of whatever form as a result of the swath cut by an advancing democratic society.[9] This is apparent in his almost socialistic enjoyment of the ruin of "old wormeaten aristocracy"[1] like the Pepperell family;[2] in his romance of

5. *Ibid.*, p. 96.   6. *Ibid.*, p. 113.
7. *American Notebooks*, p. 8. Cf. *ibid.*, pp. 22–23.
8. Hawthorne is reported to have told W. D. Howells that he wished he could find some part of America " 'where the cursed shadow of Europe had not fallen.' " Quoted from Howells by Moncure D. Conway, "My Hawthorne Experience," *The Critic*, XLV (July, 1904), 23.
9. See *American Notebooks*, pp. lxxvi–lxxxii.
1. *Passages from the American Note-Books*, p. 88.
2. *American Notebooks*, pp. 94, 116.

Colonel Pyncheon's mansion, "calculated to endure for many generations of his posterity"[3] but doomed, instead, to witness the family's self-destruction for the sake of a worthless Indian deed;[4] in Peter Goldthwaite's distorted pride and counterfeit inheritance;[5] and in unbalanced old Esther Dudley—remnant of "the decayed past . . . , with its manners, opinions, faith and feelings, all fallen into oblivion or scorn—of what had once been a reality, but was now merely a vision of faded magnificence."[6]

These ideas of precipitate social advancement now dwelt constantly in Hawthorne's mind. The leveling action of democracy was noticeable in a thousand places. He had once written of an interview with his kinsman, Eben Hawthorne: "Eben passed from the matters of birth, pedigree, and ancestral pride, to give vent to the most arrant democracy and locofocoism, that I have happened to hear; saying that nobody ought to possess wealth longer than his own life, and that then it should return to the people, &c."[7] But during the years surrounding the mid-century he himself became confirmed in the arrant democracy which had so taken him aback as a younger man. The inexorable leveling process he took from then on to be a condition of social advancement.

What Hawthorne saw in England served further to corroborate his judgment, to round it out, to cosmopolitanize it. Alice's impassioned address to Middleton, urging him to forget what was behind him and concentrate upon what lay ahead,[8] is merely a reverberation almost twenty years afterward of Governor Hancock's eloquence in "Old Esther Dudley." With a final respect paid to "the stately and gorgeous prejudices of the tottering Past," the Governor had cried, "and then, my fellow citizens, onward—onward! We are no longer children of the Past!"[9] As if he could not emphasize it enough, he had repeated his exhortation:

And I, and these around me—we represent a new race of men—living no longer in the past, scarcely in the present—but projecting our lives forward into the future. Ceasing to model ourselves on ancestral superstitions, it is our faith and principle to press onward, onward![1]

With a similar symbolic import, that failing brilliance surrounding Colcord at the close of *Doctor Grimshawe's Secret*[2] is a reflection of the iridescence which attended the passing of Esther Dudley.

With such a lingering fire, methought, with such a dying gleam, had the glory of the ancient system vanished from the Province House, when the spirit of old Esther Dudley took its flight.[3]

3. *Seven Gables*, p. 21.   4. *Ibid.*, p. 374.   5. *Twice-Told Tales*, pp. 447, 453.
6. *Ibid.*, p. 333.   7. *American Notebooks*, p. 27.
8. *The Ancestral Footstep*, p. 489.   9. *Twice-Told Tales*, p. 341.   1. *Ibid.*
2. See *Doctor Grimshawe's Secret*, p. 343.   3. *Twice-Told Tales*, p. 342.

Hawthorne was struck with the sinfulness of the past holding the present to its outmoded contracts. By refusing to let the living work out their own proper arrangements—which, Hawthorne felt, tended naturally to be democratic—it prolonged the artificial distinctions that relegated so many millions of people in the industrial nineteenth century in England to abject poverty. It was against a similar tyranny that Tom Paine had directed his attack in *The Rights of Man*.

Every age and generation must be free to act for itself *in all cases* as the ages and generations which preceded it. The vanity and presumption of governing beyond the grave is the most ridiculous and insolent of all tyrannies. . . . Every generation is, and must be, competent to all the purposes which its occasions require.

There is a great deal of Tom Paine in Holgrave's outbursts against the Past.

'Shall we never, never get rid of this Past?' cried he . . . 'It lies upon the Present like a giant's dead body! . . .

'For example, . . . a dead man, if he happen to have made a will, disposes of wealth no longer his own; or, if he die intestate, it is distributed in accordance with the notions of men much longer dead than he. A dead man sits on all our judgment-seats; and living judges do but search out and repeat his decisions. . . . We worship the living Deity according to dead men's forms and creeds. . . . And we must be dead ourselves before we can begin to have our proper influence on our own world, which will then be no longer our world, but the world of another generation, with which we shall have no shadow of a right to interfere . . . .

'. . . I doubt whether even our public edifices . . . ought to be built of such permanent materials as stone or brick. It were better that they should crumble to ruin once in twenty years, or thereabouts, as a hint to the people to examine into and reform the institutions which they symbolize.' [4]

The incumbrance of inherited estates, or of inherited traditions and habits, makes impossible each individual's working out of his own social equation—his moral obligation and privilege in a democratic state.

In a letter to Duyckinck a little over a year after his marriage, Hawthorne had cited an actual instance of the new movement in society.

A sketch—the devouring of the old country residences by the overgrown monster of a city. For instance, Mr. Beekman's ancestral residence was originally several miles from the city of New-York; but the pavements kept creeping nearer and nearer; till now the house is removed, and a street runs directly through what was once its hall.[5]

4. *Seven Gables*, pp. 219–20.
5. *American Notebooks*, p. 99; see also, Hawthorne to E. A. Duyckinck, 26 Novem-

Indications of an implacable shift in the whole social structure of the nineteenth century appeared again and again in England. He noticed, for example, that all about Tranmere the old society composed of landed gentry and cotters was tumbling into ruins, while modernity, without waiting for the complete demolition of what it dispossessed, had moved in everywhere around it. Owing to the growth of Liverpool and Birkenhead, the old manor had grown to look out of place in the midst of a modern community where taste was more fastidious than gracious, "among modern stuccoed dwellings, such as are erected for tradesmen and other moderate people, who have their residences in the neighborhood of a great city—rows of houses with such names as Belle Vue, Roslia Villas, &c . . ."[6]

Coming from a society whose self-consciousness was at that moment centered on the common man, Hawthorne was quick to discern the encroachments of "moderate people" upon the obsolescent hierarchic forms. He commended heartily the popular aspect of beautiful and recreational places like Kensington Gardens. Art had a communal function. "It is pleasant," he confessed, "to think that the people have the freedom (and therefore the property) of parks like this, more beautiful and stately than a nobleman can keep to himself."[7] In like manner he wrote of Greenwich Park that it was "the people's property and play-ground," and that as such it afforded an instance where the monarch's property actually belonged to the people, who inevitably became "sooner or later the legitimate inheritors of whatever beauty kings and queens create."[8] He saw a similar significance in the displacement of the courtly river pageants like that described by Pope in *The Rape of the Lock* by "a multitude of smoke-begrimed steamers."

An analogous change has taken place in the streets, where cabs and the omnibus have crowded out a rich variety of vehicles; and thus life gets more monotonous in hue from age to age, and appears to seize every opportunity to strip off a bit of its gold lace among the wealthier classes, and to make itself decent in the lower ones.[9]

Notwithstanding, the dismantling did not invariably proceed with sufficient rapidity to be wholly suitable to him.

Throughout the journals there may be seen what one critic has called "the mingled sense of relief and oppression which the two Englands that he saw" gave to Hawthorne—that is, "The England of

ber 1843. Cf. *Mosses*, p. 317; also, *Blithedale*, p. 529, where Hawthorne describes an old gubernatorial mansion which has been converted into a common rooming-house.

6. *English Notebooks*, p. 105.   7. *Ibid.*, p. 231.

8. *Our Old Home*, p. 266. Cf. *English Notebooks*, p. 191, where Hawthorne observes that in the public right to all footpaths "the poorest man retains a kind of property in the oldest inheritance of the richest."

9. *Our Old Home*, p. 300.

Battle Abbey, and the England of the coroner and policeman and gin shop."[1] This same compulsion to distinguish "modern England from monumental England"[2] reappears in *Doctor Grimshawe's Secret*. And in proportion as the monumental side, the England of Charlecote Hall and Nuneham Courtenay entranced him, the other aggravated so profoundly all his equalitarian instincts that it became the subject of a rather militant philanthropy.

Hawthorne had manifested all along a sympathy for the poor and oppressed—his own brothers by virtue of a common humanity. The democratic institutions of America were built on just such sympathy, and their future would stand or topple on it. On one occasion he had reproved Sophia with gentle irony for her delicate snobbishness: ". . . to think," he wrote in mock horror, "that thou shouldst have sitten an hour-and-a-half in that tobacco-smoky tavern, with those ugly people—whom, nevertheless, God made, though of course thou wilt deny it."[3] Years afterward while passing through the armory of Stirling Castle, he was especially moved, among all the feudal relics deposited there, by the mean weapons which had been employed by "poor weavers and other handicraft men," who had revolted against the government almost forty years before. "I have not the least shadow of doubt," he declared dogmatically, "that these men had a good cause to fight for; but what availed it with such weapons, and so few even of those."[4]

As much as Hawthorne had gone out of his way to become acquainted with the monumental fixtures of England, he had daily had forced upon him in Liverpool a society whose main furniture consisted of the policeman, the coroner, and the "spirit-vault." And by this society he had from the outset been wholesomely appalled. "Almost every day," he wrote in his journals shortly after reaching England, "I take walks about Liverpool; preferring the darker and dingier streets, inhabited by the poorer classes . . . there is a strong interest in such walks; and moreover there is a bustle, a sense of being in the midst of life, and of having got hold of something real, which I do not find in the better streets of the city."[5]

The ensuing entries plainly bespeak his American distress and amazement at the glimpses which he caught of English poverty.

Dec 3[d]. Yesterday—a chill, misty, December day—I saw a woman barefooted in the street; not to speak of children.[6]

1. "Hawthorne's English Note-Books," *The Nation*, XI (July 28, 1870), 60.
2. J. H. Morse, "Nathaniel Hawthorne Again," *Century Magazine*, IV (June, 1883), 311; a critical letter to the editor regarding the recent reviews of *Doctor Grimshawe's Secret*.
3. *American Notebooks*, p. 177.   4. *English Notebooks*, p. 529.
5. *Ibid.*, p. 13.   6. *Ibid.*, p. 40.

A little further on he commented somewhat wonderingly, "We have nothing parallel to these street-women, in our country."[7] However, in this and in stating that there was nothing which resembled any aspect of these uncouth throngs in "the well-dressed and well-washed multitude in an American city,"[8] he demonstrates a rather remarkable ignorance of the Irish immigrant population of Boston.

Hawthorne returned constantly to the slum districts of Liverpool throughout his first few months in England. The journals are replete with descriptions which he later welded into a chapter of *Our Old Home*, and as if these were inadequate to express his shrinking disapproval, he punctuated them by occasional ejaculations not always intended for the reading public. "My God, what dirty, dirty children!" he cried once. "And the grown people are the flowers of these buds, physically and morally."[9] Already he had ventured to formulate the theory that it would require "many generations of better life to elicit a soul in them." And he had added more than an innuendo to this when he exclaimed, "All America could not show the like."[1]

The wretchedness and squalor which he encountered on every hand, and the criminal neglect on the part of a social dispensation which disinterestedly tolerated such conditions, seldom allowed Hawthorne to forget the dual aspect that England presented. At this juncture of her civilization when feudalism, rubbing elbows with more advanced social trends, bogged down the latter by sheer weight of age, England presented a spectacle which was especially abhorrent to the eyes of Young America.

Today, I heard a dirty mother laughing and priding herself on the pretty ways of her dirty infant—just as a Christian mother might in a nursery or drawing-room. I must study this street-life more, and think of it more deeply.[2]

Hawthorne turned his efforts thereafter to a close examination and a subsequent understanding of the lives and character of the destitute people who swarmed about the slum districts of Liverpool, like "maggots in cheese."[3] Of an Irish family huddled together round a fire in the Ferry House, he wrote:

There is not much that can be caught in the description of this scene; but it made me understand, better than before, how poor people feel, . . .

7. *Ibid.*
8. *Ibid.*, p. 47. See also, *ibid.*, p. 116. "I never before felt it to be a marked characteristic of Americans, of both sexes and all classes, that every individual has a suit of Sunday clothes." 9. *Ibid.*, p. 17.
1. *Ibid.*, p. 13. Hawthorne had had an opportunity to study American poor conditions during his visit to Bridge in 1837. For his account of Irish and Canadian squatters, see *American Notebooks*, pp. 7–8.
2. *English Notebooks*, p. 17. 3. *Ibid.*, p. 18. Cf. *Ibid.*, p. 535.

and how they suffer, and yet how they have a life not quite miserable, after all; and how family love goes along with them. . . . Somehow or other, I got into the interior of this poor family, and understand, through sympathy, more of them than I can tell.[4]

And in this studious attempt to comprehend the gross, unlovely elements in a foreign society was entailed a severe condemnation of the indifference of its privileged classes toward its under-privileged ones, and an attendant feeling that democratic forces should be brought sharply to bear upon the whole dismal situation.

4. *Ibid.*, p. 35.

VI

Salutary Democracy

I . . . have heard him discuss, almost with violence, the superiority of American vegetables. Indeed, he once withered me with a scorn which was anything but mystic or melancholy because I expressed a patriotic preference for English peas.

Anthony Trollope, *The Genius of Nathaniel Hawthorne.*

HAWTHORNE applied to the English social conditions what may be called the ethic of democracy. An alliance took place—as it was fairly inevitable that it should—between his Calvinistic inheritance and his equalitarian affinities. It resulted at once in a devout democratic conscience. This conscience was painfully twinged by the social indignities of which the English lower classes were a living example. It was so elaborately sensitive, moreover, that it goaded Hawthorne into receiving the strange affection shown for him by a diseased boy in an almshouse as a reminder "that he was responsible, in his degree, for all the sufferings and misdemeanors of the world in which he lived, and was not entitled to look upon a particle of its dark calamity as if it were none of his concern: the offspring of a brother's iniquity being his own blood-relation, and the guilt, likewise, a burden on him, unless he expiated it by better deeds."[1]

With his equalitarian ideals Hawthorne was not one to shrink from the moral responsibility of brotherhood with the rest of mankind, though an innate meticulousness might occasionally prompt him to designate all farmers, yokels, gentlemen's servants, as "people akin to horses and cattle."[2] With a grimness hardly exceeded by Carlyle, whom he echoes here, he wrote of the Liverpool poor:

. . . they suffer all the ordinary diseases . . . and keep among themselves traditionary plagues that have long ceased to afflict more fortunate societies. . . . It would be a dire revenge, indeed, if they were to prove their claims to be reckoned of one blood and nature with the noblest and wealthiest by compelling them to inhale death through the diffusion of their own poverty-poisoned atmosphere.[3]

1. *Our Old Home*, p. 353. Compare Hawthorne's immediate report of this incident in the *English Notebooks*, pp. 275–77.

2. *English Notebooks*, p. 582. Cf. *ibid.*, p. 269. Hawthorne praised Jonathan Cilley as a politician who "loved the people and respected them, and was prouder of nothing than of his brotherhood with those who had intrusted their public interests to his care." *Sketches*, p. 271.

3. *Our Old Home*, pp. 339–40; cf. *Mosses*, p. 238. Compare Carlyle, *Past and Present* (Century Edition, x, 149). "One of Dr. Alison's Scotch facts struck us much.

Upon the squeamishness with which the more fortunate—including himself—were now and then afflicted at the thought of their common humanity and blood-brotherhood with beggary, Hawthorne passed orthodox Christian censure.

A poor man's breath, borne on the vehicle of tobacco-smoke, floats into a palace-window and reaches the nostrils of a monarch. It is but an example, obvious to the sense, of the innumerable and secret channels by which, at every moment of our lives, the flow and reflux of a common humanity pervade us all. How superficial are the niceties of such as pretend to keep aloof! Let the whole world be cleansed, or not a man or woman of us all can be clean.[4]

Many years prior to his residence in England the faith that stood behind this exhortation had been set forth metaphorically, in the American journals.

. . . even a human breast which may appear least spiritual in some aspects, may still have the capability of reflecting an infinite Heaven in its depths, and therefore of enjoying it. It is a comfortable thought, that the smallest and most turbid mud-puddle can contain its own picture of Heaven. Let us remember this, when we feel inclined to deny all spiritual life to some people, in whom, nevertheless, our Father may perhaps see the image of his face. This dull river has a deep religion of its own: so, let us trust, has the dullest human soul, perhaps unconsciously.[5]

This religion is a fit outgrowth of the democratic tenets and ambitions of mid-century liberals like the Young Americans. While it remained dispassionate enough, and often—as with Hawthorne—unobtrusive in America, where to disseminate it too loudly was to set the abolitionists howling, it nevertheless found England a safe and vulnerable society to attack. There is not a little exhibitionism even in Hawthorne's restrained sermonizing. As soon as three thousand miles of water lay between him and the dry tinder of the slavery question, he was ready to express his beliefs with evangelical fervor. And protected by his geographic situation, he admitted no incon-

[William Pulteney Alison, M.D., *Observations on the Management of the Poor in Scotland* (Edinburgh, 1840)]. A poor Irish Widow . . . went forth with her three children, bare of all resource, to solicit help from the Charitable Establishments. . . . At this Charitable Establishment and then at that she was refused; . . . Till her strength and heart failed her: she sank down in typhus-fever; died, and infected her Lane with fever, so that 'seventeen other persons' died of fever there in consquence. The humane Physician asks thereupon, . . . Would it not have been *economy* to help this poor Widow? She took typhus-fever, and killed seventeen of you!— Very curious. The forlorn Irish Widow applies to her fellow-creatures, as if saying, 'Behold I am sinking, bare of help: ye must help me! I am your sister, bone of your bone: one God made us: ye must help me!' They answer, 'No, impossible; thou art no sister of ours.' But she proves her sisterhood; her typhus-fever kills them: they actually were her brothers, though denying it! Had human creature ever to go lower for a proof?"

4. *Our Old Home,* p. 351.   5. *American Notebooks,* p. 148.

gruity in later dedicating to a man whose Southern sympathies had caused him to be designated "the executive tool of the slaveholding power,"[6] a book containing this superb testament regarding the oppressed peoples of a foreign land:

Unless these slime-clogged nostrils can be made capable of inhaling celestial air, I know not how the purest and most intellectual of us can reasonably expect ever to taste a breath of it. The whole question of eternity is staked there. If a single one of those helpless little ones be lost, the world is lost.[7]

Nor did he see anything incongruous, after telling his Abolitionist sister-in-law that she looked at matters "with an awful squint,"[8] in henceforth devoting himself to laying the case of the oppressed classes of Europe as well as he was able before mankind, "on whom God has imposed the necessity to suffer in soul and body till this dark and dreadful wrong be righted."[9]

Of all social and political philosophies the equalitarian ideal seemed most in accord with natural distinctions. And because Hawthorne credited it with the power to work from within the gradual and painless salvation of a society infected with the arbitrary subjugation of human beings, he was willing to be a proselytizer in its cause.

Thus he underwrote as a democrat a thesis, the inculcation of which required him to be nearly everything that he has heretofore been supposed not to be—an agitator for social reform on a basis that was essentially as religious as it was political. In this way there were allied the two antipodal phases of his nature—the fanciful and practical, the ethical and political, the part of his genius displayed in a story like "Rappaccini's Daughter" and the part which was responsible for the vivid sketches that make up the volume *Our Old Home*, or for the good taste which pervades the little biography of Franklin Pierce. The recluse of Herbert Street, who thought the most desirable mode of existence to be that of a "spiritualized Paul Pry,"[1] and the United States Consul at Liverpool, who acquired several thousand dollars under the social creed "that a man has no claim upon his fellow creatures, beyond bread and water, and a grave, unless he can win it by his own strength or skill," were one and the same man. Only they have too frequently been kept apart.

Hawthorne's ultimately profitable experience in the treacherous employ of his government had convinced him of the efficacy of the creed that all men are created free, with equal rights to the spoils of

6. New York *Times*, 13 June 1854.   7. *Our Old Home*, p. 332.
8. Hawthorne to E. P. Peabody, 13 August 1857. The original of this letter is in the Berg Collection.
9. *Our Old Home*, p. 356.   1. *Twice-Told Tales*, p. 220.

earth. Furthermore, it taught him also that the individual's position in the world together with the spoils accruing therefrom depended entirely upon his personal qualifications for obtaining them. Since America had nothing to show which even approximated the hideousness of English workhouses and slum dwellings, Hawthorne may perhaps be pardoned his easy deduction that its singular purity was owing simply to the special social and political doctrine under which it thrived.

It was not without reason, nor as usual without rancor, that *Blackwood's Magazine* in an article entitled "Hawthorne on England" trained its vituperation on this too patent prescription of democracy as a tonic for all the old ills of civilization.

There is a belief, prevalent even among intelligent Americans, men well acquainted with agricultural theories, . . . that the fertility of their native soil is owing to the Union and the Constitution, whose beneficent influences descended upon it like a rich dew. The abundance of the corn crop, the excellence of the peaches and melons, are traced in some mysterious way by these faithful Unionists to the result of the political labours of Jefferson, Hamilton, and Jay. Therefore every poor wretch whom starvation drives from Europe dwells in plenty beneath the star-spangled banner which has made the wilderness to blossom; while, on the other hand, we, living in an overpeopled island, have a deep stratum of poverty in our society because of our rotten old monarchy.[2]

As another critic once put it, Hawthorne contrasted with the English situation what appeared to him to be "the working idea of the American system, which he, both from his patriotic and his manly instinct, considered the loftier ideal."[3] The result was that he offered democracy, beneath which the new world had prospered, in solemn earnestness as a panacea for the jaded society of the old. And with a faint tinge of apostolic prescience, he wrote:

There may come a time, even in this world, when we shall all understand that our tendency to the individual appropriation of gold and broad acres, fine houses, and such good and beautiful things as are equally enjoyable by a multitude, is but a trait of imperfectly developed intelligence, like the simpleton's cupidity of a penny. When that day dawns,— and probably not till then,—I imagine that there will be no more poor streets nor need of almshouses.[4]

2. *Blackwood's Magazine*, XCIV (November, 1863), 621. This article is a critical review of *Our Old Home*. *Blackwood's*, a Tory magazine, frequently attacked America as being "the world's great object-lesson in democracy and liberalism." See Alan Nevins, *American Social History* (New York, 1923), pp. 111–12.

3. L. H. Morse, "Nathaniel Hawthorne Again," *Century Magazine*, IV (June, 1883), 311.

4. *Our Old Home*, p. 359.

Hawthorne occasionally teetered on the brink of socialism; and in truth it would have been difficult to approach more closely than this without tumbling in.

The extraordinary humility, the incurious acceptance of their lot on the part of the starving wretches who wandered about the by-ways of Liverpool made Hawthorne question all the more, he said, "whether they have all their rights."[5] Certainly in the eyes of an equalitarian they did not have. Hawthorne protested against the West Derby Workhouse, remarking with democratic indignation that "the world, that requires such an establishment, ought to be ashamed of itself and set about an immediate reformation."[6]

A year later he witnessed a mass marriage in the Cathedral at Manchester where several pauper couples had congregated on Easter, attracted by the fact that no marriage fee was required during that season. And he remembered the picture of the women in particular— "faded untimely, wrink[l]ed with penury and care; nothing fresh, virginlike, or hopeful about them; joining themselves to their mates, with the idea of making their own misery less intolerable by adding another's to it."[7] It was one of the saddest scenes he had ever looked on. Not many minutes afterward he had had an opportunity to compare this spectacle with that of an aristocratic wedding, and a bridal pair "going to live on their abundance in one of those stately and delightful English homes, . . . more exclusively and inalienably their own, because of its descent through many forefathers, each of whom had added an improvement or a charm, and thus transmitted it with a stronger stamp of rightful possession to his heir."[8]

In the face of the demoralizing facts of one-half England, this other half seemed to Hawthorne to represent, as he put it, "an insolence of riches and prosperity, which one day or another will have a downfall."[9] From scenes like those of Liverpool's, Edinburgh's, and London's poor districts he did in fact receive a premonition that the time was not far off when the old order would prove a luxury England could no longer afford to keep.

With a Calvinistic focus upon right and wrong, unsurpassed even by his own New England ancestors, Hawthorne ended by confronting the world with the problem it had so far shirked, and the fate it would some day deserve.

Is, or is not, the system wrong that gives one married pair so immense a superfluity of luxurious home, and shuts out a million others from any home whatever? One day or another, safe as they deem themselves, and

5. *English Notebooks*, p. 104. 6. *Ibid.*, p. 277.
7. *Ibid.*, p. 456. 8. *Our Old Home*, p. 362.
9. *English Notebooks*, p. 103.

safe as the hereditary temper of the people really tends to make them, the gentlemen of England will be compelled to face this question.[1]

The moral irregularity of these conditions should have been a challenge, Hawthorne thought, to every Englishman who wilfully submitted to them. No Puritan divine, no Chillingworth, was ever more merciless in his attempts to stir the conscience of a guilty wretch than was Hawthorne in trying to rouse the conscience of the British upper classes to an awareness of their social sinfulness.

A conscience thus awake to the social and political enormity of its owner's hereditary advantages was to have been cultivated in the nobleman of the unfinished English romance. Among Hawthorne's trial sketches of this aristocrat the following two are perhaps most illustrative of his unfulfilled purpose here.

The noble must have some mark upon him; some fatality; something inherited, which shall represent the strife, the bloody fear, the wrong, by which the riches of his race have been obtained.[2]

He has something on his conscience—what? Something that nullifies all his advantages; and it must be something in the common causes of things, only made to seem strange by the imaginative associations that I shall cluster about it.[3]

A similar mark and a similar injustice against the poorer element of mankind had brought the Pyncheon family, with its hereditary homestead, into prominence. In this respect the chief difference between *The House of the Seven Gables* and the English tale was that in the latter Hawthorne had nominal class delineations with which to deal. It is probable that under separate conditions, but exactly the same auspices, the English romance was meant to unfold along the lines which its predecessor had already taken.

One had only to pass the slums of Liverpool in review to be cognizant at once of the extent of the guilt which lay upon the social conscience of the other-half England, and of the fatality which relentlessly pursued it, in the shape of democracy, down the streets and byways of the nineteenth century. Hawthorne had once expressed a strong doubt as to whether anybody, nobleman or mere Colonel, was "entitled to a home, in so full a sense, in this world."[4] There was something anti-social and misanthropic, something antagonistic not only to mankind in general but to nature herself in the arrogance of a family which persisted in maintaining intact the social equation begun by its progenitor perhaps centuries ago. Among the

1. *Our Old Home*, p. 362.
2. Quoted by Davidson, *The Last Phase* . . . , Appendix xiii, from an unpublished manuscript in the Huntington Library.
3. *Ibid.*   4. *English Notebooks*, p. 104.

curious artificialities of the departed civilization, the new Adam and
Eve notice one of the stateliest private mansions on Beacon Street,
replete with luxurious furnishings which include a row of portraits
of each generation of the family that had occupied it.[5]

Thus to intrude the past upon the present, and even upon the future, was to ignore the natural law of change and growth by which
man had achieved his civilization. Such a transplantation was wholly
artificial. The true social distinctions which arise from one generation
are only pretensions when superimposed on the next. Since all forms
and guises of artificiality had been lifelong anathemas to Hawthorne,
he now saw that the political and social system which disregarded
unethically the laws of nature and Providence was doomed. Just as
a natural society had taken its revenge upon the pretensions of Gardiner, Knox, and Colonel Pyncheon,[6] so it would one day destroy the
artificial and wholly arbitrary distinctions of England. "The great
gist of this story," Hawthorne wrote of the English novel, "ought to
be the *natural* hatred of men—and the particular hatred of Americans—to an aristocracy;"[7] an antipathy, he calculated, which would
eventually "put an end"[8] to the mockery of "an artificial remoteness
between the high creature and the low one."[9]

But this had been the gist, too, of *The House of the Seven Gables.*
Because they are Americans, Maule and Redclyffe may be supposed
to entertain deep within themselves a "particular" antagonism for
aristocracy; and because both are intelligent exponents of equalitarianism they understand perfectly the ethical necessity and the
natural wisdom which ultimately compel humanity to assume a state
of society where each man of each generation must make his own
place in the world. The second speech to this effect, quoted below, is
no more than Redclyffe's elaboration upon the slightly cryptic comment of Holgrave to Phoebe Pyncheon, which had preceded it by
only a few years.

'But we shall live to see the day, I trust, [Holgrave said] . . . when no
man shall build his house for posterity. . . . If each generation were
allowed and expected to build its own houses, that single change . . .
would imply almost every reform which society is now suffering for.'[1]

'. . . One of us would be ashamed [explained Redclyffe in behalf of
Americans] to assume any distinction, except such as may be supposed
to indicate personal, not hereditary merit. We have in some measure, I
think, lost the feeling of the past, and even of the future, as regards our
own lines of descent; . . . the idea of heaping up a pile of gold, or accumulating a broad estate for our . . . descendants, is dying out. We

5. *Mosses*, p. 289.   6. Cf. *Mosses*, p. 241.
7. Quoted by Davidson, *The Last Phase* . . . , Appendix v, from an unpublished
manuscript in the Huntington Library.
8. *Ibid.*   9. *Our Old Home*, p. 351.   1. *Seven Gables*, p. 220.

wish to enjoy the fulness of our success in life ourselves, and leave to those who descend from us the task of providing for themselves. This tendency is seen in our lavish expenditure, and the whole arrangement of our lives; and it is slowly—yet not very slowly, either—effecting a change in the whole economy of American life!' [2]

For the virtue of these credences Hawthorne had found abundant demonstration everywhere. There were no such "poor-streets" as England's in America. What would have been Redclyffe's career, in comparison to the great honors he had won in the service of the United States government, if he had grown up in the almshouse whence the old Doctor had taken him to America? The answer was plain enough to Hawthorne, who had talked with the Governor of the West Derby Workhouse, and learned that because the boys were taught a trade they had a doubtful chance in the world, but that the girls were seldom able to maintain their inconsiderable lead over the evil influences of a life to which they were callously relegated.[3]

The distinction of ranks is so marked, that the English cottage damsel holds a position somewhat analogous to that of the negro girl in our Southern States. Hence comes inevitable detriment to the moral condition of those men themselves, who forget that the humblest woman has a right and a duty to hold herself in the same sanctity as the highest.[4]

It was virtually impossible, according to the social rubric to which a great portion of England still conformed, for any man or woman to improve the status inflicted upon him or upon her by the merest accident of birth. Had Redclyffe remained in England, he would have been everlastingly imprisoned within the execrable circumstances into which he had been born.

But in America there was no such automatic relegation to pauperism. Every man could rise; every man did rise, and while the ablest ones seldom achieved the material magnificence or permanence of the upper classes of Europe, the less capable ones, by the same token, never had to pollute their country with such poverty as that which defiled the society of England. This was the direct result of the equalitarian credo which, as Hawthorne himself had expressed it, made each man's worldly position conditional only upon "his own strength or skill" to win it. And so, while the pedigrees of an aristocratic society are being consumed in Earth's Holocaust, the stentorious voice of Young America is heard, shouting above the din and confusion:

2. *Doctor Grimshawe's Secret,* p. 361. This passage does not appear in the printed version, and is therefore incorporated by the editor in the notes which are appended.
3. Cf. *English Notebooks,* p. 277, and *Our Old Home,* pp. 357–58.
4. *Our Old Home,* p. 286. Cf. *ibid.,* p. 336.

'And henceforth let no man dare to show a piece of musty parchment as his warrant for lording it over his fellows. . . . If he have wit, wisdom, courage, force of character, let these attributes do for him what they may; but from this day forward no mortal must hope for place and consideration by reckoning up the mouldy bones of his ancestors. That nonsense is done away.'[5]

With democrats it was a point of honor and sportsmanship to feel as Redclyffe did, when he said to the Englishman, " 'I have a sense of meanness in not starting fair, in beginning the world with advantages that my fellows have not.' "[6] With the same sort of pride James Buchanan had written to Reid Sanders, son of the one-time American consul in London. "What a blessing it is," Buchanan said, "to be the citizen of a country where each individual may proudly feel that he is equal to his fellow man, and where merit is not eclipsed by birth and rank."[7] And Redclyffe, whose political career closely resembles Buchanan's own, takes up the sentiment from there:

'. . . what prospects—what rewards for spirited exertion—what a career, only open to an American, would I give up, to become merely a rich and idle Englishman, . . . without a possibility of struggle, such as a strong man loves, with only a mockery of a title, which in these days really means nothing . . . What has any success in English life to offer . . . to balance the proud career of an American statesman?'[8]

One rather surmises from this that Redclyffe and Hawthorne shared an inclination to see in complete individualism, in the ruthless doctrine of the survival-of-the-fittest—once they had transformed it into a categorical imperative covering man's social conduct—something eminently heroic of which democratic Americans partook in excess of all others.

From his original maladjustment Hawthorne had run a full circle. He now upheld democracy as the paragon of societies for reasons of the very opportunistic, materialistic, utilitarian proclivities from which he had at one time retired insecurely to Brook Farm. Illustrations of his about-face are numerous. For example, in 1842 he and Emerson spoke with favor, during their now famous walking trip to the village of Harvard, of the "aristocratic structure" of European society, of "that rural nobility" whose pride in their land did not allow of such shiftless pig-farms as America had to show.[9] But after actual residence in England Hawthorne deferred, over a decade later, to the contradictory opinion of an American, who proclaimed authori-

5. *Mosses*, p. 433.　　　　　6. *Doctor Grimshawe's Secret*, p. 200.
7. For excerpts from this letter, which is dated 25 January 1856, see *Political Correspondence of . . . George N. Sanders*, p. 19.
8. *Doctor Grimshawe's Secret*, p. 270.　　9. See Emerson, *Journals*, VI, 259–62.

tatively that his countrymen were fifty years ahead of the English in "agricultural science." The tendency of the English to adhere to ideas for the sake of antiquity instead of utility, "which retards them in everything else, keeps them behindhand in this matter too,"[1] Hawthorne interpolated at that time, without as much regard as he might have had for the experiments with crop fertility of men like Jethro Tull and "Turnip" Townshend.

Redclyffe felt that for " 'a simple citizen of a republic' " it would be necessary to retrogress in order to exchange the democratic scheme of living for an antiquated one like the English.[2] And Hawthorne himself agreed that a moral degradation was implicit in the class system. There was something uniformly indecorous throughout every rank in going about as Englishmen did, "always conscious of somebody above them."[3] Thus he remarked in his journals: "Hanging on the skirts of the aristocracy, a baronet probably is oftener much [more] sensible of his inferiority to the few than of his elevation over the many."[4] Even the decent job of tutor to a young nobleman had "an ugly twang of upper servitude" about it.[5] Neither Hawthorne nor his hero could comprehend the pride which Englishmen apparently felt in having others above them who were born to privileges they could never dream of attaining.[6] In the latter's words, either would have preferred to be " 'the poorest and lowest man in America than have that sentiment!' "[7] Near the close of "The Procession of Life" Hawthorne had written:

Our attempt to classify society is now complete. The result may be anything but perfect; yet better—to give it the very lowest praise—than the antique rule of the herald's office, or the modern one of the tax-gatherer, whereby the accidents and superficial attributes, with which the real nature of individuals has least to do, are acted upon as the deepest characteristics of mankind.[8]

To have transferred citizenship from the United States to England would have been to relinquish, as Redclyffe said, " 'a set of institutions which are the noblest that the wit and civilization of man have yet conceived, to enlist myself in one that is based on a far lower conception of man, and which therefore lowers every one who shares in it.' "[9] And this was but a repetition of what he had previously declared.

'I do aver that I love my country, that I am proud of its institutions, that I have a feeling unknown, probably, to any but a republican, but which

1. *English Notebooks*, p. 227.   2. *Ibid.*, p. 269.
3. *English Notebooks*, p. 62.   4. *Ibid.*, p. 54.   5. *Ibid.*, p. 189.
6. *Doctor Grimshawe's Secret*, pp. 199–200. See also *English Notebooks*, pp. 44, 385.
7. *Doctor Grimshawe's Secret*, p. 200.   8. *Mosses*, pp. 250–51.
9. *Doctor Grimshawe's Secret*, pp. 269–70.

is the proudest thing in me, that there is no man above me,—for my ruler is only myself, in the person of another, whose office I impose upon him,—nor any below me.'[1]

Not long after his arrival in England, Hawthorne attended a dinner at which two of Robert Burns's sons, a colonel and a major, were present. He entered in his journals the following report of it:

The members of this dinner-party were of the more liberal tone of thinking, here in Liverpool. The colonel and major seem to be of similar principles; and the eyes of the latter glowed, when he sang his father's noble verse—'The rank is but the guinea's stamp' &c.[2]

To this he devoutly added, "It would have been too pitiable, if Burns had left a son who could not feel the spirit of that verse."[3]

> Then let us pray that come it may
>   (As come it will for a' that)
> That Sense and Worth o'er a' the earth
>   Shall bear the gee an' a' that!
> For a' that, an' a' that,
>   It's comin' yet for a' that,
> That man to man the world o'er
>   Shall brithers be for a' that.[4]

Into this song Burns had poured his sympathy for the ostensible motivation of the French Revolution, his belief that a man's the gold whatever his stamp, that the highest of ranks is "pith o' sense an' pride o' worth." By his appreciation of those tenets Hawthorne leaves little doubt as to what he meant when, in reference to his American equalitarianism, he spoke of there being "no higher birthright," no nobler conception of man.[5] "Ay," he had written in "The Procession of Life" several years before, "this is a reality, before which the conventional distinctions of society melt away like a vapor . . . Were Byron now alive, and Burns, the first would come from his ancestral abbey, flinging aside . . . the inherited honors of a thousand years, to take the arm of the mighty peasant who grew immortal while he stooped behind his plough."[6]

Nevertheless, despite the sincerity of his encomiums Hawthorne was not blind to the momentary defects of leveling democracy. He was sensitive to the derogatory nuances which, with that peculiarly

---

1. *Ibid.*, p. 199.
2. *English Notebooks*, pp. 31–32. Hawthorne also speaks of this dinner in a letter to his publisher, 8 October 1853; *Ticknor Letters*, I, 20.
3. *English Notebooks*, p. 32.
4. For these verses, usually entitled "Is There for Honest Poverty," see *The Complete Writings of Robert Burns*, in 10 vols. The Riverside Edition, Boston; 1926, V, 185–187.
5. *Doctor Grimshawe's Secret*, p. 269.   6. *Mosses*, p. 239.

strategic aloofness of his, he overheard being directed against it during his stay in foreign lands. As a matter of fact, he habitually sought out adverse criticism and candidly recorded it in his journals. In the fall of 1856 he wrote: "I saw a decent man, of the lower orders, taken much aback by being roughly brushed against by a rowdy fellow. He looked after him and exclaimed indignantly—'Is that a Yankee?'" Hawthorne concluded somewhat regretfully, "It shows the kind of character we have here."[7]

Seldom the type of man to evade what he did not like, he frankly faced the shortcomings of his countrymen. With but a few weeks left of his sojourn in England he made the following admission in his journals:

I begin to agree partly with the English, that we are not a people of elegant manners; at all events, there is sometimes a bare, hard, meagre sort of deportment, especially in our women, that has not its parallel elsewhere.[8]

And yet, however honest he may have been in assenting to such things, he was too concerned over the reputation of his fellow democrats to allow the charge of bad manners to be brought against them unopposed or unqualified. "But perhaps what sets off this kind [of] behavior, and brings it into *alto relievo*," he suggested partly to alleviate his personal chagrin, "is the fact of such uncultivated persons travelling abroad, and going to see sights that would not be interesting except to people of some education and refinement."[9]

Actually, the moments during which Hawthorne stood embarrassed before the rustic conduct of his fellow Americans were few and fleeting. More numerous by far are the instances of his repeated insistence that Americans were as capable of delicate breeding as any people of Europe; though, as he rather lamely confessed, "what with the circumstances amid which we grow up, and the peculiar activity of our minds, we certainly do often miss it."[1] On the other hand his diagnosis of Englishmen's behavior led him to say:

. . . if we can take it as compensatory on our part (which I leave to be considered) that they owe those noble and manly qualities to a coarser grain in their nature, and that, with a finer one in ours, we shall ultimately acquire a marble polish of which they are unsusceptible, I believe that this may be the truth.[2]

From a hearty reluctance to see the members of a democratic society accused of *gaucherie,* Hawthorne was driven to exonerate them on the basis of youthfulness. American manners, he contested, "being in a transition state between those of old monarchies and what is

7. *English Notebooks*, p. 428.   8. *Ibid.*, p. 568.
9. *Ibid.*   1. *Ibid.*, p. 229.   2. *Our Old Home*, p. 287.

proper to a new republic,—it necessarily followed that the American, though really a man of refinement and delicacy, is not just the kind of gentleman that the English can fully appreciate."[3] Still, it was his hope, not to say his prognosis, that from this transitional state, this national adolescence half-way between puberty and maturity, the American would emerge "into a higher mode of simplicity than has ever been known to past ages."[4]

At the same time that Hawthorne acknowledged a certain sense of propriety to be inbred in the people who lived by the older social system, he remarked: "But this kind of fitness is evidently not to be expected in the future; and something else must be substituted for it."[5] Abuse of the doctrine of equality, and the freedom from nominal class distinctions in America often resulted in the self-conscious assumption of "aristocratic airs" by moonstruck democrats, whose faulty logic led them to think that the prerogative which made them equal to those above them conversely made them superior to those below.[6]

But if unsurmountable class barriers prohibited the English servant girl from affecting to be what she was not,[7] they also prevented the successful middle-class Englishman from being gracefully all that he had become.[8] The handicap which the mores of his society imposed upon a self-made Englishman was virtually inescapable, while in America it simply did not exist. Thus Hawthorne observed that an American "comes naturally to any distinctions to which success in life may bring him; he takes them as if they were his proper inheritance, and in no wise to be wondered at."[9] Whereas the Englishman, accustomed to the concept of his proper inheritance as a thing fundamentally unalterable, is not in the end made "a whit more refined, either outwardly or inwardly"[1] by what, in the opinion of his betters and more or less of himself, is something of a rogue's progress. He was distinctly a *parvenu*, a thing almost impossible to become in a society where all men would presumably start from scratch, with no inheritance save their own good or bad qualities. Like all upstarts he could hardly refrain from taking a "childish delight in his position, and . . . a childish wonder in having arrived at it."[2]

In the end the arguments which favored the special fitness and

3. *Doctor Grimshawe's Secret*, p. 209.
4. *Our Old Home*, p. 336.   5. *English Notebooks*, p. 117.
6. Cf. *ibid.*, p. 107. Hawthorne speaks of Lord Derby as being " . . . entirely simple, and free from all the pretence and self-assertion which persons of lower rank can hardly help be-devilling themselves with."
7. See *ibid.*; also *Our Old Home*, pp. 335–36.
8. See *Doctor Grimshawe's Secret*, p. 208. ". . . a plebeian Englishman, who rises to eminent station, never does credit to it by his manners."
9. *English Notebooks*, p. 325.   1. *Ibid.*   2. *Ibid.*

decorum of the democratic way far outweighed those that upheld the fast failing proprieties of the caste system. To be sure, there was, as the Englishman inferred to Redclyffe, "a force and efficacy in the blood" when a man distinguished himself among the "grimy order" of American commonalty, all members of which had equal rights to prominence before the law.[3] After examining closely a group of charity urchins Hawthorne decided that nothing else was needed to convince him that "birth and blood do produce certain characteristics."[4] But in a democracy this tended toward the common good. A man did not have to be born to an earldom as a prerequisite for exerting the efficacy of his blood. His origins could be as obscure as Redclyffe's. Of the letters of statesmen and warriors in the British Museum, long as it had taken Europe to produce them, Hawthorne wrote, "I saw none so illustrious as that of Washington, nor more so than Franklin's, whom America gave to the world in her non-age."[5] Many years earlier, in "The Procession of Life," he had exclaimed: "Indiscriminately let those take their places, of whatever rank they come, who possess the kingly gifts to lead armies or to sway a people—Nature's generals, her lawgivers, her kings."[6] The only requirement for success was the blood itself, and it might perhaps be discovered in any man's veins in America, where people were not classified arbitrarily as in England. And, as Hawthorne wrote, "they cross-breed together, amid the continual ups-and-downs of our social life; and so, in the lowest stratum of life, you may see the refining influence of gentle blood."[7] One suspects that from this communal distribution of hereditary grace Hawthorne expected America to realize a race of supermen—nature's generals, lawgivers, and kings!

As a matter of fact, this is not an unpermissible exaggeration of his frame of mind. No men were ever in a more advantageous position for acquiring elegant manners and a beautiful deportment than the English aristocracy. "If any," Hawthorne said, "they must be Americans; and really," he continued, "I hope there may come a time when we shall be so, and I already know Americans whose noble and delicate manners may compare well with any I have seen."[8] But for Hawthorne this was only the start. Referring to the Earl of Derby, he said blandly: "Hundreds of American gentlemen, sons of their own good works, have full as noble an air, so far as that goes."[9] After this it was not long before he had become so assured of the su-

3. *Doctor Grimshawe's Secret*, p. 183.   4. *English Notebooks*, p. 192.
5. *Ibid.*, p. 613.   6. *Mosses*, p. 239.
7. *English Notebooks*, p. 192. Cf. "The Ontario Steamboat," *The American Magazine of Useful and Entertaining Knowledge*, II (March, 1836) 270. "In our country at large, the different ranks melt and mingle into one another, so that it is as impossible to draw a decided line between any two contiguous classes, as to divide a rainbow accurately into its various hues."
8. *English Notebooks*, p. 408.   9. *Ibid.*, p. 107.

periority of Americans that he began to express astonishment at the attitude of the British toward them.

It is very queer, this resolute quizzing of our manners, when we are really and truly much better figures, and with much more capacity of polish, for drawing-room or dining-room, than they themselves are.[1]

There was something almost absurd to Hawthorne in the fact that the British failed singly to understand how a natural sensitivity enabled most Americans to acquire through education the culture and grace which was an Englishman's only by right of birth and by virtue of a long line of ancestors, whose stolid characters had gradually become imbued with the qualities of refinement after successive centuries of exposure.[2] This marvelous impressibility belonged to the beautifully behaved Redclyffe; though the reader must accept Hawthorne's rather extended say-so, since Redclyffe is hardly developed enough to show it for himself.

In manners, I cannot but think that he was better than the generality of Englishmen, . . . he was quicker to feel what was right at the moment, than the Englishman; more alive; he had a finer grain; his look was more aristocratic than that of a thousand Englishmen of good birth and breeding; he had a faculty of assimilating himself to new manners, which . . . was what perhaps chiefly made the Warden think him so like an Englishman. When an Englishman is a gentleman, to be sure, it is as deep in him as the marrow of his bones . . . An American often gets as good a surface of manners, in his own progress from youth, through the wear and attrition of a successful life, to some high station in middle age . . . Often you would not know the American ambassador from a duke.[3]

It was thus that Hawthorne controverted the old nobleman of "Earth's Holocaust," who had desperately pleaded for his kind with the statement: " 'In abolishing the majestic distinctions of rank, society loses not only its grace, but its steadfastness . . . . ' "[4]

Nowhere was the narrow insularity of their view more apparent than in the unique habit which English people had of presuming that all Americans who exhibited gentlemanly manners had profited from an English breeding. Hawthorne, notwithstanding, was rather proud of being mistaken for an Englishman by Englishmen.[5] It was

1. *Ibid.*, p. 197.

2. See *Doctor Grimshawe's Secret*, p. 38. See also *English Notebooks*, p. 408. "The surest way to give him [an Englishman] good manners is, to make a lord of him—or rather, of his grandfather, or great-grandfather. In the third generation—scarcely sooner—he will be polished into simplicity and elegance, and his deportment will be all the better for the homely material out of which it is wrought and refined."

3. *Doctor Grimshawe's Secret*, pp. 207–08.   4. *Mosses*, p. 433.

5. He took the trouble to record instances of being thus mistaken in the journals. See, for example, *English Notebooks*, p. 416 (an entry later employed in *Our Old Home*, pp. 217–18).

not so much that he was an ordinary Anglophile, as it was that he recognized how great a compliment the English were paying him when they mistook him for one of themselves.[6]

He was just aristocratic enough by temperament to endorse the fine manners of aristocrats, and enough of a democrat at heart to desire these traits for a democratic society, and to believe it capable of achieving them naturally. As a result, he belonged with those people who, unlike Henry James for example, were willing to see the full capabilities and potentialities of Americans for cultivation and refinement, and who were anxious to develop and promote them. In *Doctor Grimshawe's Secret* he thus defined his position:

. . . we are bold to say, when our countrymen are developed, . . . they will show finer traits than have yet been seen. We have more delicate and quicker sensibilities; . . . and these are surely requisites for perfect manners; and, moreover, the courtesy that proceeds on the ground of perfect equality is better than that which is a gracious and benignant condescension,—as is the case with the manners of the aristocracy of England.[7]

He was too much of a traditionalist to celebrate, as Whitman largely did, America as it was. He saw it, so to speak, as an adolescent society. And he visualized its maturity as being not that of a great, overgrown boy, but of a wholly cultivated and refined character which would embrace the best that all societies had to offer, and embrace it better than they because more naturally.

Simultaneously, it is worth noting that Hawthorne was not motivated by any common sentiment of patriotism, but rather by a faith in the innate, natural rightness of the new American mode of life, and by a confidence that it could realize as well and even better whatever he found admirable in different, older social systems like England's. "My mind had been considerably enlivened, and my sense of American superiority renewed," he once said, referring to the Americans who lived at Mrs. Blodgett's boarding-house, "by intercourse with these people." And he continued as though he had been taken aback himself by the discovery, "Really, I do not know any other place in England where a man can be made so sensible that he lives in a progressive world, as here in Mrs. Blodgett's boarding-house."[8] And on the next day he returned to his journal to add to what he had already said about these products of the new social environment:

. . . they are alive, to an extent to which the Englishman never seems conscious of life. It would do John Bull good to come and sit at our table, and adjourn with us to our smoking-room; but he would be apt to go away a little crest-fallen.[9]

[handwritten marginalia: Hawthorne believe]

6. *Doctor Grimshawe's Secret*, p. 206.   7. *Ibid.*, p. 208.
8. *English Notebooks*, p. 227.   9. *Ibid.*, p. 228.

In a democracy, Hawthorne thought, men met each other on a more actual basis, and he felt, also, that their relations allowed greater efficiency because there were not arbitrarily submerged huge sectors of the population from which excellent talent might otherwise have been forthcoming. Just as there were unheard of quantities of natural resources to be exploited in America's wild forests and vast plains, so were there in her large, unassorted multitudes. The pioneer instinct which drove Americans to penetrate the deep wildernesses of their continent existed in a less muscular and more intellectual form in Hawthorne. The outcome of it was that he set out to explore the exciting social frontiers of democracy, still in the early stages of their expansion, with an intuitive sense of the greatness of the possibilities which they contained.

To a certain extent, and in some of his less guarded outbursts, it is impossible not to reckon with antagonism in Hawthorne's state of mind, an antagonism swollen by no inconsiderable lump of national conceit. He was not merely talking to cover up a feeling of inferiority when he wrote, "I shall never love England till she sues to us for help;" or when he added, as if this were not already enough:

There is an account to settle between us and them for the contemptuous jealousy with which (since it has ceased to be unmitigated contempt) they regard us; and if they do not make us amends by coming humbly to ask our assistance, they must do it by fairly acknowledging us as their masters.[1]

Nevertheless, it was not entirely in a spirit of bravado that Hawthorne had toyed wishfully with the notion of annexing England, or had visions of an American fleet sailing up the Mersey, or a Yankee Commodore in his consulate at Liverpool. As always, he interpreted whatever national rivalry existed between the United States and England as a symptom of the inevitable displacement of an antiquated but still hale society by an unseasoned, yet thriving one.

He had fairly diagnosed those qualities which had served England's turn in so many of her past successes, when he spoke of their being "rather fit for resistance than for progress."[2] It was no baseless intuition of a vast social readjustment, nor an unwarranted confidence in the superiority of America's contribution to it, that caused him to write proleptically:

The truth is, there is a spirit lacking in England, which *we* do not lack, and for the want of which she will have to resign a foremost position among the nations, even if there were not enough other circumstances to compel her to do so. Her good qualities are getting out of date;—at all events, there should be something added to them, in the present stage of the world.[3]

1. *Ibid.*, p. 92. 2. *Ibid.*, p. 108. 3. *Ibid.*

Hawthorne looked ahead expectantly to the time when America would prove itself the Gamaliel of a greater social order. Then the security and richness of the aristocratic past would have to be re-invigorated by being absorbed into the promise and brilliancy of the democratic future. "The time will come, sooner or later," Hawthorne had said grimly of John Bull, "when the old fellow will look to us for his salvation."[4] In a note written on the verge of his departure from England in 1858, he gave instructions to his friend Henry Bright for breaking the seals of the English journals in the year 1900. "By that time, probably," he blandly wrote, "England will be a minor republic, under the protection of the United States."[5] This note to Bright, which would have seemed preposterous to any of his readers in 1900, will seem only exaggerated today.

4. Hawthorne to Ticknor, 16 February 1855. *Ticknor Letters*, I, 80.
5. Hawthorne to Bright, 2 January 1858. *Hawthorne and His Wife*, II, 168.

VII

Sixes and Sevens

*I sometimes apprehend that our institutions may perish before we shall
have discovered the most precious of the possibilities which they involve.*
                                                                Our Old Home.

IT mattered little to Young America or to Hawthorne that the
Democratic tacticians had adopted their vigorous foreign policy at Baltimore in 1852 as much to divert attention from the
smoldering problem of slavery as from any deep-seated conviction
compelling them to assert "our national progressive power before
the world . . ."[1] As a political ruse it proved supremely successful
with the youthful progressive wing of the party and with Hawthorne,
both of whom shared a strange moral and political blindness in their
almost wilful indifference toward the agitation over slavery. Both
were looking abroad in premature anticipation of the world-wide
greatness of the American future, at a time when it was growing increasingly evident that that greatness and that future would meet
their first supreme test from within. In their haste to witness the
triumph of democracy over social circumstances morally inferior,
they shirked the first step. They overlooked the inevitability of the
fact—all too obvious later on—that America had first to put her own
house in order before she could begin the direct work of building
her career among the foremost nations of the world.

In the summer of 1854 Hawthorne complained to Ticknor in disgust that the United States seemed to be "in such a confounded mess"
that he found it "impossible to read American newspapers (of whatever political party) without being ashamed of my country." And
he continued: "No wonder . . . if Englishmen hate and despise us,
taking their ideas of us and our institutions from such sources."[2]

What had unsettled Hawthorne in the newspapers was the political confusion which followed President Pierce's action on the
Kansas-Nebraska Bill. William Lloyd Garrison set his scathing
anathema upon the bill in *The Liberator*. "A thousand times accursed
be the Union which has made this possible!"[3] he wrote with a cold

---

1. *Democratic Review*, xxx (June, 1852), 491.
2. Hawthorne to Ticknor, 7 July 1854. *Ticknor Letters*, I, 55. Compare a similar
sentiment expressed in a letter to Mrs. Hawthorne on 12 September 1854. *Love
Letters*, II, 228-29.
3. *The Liberator*, 26 May 1854.

fury. In Haverhill, Massachusetts (not far from Salem), Pierce, Cushing, Senator Douglas, and Loring "the slave-catcher" were hanged
in effigy across Merrimack Street.[4] The New York *Times* vociferously
denounced the President as "the tool of the slave-holding power"[5]
and asserted in an editorial that "not a single Northern Whig voted
for the Nebraska bill—one-half of the Northern Democrats against
it—and the other half through whose help they succeeded, voted
against the wishes of the majority of their constituents—tools of
Executive influence wrongfully used to control the legislation of the
nation."[6] The general opprobrium was so great that neither Pierce
nor his reputation ever managed to outlive it.

Meantime, Americans in Europe who had the faith in equalitarianism which Hawthorne held suffered tremendous anxiety over the
internal convulsions that rocked their democracy to its base. Their
immediate fear was that the country and its way of life would shortly
discredit itself abroad if dissension from within broke forth uncon-
trollably, as it gave every evidence of doing, over the slavery question.

It was in anticipation of something like this that George Sanders
published in the English newspapers a lengthy letter in which he
stated paradoxically enough that it was not the policy of the radicals
who upheld the equal rights of European peoples to interfere in the
particular instance of American slavery. Regarding the position of
these men Sanders wrote:

They know that strife and ill-blood between the Northern and Southern
people of the United States are music and luxury to the enemies of Democracy, . . . and must feel that, at this moment, . . . it is most urgently important that their only unshackled friends on earth—the people
of the United States—should harmonize all differences, so that they may
present to Europe an unbroken front . . .[7]

For this interesting indifference of the leading advocates of universal
political and social liberty Sanders offered the lame defense that the
United States, slave-holding and otherwise, were advancing "a benighted race . . . to a highly respectable grade of civilization and
Christianity: the visible proof of which is shown in the prosperity
and good government of the American Negro Republic of Liberia, whose respectable President is a manumitted American slave,
from the Southern State of Virginia."[8] In a like strain Kossuth himself,
crusader for Hungarian political freedom, wrote:

4. *Ibid.*, 2 June 1854.   5. See The New York *Times*, 5 June and 13 June 1854.
6. *Ibid.*, 5 June 1854.
7. This letter, dated 2 June 1854, was reprinted in The New York *Times*, 24 June
1854.
8. *Ibid.* Hawthorne had met President Roberts of Liberia at his Consulate. Of his
interview with him he wrote: "I was rather favorably impressed with him; for his de-

. . . I consider the strength and prosperity of the only republican power on earth so important to the future destinies of the world that I certainly would never contribute anything to its internal divisions.[9]

The same curious paradox is apparent in Hawthorne's reply to a letter from Sanders requesting his opinion on the sentiments expressed in this public correspondence. "It was certainly pertinent in you," he told Sanders, "to write the article you now send me . . . I do not see how you could have performed the task better, or more nobly . . . It entirely satisfies me."[1] But of Kossuth's letter he said: "I do not like it well enough to be glad that he has written it. . . . Does he not trim and truckle a little? . . . I wish he had commenced his reply with a sturdier condemnation of slavery . . . "[2] Hawthorne's intellectual integrity was too thorough-going for him ever to ignore the extreme incongruity in the fact that a society based on the equality of human rights harbored the institution of slavery. Nor could he overlook the wilful inconsistency of men like Sanders and Kossuth in winking at such a fact for fear of discommoding their ideal. In the very words Hawthorne had used, the *National Anti-Slavery Standard* accused Kossuth of "truckling," and of being a "political trimmer;"[3] and that arch-abolitionist William Lloyd Garrison himself condemned him for not regretting that American practice was "so glaringly at variance with our theory of human rights."[4]

It was as clear to Hawthorne as it was to these anti-slavery people, then, that slavery was a social sin for which democracy in America ought plainly to be indicted. To this single ethical fact upon which abolitionism took its stand—though not to the principle of abolition itself—Hawthorne had acquiesced early in his career.[5] On the other hand, his conception of the problem was akin to that of the historian Jared Sparks. Slavery in the abstract he judged calamitous, a reproach to democratic society, and something that any honest democrat should wish to see adjusted as expeditiously as possible. But like Sparks, and unlike the abolitionists, he also realized that under the circumstances the United States had little to do with the matter in the abstract.[6] However ethical an affair slavery was to the North, to the South it was an economic condition with too many practical implications to be rooted out with theoretical impatience.

portment was very simple, and without any of the flourish and embroidery which a negro might be likely to assume, on finding himself elevated from slavery to power." *English Notebooks*, p. 349. 9. The New York *Times*, 24 June 1854.

1. Hawthorne to Sanders, 14 June 1854. The original is in the Berg Collection.

2. *Ibid.* 3. Quoted in *The Liberator*, 21 July 1854.

4. *Joseph Mazzini, His Life, Writings, and Political Principles,* with an Introduction by William Lloyd Garrison (New York, 1872), pp. xiii-xiv.

5. See *American Notebooks*, p. 48.

6. See Herbert B. Adams, *The Life and Writings of Jared Sparks* (Boston and New York, 1893), I, 263.

Once again, and this time in abolitionism, Hawthorne believed that he had found an instance where reformers were proceeding with their usual devastating narrow-mindedness. "I do assure you," he told his sister-in-law, Elizabeth Peabody, "that, like every other Abolitionist, you look at matters with an awful squint, which distorts everything within your line of vision; and it is queer, though natural, that you think everybody squints except yourselves." And he added, "Perhaps they do; but certainly *you* do."[7] Several years before, he had written to his friend of the Salem Custom House, Zachariah Burchmore, "I have not . . . the slightest sympathy for the slaves; or at least, not half so much as for the laboring whites, who, I believe, as a general thing, are ten times worse off than the Southern negroes."[8] The cause of the laboring whites was, as we have seen, one of the "hundred modes of philanthropy" in which, as he wrote to Longfellow, he was able to "blaze with intenser zeal"[9] than in the case of slavery. It was, in fact, his own "awful squint," and he had once had the audacity to ask Charles Sumner to adopt it in *lieu* of abolitionism. But despite the fact that, apropos of Sumner's election to the Senate, Hawthorne disclaimed "any pre-eminent ardor" for the cause which he advocated,[1] he was so far aroused by the Fugitive Slave Law as to sign a Free Soil document jeopardizing his own chances of political employment thereafter. He had expressed his intention when "absolutely cornered" of going for New England "rather than the South," and he felt that the Fugitive Law had truly cornered him.[2]

Notwithstanding, he doubted whether slavery, though possibly the most engrossing subject of the day, was the great one that so many reformers claimed it to be,[3] and he suspected that much of the philanthropic concern over the negro in the cotton fields was misguided. From his personal observation it appeared that the negro in the South was far better off than his brothers who fled North to freedom. Without risking a word in extenuation of the institution of slavery, he nevertheless confessed his opinion that the slaves themselves would have been more happily advised to stay at home, "performing their moderate share of the labors of life, without being harassed by its cares."[4] And after the active struggle for the emancipation of the negro had for some time been under way, he gradually

---

7. Hawthorne to E. P. Peabody, 13 August 1857. The original is in the Berg Collection. See also his letter to the same, 8 October 1857.

8. Hawthorne to Burchmore, 10 July 1851. Published in the *Saturday Evening Gazette*, 2 September 1883.

9. Hawthorne to Longfellow, 8 May 1851.   1. *Ibid.*

2. See his letter to Burchmore cited above. Even Franklin Pierce, as Hawthorne points out (*Life of Franklin Pierce* [Works, xii], 419), resented this law, despite his endorsement of Compromise.

3. See his letter to Longfellow just cited.   4. *Snow Image*, p. 539.

became more stubborn in this belief. "I think," he remarked in "Chiefly About War Matters," "my prevalent idea was, that, whoever may be benefited by the results of this war, it will not be the present generation of negroes, . . . who must henceforth fight a hard battle with the world, on very unequal terms."[5]

Again Hawthorne returned to the idea that by meddling in a business with which they neither had nor desired to have a scientific outlook or a practical familiarity, the reformers would once more demonstrate their power to engender retroactively more wretchedness than they were able to expel. In opposition to Emerson on the subject of John Brown's martyrdom, he had cried with a controversial directness that was unusual and therefore rather terrible in him: "Nobody was ever more justly hanged."[6] Of all the reformers throughout history John Brown offered perhaps the best illustration of philanthropy overshooting itself.

As on other occasions, Hawthorne was naturally unsympathetic toward those who were tampering with a matter of such far-reaching social consequences as the institution of slavery. He was particularly averse to the drastic prescriptions of the abolitionists, which he was certain fell outside the sphere of man's right to interfere in his destiny. And that is one of the reasons why, at the mid-century, he sanctioned publicly the view that looked upon slavery as "one of those evils which divine Providence does not leave to be remedied by human contrivances, but which, in its own good time, by some means impossible to be anticipated, . . . it causes to vanish like a dream."[7]

Before the nightmare had begun in which slavery was destined to disappear, Hawthorne had clung at times feebly to the old idea of the Union, and to the men like Pierce who stood for it. "Is there not a prospect of a compromise," he inquired of his friend Burchmore in 1851, "between the Whigs and Freesoilers in favor of the Union?"[8] In his biography of Pierce he frankly revealed a predilection for the series of measures known under the collective title of The Compromise, and an almost sanctimonious approval of Franklin Pierce's support of them.[9]

The Compromise followed Hawthorne to England, where his

5. *Sketches*, p. 319.
6. *Sketches*, p. 327. In a lecture on Courage which was given in Boston, November, 1859, Emerson had called John Brown, then waiting execution, "the new saint awaiting his martyrdom, and who, if he shall suffer, will make the gallows glorious like the cross." (J. E. Cabot, *A Memoir of Ralph Waldo Emerson* [London and New York, 1887], II, 215.) No prude, and capable of sacrilege himself on occasion, Hawthorne's frank disgust over Emerson's rather indiscreet eloquence seems to have been roused chiefly by its breach of good taste.
7. *Life of Franklin Pierce* (Works, XII), 417.
8. Hawthorne to Burchmore, 17 September 1850. Published in the *Saturday Evening Gazette*, 12 August 1883.
9. See *Life of Franklin Pierce* (Works, XII), 414-19.

earlier suspicion of anti-slavery reform became coupled with a new sense of America's international function as the hope of democracy. The result was that he shied away from the slavery controversy more nervously than before. For like Sanders and his Young Americans, he knew only too well how injurious to the prestige of the United States and of democracy itself would be dissension from within. Thus it was that he wrote exasperatedly to Ticknor: "I sympathize with no party, but hate them all—free-soilers, pro-slavery men, and whatever else—all alike." His anxiety over democracy's none too secure reputation drove him to add: "The English expect to see the republic crumble to pieces, and are chuckling over the anticipation. This is all nonsense, of course; but it grinds me, nevertheless."[1] At the Christmas Banquet was a befuddled gentleman who, having once prided himself on his consistent adherence to a single political party, "in the confusion of these latter days, had got bewildered and knew not whereabouts his party was." Here Hawthorne added a strongly autobiographical touch. "This wretched condition," he interpolated, "so morally desolate and disheartening to a man who has long accustomed himself to merge his individuality in the mass of a great body, can only be conceived by such as have experienced it."[2] No man felt more keenly than Hawthorne the necessity for America's preserving serried ranks if she were ever to impress her virtues upon incredulous foreign nations; and no reformer was more eager to have her do so.

All this overseas ambition was, in a sense, a symptom of the growing internal disease of the country. The Young Americans were unwilling that the United States should be delayed in its career by internal difficulty. The notion that the Union had nourished a monster which would have to be disposed of before other matters could be taken in hand was abhorrent to them. And so it came to be a part of the subtle distress of the nation, this overwrought and almost frantic insistence upon the illustrious destiny of democracy throughout the world at large. It was not the rambunctious optimism of the thirties. Rather, it was a half-desperate attempt to pass over the discomfort of the moment. As a matter of fact this had been precisely the strategy of the Democratic party in 1852, when they decided at the Baltimore Convention to offer a spectacular foreign policy for the sake of distracting attention from the inflammable issues certain to be ignited by any reference to the problem of slavery. It was, of course, about as successful as Dimmesdale's efforts to evade Chillingworth. The Young Americans had been naturally, and by their very aspirations, susceptible to such distraction, and for their temporary peace of mind they were willing enough to cooperate in deluding themselves

1. Hawthorne to Ticknor, 10 October 1856. *Ticknor Letters*, ii, 29.
2. *Mosses*, p. 343.

until it seemed almost hopeless that the country itself would be diverted in the same way.

Upon his return to America amid the gathering clouds of war, Hawthorne was forced at the last to relinquish Young America's idea once so heartily commended, that the "sacred Union" was an immovable basis from which not only America's destiny but that of all mankind might be "carried upward and consummated." It was a particularly hard fate for one who, never too ebullient or optimistic, had but recently acquired some of the *élan* that was the most abundant of all America's spiritual resources. No sooner had he recognized the tremendous sufficiency of the democratic way of living and the equally enormous potentialities of his country for promoting it, than he was obliged to anticipate a sudden debilitation of that power. There arose all at once before his mind's eye the tragic spectacle of a strong nation at terrible odds within itself.

In London there had come to his ears the noise of the old foundations of society crumbling away, presaging the scheduled ruin of "a heterogeneous pile of institutions" which had somehow survived their vitality.[3] And at that time he had had a sanguine faith that the fresh and vigorous institutions of America would do better than merely replace the old world's outworn ones. But it was a beclouded faith almost from the moment of its inception, and he sensed not quite simultaneously, perhaps, that the disruption of his own land was about the only cataclysm he was destined to witness.[4] Disunion would be a sorrowful course indeed for a people who, he believed, were good for at least a thousand years of sturdy national existence.[5] It would be a social catastrophe of universal importance, for the stronghold of the rights and liberties of man would be whirled away in the debacle. "Methinks the true patriots and martyr-spirits of the whole world should have been conscious of a pang near the heart," he wrote sadly, "when a deadly blow was aimed at the vitality of a country which they have felt to be their own in the last resort."[6]

So it was that the Civil War dispelled his reminiscences of Frank Pierce as the President of Young America, and all his best dreams of democracy's future, and deprived him not only of the faculty but of the desire to create. It left him, in fact, with little more than the tattered fabric of a Romance that would have set forth the illustriousness of America, to be made over later on into another theme which also failed to materialize. Such was the effect upon him, as he him-

---

3. See *Our Old Home*, p. 111. Cf. *ibid.*, p. 290.

4. *Ibid.*, p. 111. See also Hawthorne to Ticknor, 10 October 1856. "The wise ones prophesy great commotions in France, and all over the Continent. . . . But there seems to be no stormier prospect any where, than in our own country . . ." *Ticknor Letters*, II, 29.

5. *Our Old Home*, p. 111.   6. *Ibid.*, p. 24.

self described it, of "the hurricane that is sweeping us all along with it, possibly, into a Limbo where our nation and its polity may be as literally the fragments of a shattered dream as my unwritten Romance."[7]

Undeniably the matter of slavery is an instance unique in Hawthorne's thinking, where he seems to have been more concerned with the external than with the internal development of virtue. But the situation was not such a simple choice between right and wrong, humanity and inhumanity, as William Lloyd Garrison and other absolutists obviously thought. How was the United States to set the world an example of social equity, propriety, and enlightenment if she harbored a vice of the dark ages like slavery? At the same time, how could she set that example if the people of her enlightened brotherhood, in removing the discrepancy, were fighting savagely among themselves in one of the worst civil disorders in the history of any country?

Hawthorne felt that such a war was not the proper or effective course. Moreover, like many Americans who were capable of some detachment he sensed that the abolitionists were far from being exclusively humanitarian, after the fanatical religious style and zeal of Garrison. The realists of the day saw that the slavery question had become involved with the program of territorial expansion, introducing with Free-Soilers and the like the motive of political exploitation.

But regardless of whether their motives were good or bad, those who undertook the extirpation of slavery flouted one of the primary principles of the democratic code, in disregarding the minority rights of the South and in using their temporary ascendancy in the government to enforce, irrespective of those rights, the majority will. This, as far back as the days of Tom Paine, had been clearly recognized and plainly branded by Americans as only a refined and subtle form of the same tyranny which had driven men to settle the new world and fight for its independence. The argument here is not intended to imply that the indignation against slavery, where it was sincerely moral, should not have been audacious enough to manifest its abhorrence in some sort of political action. But it should indicate the ethical and political complexity of the problem which Hawthorne had thrust upon him—a complexity to which the wary nature of his mind made him especially susceptible.

For a while he toyed morosely with such retributive ideas as that in which he fancied the enemies of the American peace and Union clapped up together within the subterranean confines of the Thames tunnel, whence they would one day emerge to view their country redeemed in its own blood, "feel it to be a better land than they deserve,

7. *Ibid.*, p. 16.

and die!"[8] But little by little he began to face the situation squarely. It was the duty of each true democrat to see that affairs be made to work out for the best possible advantage of democracy. Much might yet be salvaged regardless of whether, as he said himself, "the Union is to be henceforth a living giant, or a mangled and dismembered corpse."[9] And it is to Hawthorne's everlasting credit that his lately established faith in democratic America was hardy enough, and his own interest in the making of the United States so vital that at the very close of his career, in the consciousness of age and the confusion of a nation that seemed bent either on destroying itself or starting all over again, he did not throw up his hands and take an old man's refuge in the past. Instead, he trained his faculties as strenuously as he now could upon the future, for it had not ceased to be of utmost importance to him still.

Hawthorne's attitude toward embattled democracy was as realistic as his earlier notions had been visionary. It was not a new set of ideas that occupied him; it was an obstinate clinging to such of the former as promised to remain in some degree practicable. In other words, his reaction to the latest trend in events was resuscitative rather than creative. Though he had the stamina to look forward at what might be ahead, he lacked the uncompromising idealism which as a younger man he might have been expected to possess. He concerned himself mainly with schemes for salvaging as much as possible of his country's best and soundest institutions.

Hawthorne had always felt subconsciously that slavery was a stigma to any society which permitted it, and that to a democratic society in particular it was an incredible anomaly. But there were as many practical economic reasons why it could not be quickly uprooted and annihilated as there were practical sociological reasons why it could not long endure in the midst of democracy without directly or indirectly causing trouble. Consequently, he was reduced at last to the conviction that "the North and the South were two distinct nations in opinion and habits, and had better not try to live under the same institutions," and that "Southerners were not his fellow-countrymen!"[1] With this theory in mind he told his publisher, "I go for a dissolution of the Union; and, on that ground, I hope the Abolitionists will push matters to extremity."[2] The old idea of the

8. *Ibid.*, pp. 296–97.
9. From the original conclusion to the dedicatory letter of *Our Old Home*, printed by Randall Stewart, "Hawthorne and the Civil War," *Studies in Philology*, xxxiv (January, 1937), 101.
1. F. B. Sanborn, *Hawthorne and His Friends* (Cedar Rapids, 1908), p. 61.
2. Hawthorne to Ticknor, 10 February 1860. *Ticknor Letters*, ii, 94. Hawthorne's attitude here bears an interesting resemblance to that of his friend, Dr. Charles Mackay, who suggested a "pacific dissolution of the Union" into a realm which he called the "United Republics of America." (*Life and Liberty in America, or Sketches of a Tour in*

"sacred" Union now seemed a wholly false basis upon which to erect American democracy. Even Franklin Pierce appeared in the end to be "bigoted"[3] to a concept that was worthless.

It is not an easy thing for a man of threescore to forego an ideal he has cherished in respect to the world about him. While he was still in England Hawthorne had written to Bridge: "I regret that you think so doubtfully of the prospects of the Union; for I should like well enough to hold on to the old thing."[4] And to his sister-in-law he remarked six years later, "I am very often sensible of an affectionate regard for the dead old Union."[5] For all his undoubted intellectual courage he could not help withdrawing now and then into a solitude like that of his post-college years, or like that of the stern and remote Septimius Felton. "Are times so terribly bad as people say?" he asked Ticknor. "I have left off reading newspapers and only know by hearsay that the Union is falling asunder."[6]

On the whole, however, Hawthorne adapted himself to circumstances with some resilience and flexibility. He pursued his examination of the motives and the probable outcome of the war with as clinical an interest as ever. "What ever happens next," he wrote to Bridge in the spring of 1861, "I must say that I rejoice that the old Union is smashed. We never were one people, and never really had a country since the Constitution was formed."[7] But he had not yet determined in his own mind upon the best excuse for fighting a war. "If we are fighting for the annihilation of slavery," he argued, ". . . it may be a wise object, and offers a tangible result, and the only one which is consistent with a future Union between North and South."[8] In this case he advocated arming the slaves, a policy abhorrent even to the North's most fanatical reformers. On the other hand, he told Bridge, "If we pummel the South ever so hard, they will love us none the better for it; and even if we subjugate them, our next step should be to cut them adrift."[9]

In the final analysis Hawthorne thought that the only constructive purpose which the war might serve would be to establish some free territory where democracy could once and for all impregnably entrench itself. Thus he wrote to his friend Henry Bright in England:

the United States and Canada in 1857–8 [New York, 1859], p. 324). It was Mackay's notion that the United States was too vast to be a single country under one system of manners and morals.

3. Hawthorne to Bridge, 14 February 1862. In *Personal Recollections*, p. 172.

4. This letter, dated 9 January 1857, is printed in part by Lathrop, *Biographical Sketch*, p. 542.

5. Hawthorne to E. P. Peabody, 20 July 1863. Printed in the Boston *Post*, 18 April 1887.

6. Hawthorne to Ticknor, 28 December 1860. *Ticknor Letters*, II, 111.

7. This letter, dated 26 May 1861, is printed in part by Lathrop, *Biographical Sketch*, pp. 542–43.

8. *Ibid*   9. *Ibid*.

When we have established our boundary lines to our satisfaction, and demonstrated that we are strong enough to subjugate the whole South, I trust we shall cast off the extreme Southern states, and giving them a parting kick, let them go to perdition in their own way. I want no more of their territory than we can digest into free soil; but now that we have actually come to swords' points, it would be a sin and shame to take less.[1]

The moral heritage of democracy was at stake. Any amalgamation along the lines of the old Union might tend to prolong slavery, Hawthorne believed, for another hundred years. The North might thus have shed its blood in vain in the battle against the evil of slavery, and still democracy would have no real bulwarks against it. "Free soil," he exclaimed, "was never in so great danger as now."[2] So he held to his idea of amputation and viewed the war as a struggle mainly over the privilege of "selecting the point where our diseased members shall be lop't off."[3] To this end he urged that the North push on for the sake of preserving to democracy as much territory as was capable of being made into free soil.[4] "I might even deem it allowable for myself, in the last resort," he admitted reluctantly, "to be content with half the soil that was once our broad inheritance."[5] It was his hope that democracy would be democracy still, as heaven had remained heaven in *Paradise Lost*, "after Lucifer and a third part of the angels seceded from its golden palaces."[6]

Yet despite all his endeavors to the contrary, he could not keep a steadfast faith in the ultimate career of democracy once the turmoil into which it had been so prematurely plunged should have subsided. Brief as was the war's duration, he was not to be there on the day when reconstruction was begun. "I truly regret," he confided to Bright, "that my youth was not cast in these days, instead of in a quieter time."[7] But there is a certain fitness in the fact that a period in the history of America passed away with him. The day of expansion and annexation, of Jackson and the spoils, of Clay, Calhoun, and Webster, and the rivalry of Whigs and Democrats, the first tide of democracy rising and overflowing the pretensions of aristocrats—this day went out with the Civil War. As a young man Hawthorne had seen the popularity of Irving and Cooper, he had known the New England

1. Hawthorne to Bright, 14 November 1861. The original is in the possession of the Marquis of Crewe, K.G.

2. From the letter to E. P. Peabody just cited.

3. Hawthorne to Bridge, 12 October 1861. *Personal Recollections*, p. 170. Compare his letter to the same, 14 February 1862, *ibid.*, p. 172.

4. See his letter to Bright already cited.

5. From the excised conclusion to the dedicatory letter of *Our Old Home*, cited above.

6. *Sketches*, pp. 344–45.

7. This letter, dated 14 November 1861, is in the collection of the Marquis of Crewe, K.G.

Brahmins in his prime, and had been a member of the Saturday Club[8] in his early old age. He would have been too old a man to adjust himself comfortably to post-war conditions. The job of reconstruction was a young man's work, and there is a singular timeliness in Hawthorne's death which made his life much more of an integrated work of art on the part of Providence than those of Emerson, Longfellow, and Lowell, which overlapped awkwardly the world of Mark Twain, William Dean Howells, and Sidney Lanier.

Hawthorne and the America in which his genius grew to maturity had, in the words of Hosea Biglow, "kind o' gin out." No one realized this better than he. "The war continues to interrupt my literary industry,"[9] he told Ticknor, while he vainly and pathetically strove to turn a hundred ill-conceived ideas to some account. He confessed to Fields regarding the romance which remained uncompleted through four separate attempts to bring it off: "I linger at the threshold, and have a perception of very disagreeable phantasms to be encountered if I enter."[1] Similar phantasms appear also to have stood in the way of his prospectus of the collective destiny of his people. Appended to a letter which he sent to Charles Sumner in the spring of the year 1861 is a single eloquent question: "P.S. What are we coming to?"[2] Two years later he informed Bridge that on the score of the depressing and miserable conflict, he himself had been beaten to insensibility.[3] Then, quite unexpectedly, he wrote to Fields in October: "Those verses entitled 'Weariness,' in the last Magazine seem to me profoundly touching. I too am weary, and begin to look ahead for the Wayside Inn."[4] The verses which he referred to were Longfellow's. The Wayside Inn was not.

It is to Hawthorne's supreme credit that in his appraisal of the political and social upheaval of the war he had the courage to face the facts. He was more accurate and realistic than Emerson, who after having taken up the hue and cry spent the post-war years obeying the voice of pre-war America as though nothing had intervened which had changed the tune; or Whitman, whose rehabilitation did not include coming to grips with America's most pressing sociological problem, which abolition still left unsolved as Hawthorne knew it would.

Portents of some great impending change recurred frequently to Hawthorne in the last few months of his life. "You will live to see the

8. See Edward Waldo Emerson, *The Early Years of the Saturday Club, 1855–1870* (Boston and New York, 1918), pp. 207–17.

9. Hawthorne to Ticknor, 16 May 1861. *Ticknor Letters*, II, 114.

1. Hawthorne to Fields, 18 October 1863. See Fields, *Hawthorne* (Boston, 1876), p. 107.

2. Hawthorne to Sumner, 11 April 1861. The original is in the Sumner Collection of the Widener Library at Harvard.

3. Hawthorne to Bridge, 21 January 1863, in the collection of Miss Maurice.

4. This letter, dated 24 October 1863, was printed in part in *Yesterdays*, pp. 109–10.

Americans another people than they have hitherto been,"[5] he promised Henry Bright; and in the same vein he wrote to Ticknor with a
kind of simple assurance, "We are going to have great changes in our
institutions."[6] But his comprehension of these alterations in the American social system was beset with doubt. He could not forget that he
had not wanted war, that he had approved of it only because, having
once commenced, it would have proved a futile carnage unless carried through to a definite end. In a letter to Elizabeth Peabody he
revealed his qualms without compunction and certainly without any
idea of gratifying his correspondent:

. . . I have always thought that it should have been avoided . . . I agree
with your friend —— ——, who thinks that the war will only effect by a
horrible convulsion the self-same end that might and would have been
brought about by a gradual and peaceful change. Nor am I at all certain
that it will effect that end. Even these recent successes have not as in-
dubitable a tendency in that direction.[7]

At the very last, with his old questioning habit of mind, he became
skeptical not only of events but of his own faculties for interpreting
them. In that portion of the dedication of *Our Old Home* which he
had been prevailed upon to strike out—that last creative effort linking
him to the past and his earlier criticism—he said: "I can judge little
of these matters, and know not well what to hope, although I can see
much to fear."[8] The uncertainty in that statement belonged to a spirit
no longer at ease in contemplating the objectives of progress, and to
a mind not young enough to accept with equanimity the unsettled
configurations of a changing American society.

5. Hawthorne to Bright, 14 November 1861, in the possession of the Marquis of
Crewe, K.G.
6. *Ticknor Letters*, II, 121. This letter is dated 8 February 1863.
7. Hawthorne to E. P. Peabody, 20 July 1863, cited above. Hawthorne's attitude
bears a striking resemblance to that of the South's great sectionalist, John C. Calhoun.
"It has been lately urged . . . that it is the mission of this country to spread civil
and religious liberty over all the globe, and especially over this continent—even by
force, if necessary. It is a sad delusion. . . . To preserve . . . liberty it is indispensable to adopt a course of moderation and justice toward all nations; to avoid war whenever it can be avoided; to let those great causes which are now at work, and by which
the mere operation of time, will raise our country to an elevation and influence which
no country has ever heretofore attained, continue to work. By pursuing such a course,
we may succeed in combining greatness and liberty . . . and do more to extend liberty
by our example over this continent and the world generally, than would be done by a
thousand victories." (R. K. Cralle [ed.], *The Works of Calhoun,* [1867], IV, 416, 420.)
8. See the original conclusion to the dedicatory letter of *Our Old Home*, cited above.

VIII

The Social Ethic

The creation of tragedy demands of its author a mature understanding of the relation of the individual to society . . . He must have a coherent grasp of social forces, or, at least, of man as a social being . . . For the hero of tragedy is never merely an individual, he is a man in action, in conflict with other individuals in a definite social order.
[F. O. Matthiessen, *American Renaissance.*]

THE moral problem to be found wherever the individual's maladjustment to society culminates in sin furnished Hawthorne with his major tragic themes. In the main this problem is worked out through some resolution by the individual of his maladjustment, an expiation of his sin, by coming to terms with society—by coming to terms with a democratic society. Such in fact is the central action of *The Marble Faun, The Scarlet Letter, The House of the Seven Gables.* It remains to be seen from these tragedies what Hawthorne conceived to be the moral interplay between the individual and those forces of society which he saw at work in and about him.

The House of the Seven Gables constitutes Hawthorne's most forthright use of American democratic philosophy as a basis for a social ethic. The theme of this romance has to do with inherited sin, the sin of aristocratic pretensions against a moral order which, in the judgment of an equalitarian like Hawthorne, calls for a truer and higher evaluation of man. For the inheritance of the Pyncheon family proves to be no more than the antagonism of the old Colonel and his world toward things democratic.

Hawthorne was a shrewd enough student of history to be aware that the Puritan society of New England had been as aristocratic in its way as the feudal society of Europe, with which he was later to have a first hand acquaintance. He saw clearly the sharp cleavage that existed then between the various members of the social group. The servants who stood inside the entrance to the House of the Seven Gables directing one class of people to the parlor and the other to the kitchen preside likewise over the social distinctions of the whole story, separating the Pyncheons from the Maules and gentility from democracy until the very end.[1] It is Hawthorne's symbolism at its best.

In the days of the theocracy, Hawthorne is willing to admit, there

1. *Seven Gables*, p. 25.

may have been some "temporary advantage"[2] to the division between high and low and the suppression of the one by the other. Though such suppression was wrong-doing regardless of extenuating circumstances, it was a type of evil that was less apparent in the days of the Colonel than it had since become.

There is something so massive, stable, and almost irresistibly imposing in the exterior presentment of established rank and great possessions, that their very existence seems to give them a right to exist; at least, so excellent a counterfeit of right, that few poor and humble men have moral force enough to question it, even in their secret minds. Such is the case now, after so many ancient prejudices have been overthrown; and it was far more so in ante-Revolutionary days, when the aristocracy could venture to be proud, and the low were content to be abased.[3]

The Colonel who perpetrated the original wickedness belonged to a world whose social ethic was imperfectly developed. This fact makes his sin more normal than that of his heirs, yet no less culpable in the eyes of Holgrave or Hawthorne, both of whom measure it by an ethical absolute without reference to temporal variants. Meanwhile, each heir who accepts the Colonel's ill-gotten gain is an accessory after the fact. In times of growing social enlightenment when the heir cannot help knowing that his ancestor violated the rights of the commoner Maule, he is the wilful recipient of stolen goods. If he would share the spoils he must share the guilt.

For various reasons, however, and from impressions often too vaguely founded to be put on paper, the writer cherishes the belief that many, if not most, of the successive proprietors of this estate were troubled with doubts as to their moral right to hold it. Of their legal tenure there could be no question; but old Matthew Maule, it is to be feared, trode downward from his own age to a far later one, planting a heavy footstep, all the way, on the conscience of a Pyncheon. If so, we are left to dispose of the awful query, whether each inheritor of the property—conscious of wrong, and failing to rectify it—did not commit anew the great guilt of his ancestor, and incur all its original responsibilities.[4]

It was to a consciousness of similar sin against the democratic morality, which he felt was the only true social ethic, that Hawthorne later tried to arouse the British upper classes. Democracy, like Maule, should plant "a heavy footstep" on the conscience of any aristocracy.

The social sinfulness of aristocracy became specific, took on symbolic expression for the purposes of art in the crime which the arrogant old Colonel committed in usurping the home of the commoner Maule. It became more explicit still in the Colonel's effort to appropriate for himself and his heirs a tract of land somewhere in Maine. The fate

2. *Ibid.*, p. 14.   3. *Ibid.*, p. 40.   4. *Ibid.*, p. 34.

of this abortive estate is especially significant. It reveals the natural destruction by democracy of the artificial, unethical arrangements of feudalism.

But, in course of time, the territory was partly regranted to more favored individuals, and partly cleared and occupied by actual settlers. These last, if they ever heard of the Pyncheon title, would have laughed at the idea of any man's asserting a right—on the strength of mouldy parchments, signed with the faded autographs of governors and legislators long dead and forgotten—to the lands which they or their fathers had wrested from the wild hand of nature by their own sturdy toil.[5]

The family ambition to possess such an estate is so persistent that it even haunts the ascetic daydreams of poor Hepzibah, who clings wistfully to the hope that some sort of deed may yet appear to establish arbitrarily the claim of one family in default of the rights of all those common folk who have broken, cultivated, and inhabited the land for their livelihood. There is likelihood that Hawthorne was influenced here by Rousseau, whose works he had read extensively during June, July, and August of 1848.[6] The following passage from *The Social Contract* can conceivably have had a strong conditioning effect on his thinking in connection with the land in Waldo County, Maine.

In general, to authorize the right of the first occupant upon any territory, the following conditions are necessary: first, that the land shall never have been occupied; second, that only such a quantity be occupied as will be necessary for subsistence; third, that it be taken possession of not by an empty ceremony but by labor and cultivation, for this is the only sign of ownership which, in default of legal title, should be respected by others.[7]

By rendering the Pyncheon claim to such territory a snare and a delusion, Hawthorne signified the baselessness of the pretensions of gentility and its gradual absorption in the morally inevitable progress of society toward democracy.[8]

But the Pyncheon family itself (like the illusion of property upon which still depended much of the pride that was the mainstay of their spirit) gradually became more and more attenuated as the falseness of their position was made clearer by the great movement of society toward the equalitarian ideal. In fact, by the time the story proper opens, the process by which their proudly accumulated mass of possessions (spiritual and material) "shall be scattered abroad in its

5. *Ibid.*, p. 33.

6. See *Essex Institute Historical Collections*, LXVIII (1932), 65–87.

7. Edward L. Walter (ed.), *The Social Contract*, translated by R. W. Harrington (New York, 1893), I, ix.

8. This is likewise the gist of the tale "Peter Goldthwaite's Treasure."

original atoms"[9] is nearly complete. Their coveted estate is occupied by common people who wrest a living from it with manual labor. One of their scions has married "a young woman of no family or property," died and left as only heir to the Pyncheon prejudices and delusions a daughter of democracy.

There are but two developments left before the final absorption of the family can be achieved; the working out of each of these is the schedule for the story. By marrying Holgrave, Phoebe must merge, under the healthy and joyous auspices of equalitarianism, the blood of the old Colonel with the blood of the commoner whom he wronged. Thus she will expiate the old social guilt by dissipating the false distinctions that underlay it. Simultaneously the grim pride of the Pyncheons, which has erected as its monument the House of the Seven Gables and maintained the house as a token of inviolateness and aloofness for generations, must be punctured and all its vital juices drawn off until there remains only a monstrous emptiness.

The undemocratic pride of the Pyncheons first manifested itself as a sin against society when the Colonel usurped the land of Matthew Maule, the commoner, on which to build a mansion to house his ill-founded pretensions. A self-destructive element in his behavior is implicit in the legend, which attributes his death to the fact that by his conduct he drew on his own head the curse of old Maule. Allegorically considered, Maule's curse is the moral sentence of society which a man inevitably brings on himself in sinning against his fellow. If we read from the legend, then, the sin of pride may be seen to contain the germ of its own annihilation.[1] And if we translate from the legend to the fact in terms of the action of the romance, we shall further see that it is the factor of isolation in the pride of the Pyncheons which automatically effects their ruin.

Like the chickens in the yard who pointedly resemble them, the Pyncheons had "existed too long in their distinct variety."[2] In this parable is contained all the significance of an overweening self-interest operative within the carefully prescribed limits of one family for generation after generation. Deterioration is obvious in the blighted spinster who, with her hens and her brother, still clings to the last shreds of gentility.

Uncle Venner, the commoner, once remarked to Hepzibah that her family "never had the name of being an easy and agreeable set of folks. There was no getting close to them," he said.[3] In the absence of a claim to anything more tangible except the house itself, this is the

9. *Seven Gables*, p. 14.
1. The fact that Judge Pyncheon is supposed to have ruined Clifford furthers the allegory of the family self-destruction.
2. *Seven Gables*, p. 113.   3. *Ibid.*, p. 84.

only inheritance of the last two inhabitants of Colonel Pyncheon's mansion. "'Miss Hepzibah,'" observed Holgrave, "'by secluding herself from society has lost all true relation with it, and is, in fact, dead . . .'"[4] "She had dwelt too much alone,—too long in the Pyncheon House—until her very brain was impregnated with the dry-rot of its timbers."[5] "In her grief and wounded pride, Hepzibah had spent her life in divesting herself of friends; she had wilfully cast off the support which God has ordained his creatures to need from one another . . ."[6] Over against her gaunt and decadent individualism is set the contrasting figure of lively Phoebe, "a fair parallel between new Plebeianism and old Gentility."[7] It is she who brings life into the dark house and hearts of Clifford and Hepzibah, and takes it away with her when she leaves.

But it is impossible in the present state of society even for the dark old sanctuary of Pyncheon gentility to preserve its insularity intact.

Let us behold, in poor Hepzibah, the immemorial lady,—two hundred years old, on this side of the water, and thrice as many on the other,—with her antique portraits, pedigrees, coats of arms, records and traditions, in Pyncheon Street, under the Pyncheon Elm, and the Pyncheon House, where she has spent all her days,—reduced now, in that very house, to be the huckstress of a cent-shop.[8]

The opening of the cent-shop to let the outside world into the stifling interior of the secluded house is a symbol of the salutary virtues of the Maule forces, or the forces of democracy, in contrast to the moribund condition of the Pyncheons. "In this republican country, amid the fluctuating waves of our social life," wrote Hawthorne, "somebody is always at the drowning point."[9] The Pyncheons were drowning in their own separateness, unable to draw the breath of life because they had so entirely shut themselves away from it. The cent-shop is a kind of pulmonary connection from humanity to the almost strangled existence of the House of the Seven Gables.

Hitherto, the life blood has been gradually chilling in your veins as you sat aloof, within your circle of gentility, while the rest of the world was fighting out its battle with one kind of necessity or another. Henceforth, you will at least have the sense of healthy and natural effort for a purpose, and of lending your strength—be it great or small—to the united struggle of mankind. This is success,—all the success that anybody meets with![1]

4. *Ibid.*, pp. 257–58.   5. *Ibid.*, p. 80.
6. *Ibid.*, p. 290.   7. *Ibid.*, p. 104.
8. *Ibid.*, pp. 55–56. Hepzibah's resemblance to old Esther Dudley in the tale of that name is patent.
9. *Ibid.*, p. 55.   1. *Ibid.*, p. 63.

Holgrave was right; Hepzibah did undergo "the invigorating breath of a fresh outward atmosphere, after the long torpor and monotonous seclusion of her life."[2] But the experience was transitory. She retained her aristocratic arrogance, and inwardly despised the people by whose pennies she hoped to be sustained. The democracy she still repudiated failed to provide for her because she tried to take it in on her own conditions, to pervert it to her own undemocratic ends. Hepzibah, "the recluse of half a lifetime," proved pathetically incapable of merging with humanity in the common struggle for existence. It is Phoebe who takes over the cent-shop.

The childish, ineffectual Clifford exemplifies if possible a worse maladjustment than his sister. He has what remains of the exquisite nature that Hawthorne describes as "always selfish in its essence."[3] A person of his stamp "can always be pricked more acutely through his sense of the beautiful and harmonious than through his heart."[4] Had his character been allowed an opportunity for full natural development his taste or aesthetic temper might have been so perfectly cultivated as to have "completely eaten out or filed away his affections,"[5] thus making even more complete his isolation from the human heart by which men live.

But Clifford too had moments in which he felt the regenerative urge to burst from the inner prison of himself into the stream of life. "With a shivering repugnance at the idea of personal contact with the world, a powerful impulse still seized on Clifford, whenever the rush and roar of the human tide grew strongly audible to him."[6] On one such occasion he was watching from a window of the House of the Seven Gables when a political parade went by in the street below. It seemed "one broad mass of existence,—one great life,—one collected body of mankind, with a vast, homogeneous spirit animating it—a mighty river of life, massive in its tide, and black with mystery, and, out of its depths, calling to the kindred depth within him."[7] So strong was the influence upon him to join in the march of his fellow men that it affected him as a sort of primal madness, and he could "hardly be restrained from plunging into the surging stream of human sympathies."[8] He was impelled, Hawthorne suggests, by "a natural magnetism, tending towards the great centre of humanity."[9] Breathlessly he remarked to the terrified Hepzibah that had he taken the plunge and survived it, it would have made him another man. Hawthorne interpolates again by saying that he "required to take a deep, deep plunge into the ocean of human life, and to sink down and be covered by its profoundness, and then to emerge, sobered, invigorated, restored to

2. *Ibid.*, p. 71.   3. *Ibid.*, p. 136.   4. *Ibid.*, p. 139.
5. *Ibid.*, p. 140.   6. *Ibid.*, p. 199.   7. *Ibid.*
8. *Ibid.*, p. 200.   9. *Ibid.*

the world and to himself."[1] In his desire shortly after this incident to join the villagers going to church on Sunday, he displayed a "similar yearning to renew the broken links of brotherhood with his kind."[2] Yet he and Hepzibah were unable to go through with it once they stood on the front step in plain sight of the whole town and all its citizens. They retreated into the gloom of the house which was the historical and material symbol of the isolation of their hearts. "For, what other dungeon is so dark as one's own heart! What jailer so inexorable as one's self!"[3]

Living arrangements like those of the later Pyncheons, as Hawthorne noted elsewhere, "assumed the form both of hypocrisy and exaggeration, by being inherited from the example and precept of other human beings, and not from an original and spiritual source."[4] The point Hawthorne is trying to make is the same one which Thoreau attempted to demonstrate by his life, and Emerson by his philosophy: namely, the moral necessity for all men to establish—as Emerson put it in *Nature*—"an original relation to the universe."

In one form or another this idea had dogged the subtler American democratic thinkers since Jefferson and Tom Paine insisted that each generation not only should be able but should be made to set up its own laws and contracts. Paine thought that to escape the infelicitous prejudices of the past it was necessary for men to think as though they were the first men who thought. We have already seen from the English romance that Hawthorne felt about his own generation as Holgrave feels about his. They must slough off the second-hand arrangements of the defunct past and work out their own relation to the world. This was their responsibility according to the best theories of democratic individualism. To fail in it as the Pyncheon progeny had was "sinister to the intellect, and sinister to the heart." It inevitably brought about "miserable distortions of the moral nature."[5]

Thus the selfish individualism of a family so jealously guarding its interests through successive epochs, in defiance of newer trends and mores to which men at large are susceptible, is shown to be self-destructive. By preserving Colonel Pyncheon's proud egocentricity, the heirs cherished the very corrosive evil which eventually ate away their humanity. " 'The truth is,' " says Hawthorne's spokesman Holgrave, " 'that, once in every half-century, at longest, a family should be merged into the great, obscure mass of humanity, and forget all about its ancestors.' "[6] Only in this way is it possible to avoid the arro-

1. *Ibid.*, p. 201.   2. *Ibid.*   3. *Ibid.*, p. 204.
4. *Snow-Image*, p. 460. These comments occur in the sketch "Main Street," which was first published in Elizabeth Peabody's *Aesthetic Papers*, 1849, about a year before *The House of the Seven Gables* was begun.
5. *Ibid.*   6. *Ibid.*, p. 222.

gance which represents a sin against society, morally punishable by a fearful and hopeless ostracism.

This ostracism is the real legacy which Colonel Pyncheon left to his redoubtable progeny. "A man will commit almost any wrong," said Clifford, "—he will heap up an immense pile of wickedness, as hard as granite, and which will weigh as heavily upon his soul, to eternal ages,—only to build a great gloomy, dark chambered mansion, for himself to die in, and for his posterity to be miserable in."[7] The dark chambered mansion is the human heart in isolation.

Maule's curse—the moral sentence passed by society—is that the Pyncheons shall be destroyed by their sin of selfishness against him and his class. But they shall meet destruction under the special and significant circumstances which are the consequences of their sin against the commoner. They shall ultimately be destroyed by the solitude which they built for themselves at Maule's expense in the shape of the House of the Seven Gables, where the Colonel died alone at the beginning of the story and where (reincarnated in the character of the Judge) he returns to die alone at the end.

A few hours earlier while impotent, friendless old Hepzibah cast futilely about, like someone in a nightmare, for succor from the wicked Judge, it seemed "as if the house stood in a desert, or, by some spell, was made invisible to those who dwelt around, or passed beside it."[8] Here is the tragic crux of the story. This is the bitter atonement which the family has made for the guilt which it wilfully assumed for so many generations. And a few hours later—"The gloomy and desolate old house, deserted of life, and with awful Death sitting sternly in its solitude, was *the emblem of many a human heart*, which, nevertheless, is compelled to hear the thrill and echo of the world's gayety around it."[9] The House is Hawthorne's master symbol of isolation. It stands for the spiritual condition of those who by their hostility to democracy sin against what he believed to be the true moral order, and as a result become evanescent through their utter separateness from mankind.

The theme of *The Scarlet Letter* is also that of the isolation of the human heart. But unlike *The House of the Seven Gables* it contains no balance between those characters who belong to the world at large and those cut off from it. There is no Phoebe opposite a Hepzibah, no light to offset the dark. The unrelieved painfulness which distressed even Hawthorne in this story results from the fact that every one of the chief characters is segregated from the common life. The moral action of the book therefore, instead of developing between

7. *Ibid.*   8. *Ibid.*, p. 290.   9. *Ibid.*, p. 348. The italics are mine.

the outcasts and the life from which they are shut away, takes place wholly within the unhappy souls of the individuals whose guilt imprisons them within themselves. The outside world is seen chiefly through their tormented vision, and then only as a sort of dark projection of their own consciences.

In this way the recoil of the townspeople at the sight of the scarlet letter on Hester's bosom is really no more than the impressionistic portrayal of her own state of mind, her conscience flinching before the inescapable acknowledgment of her sin. Dimmesdale attempts to hide his guilt, but the acknowledgment of it is still there, ingrown, Hawthorne would have us believe, on his very flesh. In this manner Hawthorne symbolizes the great difference between the minister and Hester. The world does not recognize him for what he is. But that very fact renders his own consciousness of his state more morbid than ever, until concealment of the guilty condition of his true self secretly destroys his moral tissue. As a result his suffering is far more intense and sickly than Hester's.

Hester wears her shame somewhat as though it were a badge of honor which she has earned by appearing in her true light before the world. By thus righteously acknowledging her guilt she is able to bear herself with honesty before society. Dimmesdale rejected the true relationship to society that would have saved him.

Though Hester, too, might have made the same rejection by running away to a land where she was unknown and could live under false pretenses, it is testimony of her strength of character that she refused to turn herself into such a moral impostor. Only once was she on the verge of joining Dimmesdale in hypocrisy, and then only momentarily when she threw away the embroidered symbol of her free acknowledgment of guilt, thereby divesting herself of the honesty through which she had wrought with pain and courage whatever salvation she could claim. When the elfish Pearl unpredictably returns it to her, insisting that she replace it on her breast, the symbolism—which here shows Hawthorne at the height of his imaginative power—is nearly perfect. For Pearl stands for Hester's obligation to society—her *moral responsibility*.

As "the effluence of her mother's lawless passion"[1] Pearl lived in the solitary state which, like her mother's, came of being outside the regulations of society. Hester's responsibility was to bring her into the fold.

Mother and daughter stood together in the same circle of seclusion from human society; and in the nature of the child seemed to be perpetuated those unquiet elements that had distracted Hester Prynne before Pearl's

1. *The Scarlet Letter*, p. 200.

birth, but had since begun to be soothed away by the softening influences of maternity.[2]

Pearl was a born outcast of the infantile world. An imp of evil, emblem and product of sin, she had no right among christened infants. Nothing was more remarkable than the instinct, as it seemed, with which the child comprehended her loneliness; the destiny that had drawn an inviolable circle round about her.[3]

Her nature appeared to possess depth, too, as well as variety; but—or else Hester's fears deceived her—it lacked reference and adaptation to the world into which she was born. The child could not be made amenable to rules. In giving her existence, a great law had been broken; and the result was a being whose elements were perhaps beautiful and brilliant, but all in disorder; or with an order peculiar to themselves, amidst which the point of variety and arrangement was difficult or impossible to be discovered. Hester could only account for the child's character—and even then most vaguely and imperfectly—by recalling what she herself had been during that momentous period while Pearl was imbibing her soul from the spiritual world, and her bodily frame from its material of earth. The mother's impassioned state had been the medium through which were transmitted to the unborn infant the rays of its moral life . . .[4]

Hester herself represented a similar ostracism, though she maintained the saving grace as best she could of being "quick to acknowledge her sisterhood with the race of men."[5]

In all her intercourse with society, however, there was nothing that made her feel as if she belonged to it . . . She stood apart from moral interests, yet close beside them, like a ghost that revisits the familiar fireside, and can no longer make itself seen or felt; . . . or, should it succeed in manifesting its forbidden sympathy awakening only terror and horrible repugnance. These emotions, in fact, and its bitterest scorn besides, seemed to be the sole portion that she retained in the universal heart.[6]

Thus alone and cast off by society, Hester regarded Pearl as the "sole treasure to keep her heart alive." To those who would take the child from her, not realizing its significance as the incarnation of her responsibility to society, her one hold upon the moral life, she exclaims, " 'She is my happiness!—she is my torture, none the less! Pearl keeps me here in life! Pearl punishes me too! See ye not she is the scarlet letter, only capable of being loved, and so endowed with a million-fold the power of retribution for my sin?' "[7]

Enjoined by Hester to take her part, Dimmesdale upholds her

2. *Ibid.*, p. 119.   3. *Ibid.*, p. 118.
4. *Ibid.*, p. 115.   5. *Ibid.*, p. 195.
6. *Ibid.*   7. *Ibid.*, p. 139.

claim with an ethical conviction and insight upon which he himself is tragically incapable of acting.

She recognizes, believe me, the solemn miracle which God hath wrought, in the existence of that child. And may she feel, too,—what, methinks, is the very truth,—that this boon was meant, above all things else, to keep the mother's soul alive, and to preserve her from blacker depths of sin into which Satan might else have sought to plunge her! Therefore it is good for this poor sinful woman that she hath an infant immortality . . . to be trained up by her to righteousness—to remind her, at every moment, of her fall,—but yet to teach her, as it were by the creator's sacred pledge, that, if she bring the child to heaven, the child also will bring its parent thither![8]

As mother and daughter leave the governor's mansion the minister's convictions are forthwith proved by the altercation with Mistress Hibbins. Through Pearl Hester has been able to resist temptation to take the evil way and join the witches against society. "Even thus early," added Hawthorne pointedly, "had the child saved her from Satan's snare."[9]

Between Pearl and the scarlet letter there is a subtle connection which is suggested by the resemblance of Pearl's dress to the embroidered token, and by the actual words of Hester and Dimmesdale during the scene before Governor Bellingham and the Reverend Mr. Wilson. The display of the letter stands for the open acknowledgment of sinfulness by Hester, and her attachment to Pearl signifies her acceptance of the consequences of her sin, her ethical obligation. Similarly the child's freakish insistence on the letter may be said to represent Hester's moral responsibility requiring the forthright recognition of her guilt as one of the inevitable consequences of wrongdoing. Here again is apparent Hawthorne's skill in portraying a state of mind in terms of the physical world.

The willing admission of wrong and willing assumption of the obligations incurred by her conduct, while they tend to ostracize Hester, provide her nevertheless with her proper role in the moral life of mankind, thereby making her isolation far less terrible than Dimmesdale's. By failing to respond to Pearl's insistence that he take her and Hester by the hand in the public square, the minister demonstrates a moral irresponsibility which makes his own retribution impossible.[1]

Dimmesdale is isolated through keeping fearfully to himself his true position with respect to society. He well knows the moral disintegration which he faces in failing to take his proper place among

---

8. *Ibid.*, pp. 141–42.   9. *Ibid.*, p. 144.
1. Hawthorne speaks in so many words of his "idea of man's eternal responsibility" in *The Blithedale Romance*, p. 545.

men. Admonishing Hester to expose the father of her child, he says, in a speech heavy with *double entendres:*

Heaven hath granted thee an open ignominy, that thereby thou mayest work out an open triumph over the evil within thee, and the sorrow without. Take heed how thou deniest to him—who, perchance, hath not the courage to grasp it for himself—the bitter, but wholesome, cup that is now presented to thy lips.[2]

Thus early Dimmesdale—whose ethical perceptions are always greater than his courage to live up to them—realized which way salvation lay for him, but lacked the strength of will to take it. Instead, he made wretched shift with the semblance of respectability, "a being who felt himself quite astray and at a loss in the pathway of human existence, and could only be at ease in some seclusion of his own."[3] He had cheated himself of a true part in life by depriving himself of the open sin and ignominy which in Hester's case were "the roots which she had struck into the soil."[4] By his deceit he was leading an existence as unreal as the lie it was based on. " 'Had I one friend [he exclaimed]—or were it my worst enemy!—to whom, when sickened with the praises of all other men, I could daily betake myself, and be known as the vilest of all sinners, methinks my soul might keep itself alive thereby.' "[5]

It is not the consciousness of sin and guilt that fills the soul of Dimmesdale with its trance-like terror; it is the sense of the growing rift between him and society, the feeling that he has somehow become detached from life and is falling into a moral limbo farther and farther from reality and the honest existence of men.

It is the unspeakable misery of a life so false as his, that it steals the pith and substance out of whatever realities there are around us, and which were meant by Heaven to be the spirit's joy and nutriment . . . And he himself, in so far as he shows himself in a false light, becomes a shadow, or indeed, ceases to exist.[6]

This is the misery which Hester escaped by assuming her proper relationship with those about her. In the case of Dimmesdale, the sin itself was not so demoralizing as the separation from life and his fellow men which his dissembling wrought.

Dimmesdale exemplifies the thesis with which Hawthorne was preoccupied in working out his character and his fate; namely, that "all the powers of nature call . . . earnestly for the confession of sin."[7] The minister's desperate attempts to swim against the natural current result in complete exhaustion of the life within him. Here Hawthorne's abhorrence of whatever runs counter to nature is again im-

2. *Scarlet Letter*, p. 89.   3. *Ibid.*, p. 88.   4. *Ibid.*, p. 103.
5. *Ibid.*, p. 230.   6. *Ibid.*, pp. 177-78.   7. *Ibid.*, p. 160.

portant to his art. Like others who make a similar mistake but in different guises, Dimmesdale succeeds only in creating for himself an intolerable state of isolation. His life could have been saved only by breaking from its imprisonment in fear and "telling its secret . . . to the great heart of mankind; beseeching its sympathy or forgiveness, . . . and never in vain!"[8] As it is, the liaison with the common heart of humanity is suspended; the seclusion and privacy of the minister's weak-willed nature is prolonged in its unnatural state so that Chillingworth can virtually accomplish his dreadful ends. "All that guilty sorrow, hidden from the world, whose great heart would have pitied and forgiven, to be revealed to him, the Pitiless, to him, the Unforgiving."[9]

Old Roger Chillingworth, the conventionally wronged husband, constitutes formal morality which, having lost the true purpose and spirit of human ethics, has become a means not of salvation but of perdition. He represents the operation of ethical precepts, which were originally designed to enable men to live harmoniously in society, so divested of their indwelling humanity that they become a force of devastation, of isolation to the human heart. The calculating, scientific, heartless righteousness of mechanical morality which gets away from the human essence and social purpose of ethics is an instrument of the devil. So Chillingworth, as the incarnation of such righteousness, becomes a fiend.

The viper which Dimmesdale more or less uncomprehendingly nourished in his bosom, his real persecutor, is this formal ethic embodied in Chillingworth, these precepts with the life gone out of them. They can cauterize the minister's guilty soul but cannot draw it into the healing heart of humanity because, like the leech, they have become detached from that heart. To submit your guilt to the direct judgment of society, as Hester did, is to participate in the saving ethic of society. To submit it privately to a merciless traditional judgment apart from the live sympathy of mankind merely to evade an original and proper relationship toward men, as Dimmesdale did, is to bring upon your head all the punitive force of morality with none of its regenerative faculties.

It is as formal morality that Chillingworth must accompany his victim in the projected flight with Hester overseas, for flight denotes that the minister still chooses to stand trial before his doctrines of righteousness that do not involve him with men. It is as formal morality, also, that Chillingworth must argue to keep his victim from confessing, because confession will bring the minister under the regenerative influence of the social ethic and the power of the false one over him will thus be shut off forever. Dimmesdale's appearance at last on the scaffold, which stands guard over the mores of the people, means

8. *Ibid.*, pp. 289–90.   9. *Ibid.*, p. 170.

that he has rid himself of the specter of technical morality and established his adjustment to the vital ethic of society. He escapes the fiend thereby.

'Hadst thou sought the whole earth over,' [said Chillingworth] . . . looking darkly at the clergyman, 'there was no one place so secret,—no high place nor lowly place, where thou couldst have escaped me,—save on this very scaffold!' 'Thanks be to Him who hath led me hither!' answered the minister.[1]

Thus is the formal morality, whose scourge Dimmesdale was vulnerable to because of his hypocrisy, finally invalidated. Without a compromising soul that shrinks from the salutary verdict of society to keep it alive, it has no alternative but to shrivel away to nothing. This, in keeping with his perfectly symbolical existence, Chillingworth proceeds to do.

Dimmesdale rationalizes his disinclination to confess his sin before the world on the grounds that from his exalted place among men he may still render a great service which any public stigma attached to him would at once prevent. But he is soundly rebuked by the theoretical Chillingworth, who says truthfully of those who attempt to justify their hypocrisy on this basis that " 'if they seek to glorify God, let them not lift heavenward their unclean hands! If they would serve their fellow men, let them do it by making manifest the power and reality of conscience, in constraining them to penitential self-abasement!' "[2] This manifestation of the power and reality of conscience is what Hawthorne attempted in *The Marble Faun*.

In certain respects *The Marble Faun* is the complement of *The Scarlet Letter*. The latter contains the study of a man outwardly accepting social taboos, sinning against them, and then shunning judgment according to them. The former is the story of a man untrained in social decorums, sinning against them, and then actuated by conscience to accept them and their judgment as the way of growth and salvation. Dimmesdale half pleads with Hester to reveal the father of her child so that he too may share in the punishment and regeneration of a public acknowledgment of guilt. But Hester steadfastly refuses, intuitively aware that the regenerative purposes of morality are served only when that great moral instrument the conscience initiates behavior. Dimmesdale's conscience thereupon proves insufficient until the scene on the scaffold at the very end. Donatello on the other hand demonstrates the perfect adequacy of the conscience in assuming without further compulsion his full obligation to society and the moral order.

Donatello is a product of American social thought during an era

1. *Ibid.*, p. 300.   2. *Ibid.*, p. 162.

which was trying to determine, as Whitman put it, how much liberty men were able to bear. The question which had to be settled by each American who subscribed to the individualism of democracy was what sort of control is there which, without being incompatible with liberty, will yet be effective in preventing freedom from running to the absolute license of anarchy. In social circumstances where the individual and not the state is supreme, what is to keep a man from all kinds of lawless excesses in the indulgence of his self-interest? Like Tom Paine, those offspring of the Enlightenment who framed our Constitution put their somewhat worldly trust in the power of reason as an inner check upon the conduct of the free individual. But the adequacy of the mere faculty of reason came to be suspected. And it was suspected on the grounds that a certain amount of formal instruction and artificial training was necessary before human reason could be relied upon to distinguish between right and wrong.[3]

This necessity for education of some sort naturally clashed with the political emphasis which Jacksonian Democracy wanted to put upon the common untutored man, the bugbear of Federalists like James Fenimore Cooper and the Hartford Wits. Therefore it happened that the democratic movement of Evangelical Protestantism was prompted to advertize another control—the conscience. Unlike the faculty of reason, the conscience did not depend in the slightest upon education; on the contrary, it was itself the educating factor. "So long as an unlettered soul can attain to saving grace," Hawthorne wrote in his introduction to *Mosses*, "there would seem to be no deadly error in holding theological libraries to be accumulations of, for the most part, stupendous impertinence."[4] This belief in some faculty through which the moral law could be apprehended by the individual regardless of his background and training is fundamental to equalitarian philosophy in the first half of the century.

In effecting a liaison between the individual and the moral structure of the universe, conscience regulated men's behavior so that under the condition of freedom they did not turn to licentiousness and discord. What is more, it supplied the means of their exaltation.

The whole Universe is absolute Law [asserted Whitman]. Freedom only opens entire activity and license *under the law* . . . Great—unspeakably great—is the Will! The free Soul of man! At its greatest, understanding and obeying the laws, it can then, and then only, maintain true liberty. For there is to the highest, that law as absolute as any—more absolute than any—the Law of Liberty. The shallow, as intimated, consider liberty a release from all law, from every constraint. The wise see in it, on

3. See L. W. Marston, "Locke's Metaphysics Illustrated by Owen's Socialism," *The Monthly Magazine* (John A. Heraud, ed.), ser. 3, IV, 210.
4. *Mosses*, p. 29.

the contrary, the potent Law of Laws, namely, the fusion and combination of the conscious will, or partial individual law, with those universal, eternal, unconscious ones, which run through all Time, pervade history, prove immortality, give moral purpose to the entire objective world, and the last dignity to human life.[5]

"Once banish the internal law from the soul," proclaimed an obscure contemporary of Whitman's, ". . . and redemption is an impossibility."[6]

Whitman, Emerson, Thoreau, and most democratic thinkers of the time saw morality operative in human conduct and were convinced that human beings can achieve true liberty and happiness through living out the moral impulse which, as the pervasive principle of the universe, is innate within them. "Believe us, reader," wrote our typical commentator, "that where in earth's remote districts, an untaught heathen shall have faithfully acted out the injunctions of conscience in his breast, . . . *that* man shall be accepted by our common Father . . ."[7] This is exactly the situation of Donatello, the untaught individual who, through demonstrating the validity and effectiveness of conscience, attains a state of grace.

The doctrine of the inner check was indispensable to the social and political philosophy of the century's serious democratic thinkers. In one form or another it lay at the root of such typical works as Thoreau's essay *On the Duty of Civil Disobedience,* Emerson's *Self-Reliance.* It furnished the ethical justification for the *laissez faire* spirit of government. The regulatory and policing interference of the state in the lives of individuals could be kept at a minimum since each man's behavior was policed by his own conscience in direct accordance with the immutable laws of the universe. More than this, state supervision of private citizens had to be kept at a minimum if the full value of democracy in facilitating the growth of the human being were to be realized. Moral responsibility was seen to develop the individual's character, and such responsibility is impossible where virtue is not a matter of conscience but of constraint, of outer rather than inner compulsion. That is the reason Hawthorne takes care to have no policemen dogging the steps of Donatello, no fear of apprehension and punishment by the civil authorities. Donatello can achieve maturity only by freely choosing right conduct, and not by having it forced upon him as Dimmesdale would have had it forced on him by Hester. In seeking of his own accord to bring justice upon himself, Donatello becomes the fictional proof of Emerson's theory that formal government is rendered unnecessary by the growth of private character.

5. *Complete Prose Works* (1892), pp. 336–37.
6. L. W. Marston, "Locke's Metaphysics . . ." *loc. cit.,* p. 210.
7. *Ibid.,* p. 214.

The individual acquires moral wisdom and character through using his freedom to live conscientiously. This, in a phrase, is the theme of *The Marble Faun*. Behind it can be detected the broad teaching, which stemmed from nineteenth-century Evangelical Protestantism, that man was able to practise virtue of his own free will, and through the spiritual experience of such practice develop integrity. To show the individual's potentialities for growth Hawthorne wrote his story of the Faun, who, living as nearly as possible in a state of natural simplicity and devoid of any formal knowledge of ethical principles, is transformed and educated by the activity of an innate moral faculty into a mature and civilized being.

At the outset there is observable in Donatello, as in the statue of the faun which he resembles, a "lack of moral severity."

The being here represented is endowed with no principle of virtue, and would be incapable of comprehending such; but he would be true and honest by dint of his simplicity. . . . It is possible, too, that the Faun might be educated through the medium of his emotions, so that the coarser animal portion of his nature might eventually be thrown into the background, though never utterly expelled.[8]

Despite the homely, simple, sincere impulses of the natural man, there were in Donatello "deficiencies both of intellect and heart, and especially, as it seemed, in the development of the higher portion of man's nature."[9] In previous members of his family these defects and virtues had become grotesque with advancing age, when the licence and ebullience of youth passed and left the scion of the Monte Benis' "sensual, addicted to gross pleasures, heavy, unsympathizing, and insulated within the narrow limits of a surly selfishness."[1] The future that Donatello would have had to look forward to had he continued in the innocence with which he began is not an attractive one. And here it is important to note that from Hawthorne's point of view Donatello is fortunate to have undergone a deep moral experience, however painful and sad he may have found it.

Donatello is at first only a "poor simple boy." Those who knew him well "habitually and instinctively allowed for him, as for a child or some other lawless thing."[2] In his faun-like state he seemed to be wholly unconnected with the moral universe. "There was," Hawthorne wrote, "an indefinable characteristic about Donatello that set him outside of rules."[3] He kills on the simple instinct of natural justice, voiced by Miriam, that "innocent persons were saved by the destruction of a guilty one, who deserved his doom."[4] But not long after the crime had been committed there set in that transformation for which Hawthorne's English publishers named the romance. The passing of

8. *The Marble Faun*, p. 24. 9. *Ibid.*, p. 271. 1. *Ibid.*, p. 272.
2. *Ibid.*, p. 28. 3. *Ibid.* 4. *Ibid.*, p. 201.

the fierce primitive energy which had provoked Donatello to throw the model from the Tarpeian rock left him on the verge of manhood, and there "developed within him an intelligence which was no native characteristic of the Donatello whom we have heretofore known."[5] Moral consciousness woke within him, and as a result "he had little left of that singular resemblance, on account of which, and for their sport, his three friends had fantastically recognized him as the veritable Faun of Praxiteles."[6]

When Kenyon visits Monte Beni he observes in Donatello's character "something lost, or something gained,"[7] he cannot quite tell which. But he finds a perceptible change in his friend, and he wonders if it may not be a sign of "growth and development." Donatello somehow appears to have lost the natural impulsiveness of his earlier state and acquired the "power of dealing with his emotions,"[8] like more highly cultivated persons. The customs and restraints of society had begun to act on him, however slightly as yet. He had gained insight into the mysterious moral life of the world.

It was perceptible that he had already had glimpses of strange and subtle matters in those dark caverns, into which all men must descend, if they would know anything beneath the surface and illusive pleasures of existence. And when they emerge, though dazzled and blinded by the first glare of daylight, they take truer and sadder views of life forever afterwards.[9]

Donatello's behavior now "told of a vivified intellect, and of spiritual instruction that had come through sorrow and remorse; so that instead of the wild boy, the thing of sportive, animal nature, the sylvan Faun, here was now the man of feeling and intelligence."[1] The sculptor, Kenyon, tried to express in a bust the new soul and intellect which he felt had been inspired in Donatello by the agonizing experience he had passed through.[2] The bust proved successful, for both Hilda and Hawthorne are struck with the notion that the features have been transformed by some sort of "moral growth" which, though it is incomplete, nevertheless gives "the impression of a growing intellectual power and moral sense."[3]

It is Donatello's final action which proves the validity of the democratic faith in the individual's inner control. Miriam's words reveal the resolution of his conscience.

Here is Donatello haunted with strange remorse, and an unmitigable resolve to obtain what he deems justice upon himself. He fancies, with a kind of direct simplicity, . . . that, when a wrong has been done, the

5. *Ibid.*, p. 203. 6. *Ibid.*, p. 235. 7. *Ibid.*, p. 252.
8. *Ibid.*, p. 289. 9. *Ibid.*, p. 302. 1. *Ibid.*, p. 367.
2. *Ibid.*, p. 326. 3. *Ibid.*, p. 433.

doer is bound to submit himself to whatsoever tribunal takes cognizance of such things, and abide its judgment! [4]

Donatello's behavior, as he himself explains it, was due to " 'a sense, an impulse, an instinct . . . which sometimes leads me right.' "[5]

Such a sense, such an inward compulsion to right conduct was lacking in Judge Pyncheon, for example, in whose life there was enough false splendor "to cover up and paralyze a more active and subtile conscience than the Judge was ever troubled with."[6] The judge's prototype, too, pursued his selfish ends, trampling alike on the weak and strong of mankind, with an inveteracy that "knew neither rest nor conscience."[7] Holgrave, on the contrary, exhibits the very opposite disposition. Hawthorne points out that the most remarkable aspect of Holgrave's unsettled character lay in the fact that "he had never violated the innermost man, but had carried his conscience along with him."[8] In this respect also he might, as Hawthorne wrote, "fitly enough stand forth as the representative of many compeers in his native land."[9] Thus in this earlier romance based upon the natural and moral hostility of democracy for aristocracy does Hawthorne contrast the virtue, humanity, and conscientiousness of the first with the egocentricity and ruthlessness of the second.

But it is *The Marble Faun* that depicts the full regenerative power of conscience in bringing the individual from the purgatorial state of isolation, which is the punishment of sin, into the saving grace of brotherhood with men. The immediate effect of Donatello's crime was to set him and Miriam apart even from their closest friends, in a kind of "moral seclusion" where they became abnormally sensitive almost at once to "the immeasurable waste, that lay between them and all brotherhood or sisterhood."[1] Later on, the ethical import of Donatello's solitude comes out in his remark to Kenyon: "It is not my will, but my necessity, to avoid men's eyes."[2] Hawthorne is explicit with respect to his notion that Donatello's seclusion is a "moral estrangement" serving an ethical purpose.

For it is one of the chief earthly incommodities of some species of misfortune, or of a great crime, that it makes the actor in the one, or the sufferer of the other, an alien in the world, by interposing a wholly unsympathetic medium betwixt himself and those whom he yearns to meet.[3]

Thus perception of an infinite, shivering solitude, amid which we cannot come close enough to human beings to be warmed by them, . . . is one of the most forlorn results of any accident, misfortune, crime, or peculiarity of character, that puts an individual ajar with the world.[10]

4. *Ibid.*, p. 490.   5. *Ibid.*   6. *Seven Gables*, pp. 274–75.
7. *Ibid.*, pp. 151–52.   8. *Ibid.*, p. 212.   9. *Ibid.*, p. 217.
1. *Marble Faun*, p. 206.   2. *Ibid.*, p. 264.

3. *Ibid.*, p. 114. Merely to have secret knowledge of a crime effects a similar condition of mind and spirit, as Hilda's part in the story demonstrates.
10. *Ibid.*, p. 138.

The definitely sociological drift of Hawthorne's moral argument is further emphasized by Kenyon's pertinent suggestion that the natural punishment of sin may be to "insulate the sinner from all sweet society."[5] The owl tower—an edifice with a significance similar to that of the House of the Seven Gables except that it is only a temporary dwelling—is a perfect symbol of Donatello's segregation. The tower, as Kenyon imagines, "resembles the spiritual experience of many a sinful soul, which, nevertheless, may struggle upward into the pure air and light of Heaven at last!"[6]

Donatello, Hawthorne would have his reader believe, passes out of his isolation into a happier estate through conscientiously establishing his proper connection with men, through feeling all along the line the intimate bond between himself and his fellows. And when the idea first came to him of living for the welfare of his fellow-creatures his "original beauty, which sorrow had partly effaced, came back elevated and spiritualized" as though from the "black depths" of his suffering and isolation "the Faun had found a soul, and was struggling with it towards the light of heaven."[7] Hard on this spiritual regeneration of Donatello there follow some good American reflections by Hawthorne on the fact that Italians would seldom or never think of so typically democratic a consecration as that which pledged a man to the consideration of his brothers.

The great democratic conscience, operating through the suffering which morally educates human beings,[8] was the influence that Hawthorne saw drawing the individual out of himself into that sense of unison with all men which was the prime requisite of the social ethic. Such a democratic conscience prompted him even outside America to feel keenly his own connection with the inhabitants of slums and the inmates of workhouses and children's homes. It may be observed that Pearl, as a child, showed no trace of this conscience. "She wanted—what some people want throughout life—a grief that should deeply touch her, and thus humanize and make her capable of sympathy."[9] Hawthorne's report of the discourse of Florence Nightingale's mother on Lady Byron during the famous breakfast party at Richard Monckton Milnes's reveals that some such judgment as the one passed upon Pearl was forming in the back of his mind regarding Byron's wife. "Somehow or other," he wrote, "all this praise, and more of the same kind, gave me the idea of an intolerably irreproachable person; and I asked Mrs. Nightingale if Lady Byron was warm-hearted."[1]

He criticized the fastidious George P. Bradford in the same vein. "Good as he is," he wrote, "I cannot help thinking him rather selfish,

5. *Ibid.*, p. 350.   6. *Ibid.*, p. 292.   7. *Ibid.*, p. 309.
8. See the *English Notebooks*, p. 61. "I thought that the faces of the patients all looked remarkably intelligent, though they were evidently men of the lower classes; —suffering had educated them, for the time, morally and intellectually."
9. *Scarlet Letter*, p. 221.   1. *English Notebooks*, p. 382.

or self-involved, and tied down to self by a thousand little hair-lines; and yet he feels regard for a good many people, and is of most social tendencies." In the explanation which follows the familiar note is struck once more. "He is an old bachelor; and I suppose he might have developed into something better by marriage, and by coming into more earnest contact with the joys, griefs, and business of the world, than he has."[2]

A remarkable thing about Hawthorne is that this attitude was not something he had acquired after mature experience and deliberation. It originated when he was a boy living in Salem and editing his little magazine the *Spectator*. In an essay entitled "On Solitude" in the first issue of that modest publication, Hawthorne broached the faith which he never substantially altered in the regenerative virtues of social contact. "Man is naturally a sociable being," he argued somewhat precociously. "It is only in society that the full energy of his mind is aroused. Perhaps life may pass more tranquilly, estranged from the pursuits and vexations of the multitude, but all the hurry and whirl of passion is preferable to the cold calmness of indifference." In his well-known letter to Longfellow, sent from Salem toward the close of his long seclusion, he passed judgment upon his own life on the same grounds.

. . . I have been carried apart from the main current of life . . . I have secluded myself from society . . . I have made a captive of myself and put me into a dungeon . . . there is no fate in this world so horrible as to have no share in either its joys or sorrows. For the last ten years, I have not lived, but only dreamed about living.[3]

To be removed from the human fraternity, for whatever reason, was to step out of life into unreality.

Nearly all of the maladjusted characters in Hawthorne's fiction are expressions of states of mind resulting from some sort of estrangement from mankind. Clifford Pyncheon, for example, is a "representative of that great class of people whom an inexplicable Providence is continually putting at cross-purposes with the world: . . . making their existence a strangeness, a solitude, and torment."[4] So, of course, are the other major tragic figures whom this chapter has considered. But the theme recurs constantly in the minor works as well.[5] The tales called "Prophetic Pictures" and "Drowne's Wooden Image" dwell upon the artist's indifference to humanity. In his devotion to nothing except his art, "like all other men around whom an engrossing pur-

2. *Ibid.*, p. 76.
3. The original of this letter is in the Craigie House.
4. *Seven Gables*, p. 181.
5. For a discussion of the theme of isolation in Hawthorne, see *American Notebooks*, pp. lxviii–lxxii.

pose wreathes itself, he was insulated from the mass of human kind."[6]
"The Artist of the Beautiful" and "A Virtuoso's Collection" provide
similar instances. In the latter the Virtuoso is portrayed as a refined
and cultivated person without moral or spiritual depth. He reflects the
extreme materialism of the age when he says:

'My destiny is linked with the realities of earth. You are welcome to your
visions and shadows of a future state; but give me what I can see, and
touch, and understand, and I ask no more.' [7]

Hawthorne's full democratic sense of the Virtuoso's immorality comes
out as the latter shakes hands with the narrator without "a single
throb of human brotherhood."[8]

To the many intricate moral reasons already considered for Hawthorne's rejecting the Brook Farm experiment, another must be
added. Of the Brook Farmers Hawthorne said, "as regarded society at
large, we stood in a position of new hostility, rather than new brotherhood."[9] Brook Farm had made the error of isolation by differentiating
itself from men in general. Like the arch-reformer Hollingsworth it
manifested no deeply social conscience.[1] In the special interests of a
few experimentalists it committed the sin of indifference toward men
at large. This sin of indifference to the rest of the world—as his reaction to the poor and oppressed of Europe leaves quite clear—was one
of which Hawthorne was not guilty, nor did he ever have any idea that
it could be committed by an entire nation of his democratic countrymen.

A man's conscientious association with his brothers through the
sympathetic medium of the human heart was in Hawthorne's democratic judgment the whole basis of the real and the moral. The spectacular discovery of Ethan Brand was simply that he was "no longer a
brother man, opening the chambers or the dungeons of our common
nature by the key of holy sympathy."[2] His life exemplified "the sin of
an intellect that triumphed over the sense of brotherhood with man
and reverence for God."[3] It was the "Unpardonable Sin." In its suppression of the sense of brotherhood with all men it was the cardinal
sin against the principles of democracy—the "only sin that deserves a
recompense of immortal agony!"[4]

In *Ethan Brand, The Marble Faun, The Scarlet Letter, The House
of the Seven Gables,* and others, Hawthorne created indigenous American tragedy. It is tragedy which could have come from no one but a

6. *Twice-Told Tales*, p. 206. Compare the similar indifference of the scientist in
"Rappaccini's Daughter" and "The Birthmark."
7. *Mosses*, pp. 558–59.   8. *Ibid.*, p. 559.   9. *Blithedale*, p. 343.
1. See *Ibid.*, p. 399.   2. *Snow Image*, p. 495.   3. *Ibid.*, p. 485.
4. *Ibid.*

democratic writer. At the present time it represents about the most
satisfactory expression in art of the basic morality of democratic life.
Beside Hawthorne, Whitman was picturesque, Emerson was visionary, Thoreau was crabbed. The essential elements of the existing
democracy are harder to come at in these great democrats than in
Hawthorne. There was something procrustean about their philosophy.
They lopped off American society to fit their respective wills. Consequently, they tend to express not the actual conditions of the country, but ideas of their own which had grown out of those conditions
into something unique in each case. Their writings are projections of
three democratic egos, each different. Their work is not, in the sense
that Hawthorne's is, an imaginative probing into the depths to find
what was actually there, a fidelity of the artist instead of a conviction
of the man—as Eliot has put it. All three wrote more in the spirit of
the inventor than the discoverer. Each set up his own world and went
and lived in it. Emerson's society was made up without evil; Whitman's constituted an irrepressible promiscuity; Thoreau's consisted of
Walden and his private conscience. Hawthorne, however, drew together by his work two phases of American culture which have long
seemed quite distinct from one another, if not entirely antipathetic—
Puritan America and Democratic America. In his clinical preoccupa-
tion with the pathology of guilt and the nature of evil he was as much
a Puritan as any Calvinistic divine. But in his diagnoses and his
therapeutics he was a thoroughgoing democrat.

It may be objected that Hawthorne's world is a murky land of romance, no more typical and possibly even less so than those of his
highly original contemporaries. But that is to ignore his whole intent,
which was to portray the American state of mind and spirit, not
catalogue the American aspect or devise the ideal democratic world.
It is also to overlook the method he used to carry out his purpose. It
has to be understood that Hawthorne was a true impressionist, that
he was driven to impressionism by the nature of his theme. It was not
pure choice. He would rather have written like Anthony Trollope, he
once said. But unlike Trollope he was writing dramas of the soul and
its moral life. To do it consummately he had to project mental conditions into the physical world, to make the dominion of the mind so
complete that all of life became only a frame of reference to what
was going on within. If such a world seems uninhabitable it is not because it is an extravagance of the fancy. It is real enough, only it
represents a special phase of reality, specially treated in art. And the
world of art is always uninhabitable.

The vital action of Hawthorne's world, like that of every tragedian's,
is the unremitting contest between the good and evil of men's lives.
His development of this action is in part an artistic outgrowth of the

maladjustment, economic and philosophic, from which he himself suffered during most of his career. It was a maladjustment that his three famous contemporaries sought to evade by going into circumstances which they had made to order for themselves.

Hawthorne conscientiously faced the positive and negative elements in the American equation. In the Puritans he found bleak evidence of the contrast between man's forward-looking and his backsliding. In the society of his own day, and in himself as a member of that society, he observed the same discrepancy in newer guises between what life is and what man would have it. And in reflecting throughout his writing the maladjustments of nineteenth-century America, he achieved one of the finest and truest expressions of a democracy, where in their concern for the decency of human existence men are incessantly striving to adjust the promises of freedom to the permissions of morality.

BIBLIOGRAPHY

HAWTHORNE'S WORKS

THE first section of this bibliography lists the unpublished material which has been of primary importance to this work. The second section includes variously edited texts, and memoirs, essays, articles, etc., which quote in part or in full letters of Hawthorne. Random letters and fragments scattered through the United States and England in various libraries, museums, and collections are listed in footnotes.

A. Unpublished

Chiefly About War Matters, by a Peaceable Man: the original of the sketch printed in the *Atlantic Monthly*, July, 1862, in the possession of the heirs of Emma Collyer Hosmer, Chicago, Illinois.

The French and Italian Notebooks by Nathaniel Hawthorne, Based upon the Original Manuscripts in the Pierpont Morgan Library, an unpublished dissertation by Norman Holmes Pearson (Yale, 1941).

Trial Drafts of Hawthorne's Unfinished Romance: preliminary sketches for the uncompleted last romance, based upon the original manuscripts in the Huntington Library, the Pierpont Morgan Library, the Berg Collection in the New York Public Library, and the Concord Free Public Library at Concord, Massachusetts. Typescript copies of the originals are included in the Appendix to Mr. Edward Davidson's unpublished dissertation, *The Last Phase of Nathaniel Hawthorne* (Yale, 1940).

B. Published

The American Magazine of Useful and Entertaining Knowledge, II (Boston, 1836). Nos. 7–12, March to August, were edited and virtually written by Hawthorne and his sister.

The American Notebooks by Nathaniel Hawthorne, Based upon the Original Manuscripts in the Pierpont Morgan Library, edited by Randall Stewart (New Haven and London, 1932).

Autograph Edition of Hawthorne's Works (New York, 1900), XVII.

BACON, THEODORE, *Delia Bacon: A Biographical Sketch* (Boston and New York, 1888). Contains some twenty letters of Hawthorne, here first published.

BRIDGE, HORATIO, *Personal Recollections of Nathaniel Hawthorne* (New York, 1893).

CHORLEY, HENRY F., *Recent Art and Society as Described in the Autobiography and Memoirs*: compiled by C. H. Jones from the edition of Henry G. Hewlett (New York, 1874), pp. 229, 241–42. Also in *Personal Reminiscences*, edited by R. H. Stoddard (New York, 1874), p. 63.

The Diary of William Pynchon, edited by Fitch Edward Oliver (Boston, 1890), pp. viii–ix.

The English Notebooks by Nathaniel Hawthorne: Based upon the Original Manuscripts in the Pierpont Morgan Library, edited by Randall Stewart (London, 1941).

FIELDS, JAMES T., *Yesterdays With Authors,* (Boston, 1884) pp. 41–124, *passim.*

"Hawthorne's Contributions to the Salem Advertiser," edited by Randall Stewart, *American Literature,* v (January, 1934), 327–41.

The Hawthorne Diary of 1859, edited by William L. Reenan: privately printed (Freelands, 1931).

Hawthorne's First Diary, edited by Samuel T. Pickard (Boston and New York, 1897).

"Hawthorne in the Boston Custom House," extracts from his private letters, *Atlantic Monthly,* xxi (February, 1868), 106–11.

"Hawthorne's Spectator," edited by Elizabeth Lathrop Chandler, *The New England Quarterly,* iv (April, 1931), 288–330.

HAWTHORNE, JULIAN, "A Group of Hawthorne Letters," *Harper's Magazine,* cviii (March, 1904), 602–07.

HAWTHORNE, MANNING, "Hawthorne and Utopian Socialism," *New England Quarterly,* xii (December, 1939), 726–30. Two letters to David Mack.

HAWTHORNE, MANNING, "Maria Louisa Hawthorne," *Essex Institute Historical Collections,* lxxv, 103–34.

JOLINE, ADRIAN H., *Meditations of an Autograph Collector* (New York and London, 1902), pp. 39–41, 158.

LATHROP, ROSE HAWTHORNE, "The Hawthornes in Lenox; Told in Letters by Nathaniel and Mrs. Hawthorne," *Century,* xxvii (November, 1894), 86–98.

LATHROP, ROSE HAWTHORNE, *Memories of Hawthorne* (Boston, 1897).

Letters of Hawthorne to William D. Ticknor, 1851–1864 (Newark, 1910), 2 vols. Privately printed in a limited edition by the Cartaret Book Club.

Love Letters of Nathaniel Hawthorne (Chicago, 1907), 2 vols. Privately printed in a limited edition by the Society of Dofobs.

"Nathaniel and Elizabeth Hawthorne, Editors," *Colophon,* New Graphic series 3, nos. 1–3, 12 pp.

OSBORNE, JOHN BALL, "Nathaniel Hawthorne as American Consul," *Bookman,* xvi (January, 1903), 461–64. Analysis of two volumes of Hawthorne's official letters on file in the State Department.

The Political Correspondence of the Late Hon. George N. Sanders. Catalogue of public sale, Wednesday, 13 May 1914, under the management of the American Art Association, American Art Galleries, Madison Square South, New York. Items 69–76 represent letters from Hawthorne to Sanders.

Saturday Evening Gazette, 2 September 1883, 12 August 1883.

"A Sketch by Hawthorne," edited by Norman Holmes Pearson, *New England Quarterly,* vi (March, 1933), 136–44.

STEWART, RANDALL, "Hawthorne and Politics: Unpublished Letters to

William B. Pike," *New England Quarterly*, v (April, 1932), 237–63.

Ticknor, Caroline, *Hawthorne and His Publisher* (Boston, 1913).

Twenty Days with Julian and Little Bunny, a Diary (New York, 1904).

"Unpublished Letters of Nathaniel Hawthorne," *Athenaeum*, 10 and 17, August 1889, pp. 191, 192, 225. Reprinted in the *Critic*, xii (31 August 1889), 104, 105; xii (7 September 1889), 115–16.

The Works of Nathaniel Hawthorne, with Introductory Notes by George Parsons Lathrop and *Nathaniel Hawthorne and His Wife, a Biography by Julian Hawthorne* (Boston and New York, 1891), 15 vols.

PERIODICALS

Since biographers have had little to say of Hawthorne's social thought, I have not felt compelled to enumerate the standard critical and biographical works, most of which can be found in any adequate general bibliography of Hawthorne. The following list, while it contains most of the worthwhile articles that have appeared in the magazines up to the present day, lays special stress on publications constituting the judgment of Hawthorne by his contemporaries; such material seems a fitting codicil to a work which deals largely with a similar judgment made the other way round.

Albee, John, "Hawthorne," *The Unitarian Review*, xxiii (May, 1885), 419–31.

"American Authorship, No. 3, Nathaniel Hawthorne," reprinted from the *New Monthly Magazine* in *Littell's Living Age*, xxxviii (16 July 1853), 154–60.

"American Views of the English Character," *Reader*, ii (3 October 1863), 367–68.

Ammidon, Philip R., "Hawthorne's Last Sketch," *The New England Magazine*, n.s. i (June, 1886), 516–26.

"The Blithedale Romance," *The American Whig Review*, xvi (November, 1852), 417–24.

"The Blithedale Romance," The London *Athenaeum* (10 July 1852), 741–43.

"The Blithedale Romance," *The New Monthly Magazine*, reprinted in *Littell's Living Age*, xxxiv (14 August 1852), 327–32.

"Books Read by Nathaniel Hawthorne, 1828–1850," *Historical Collections of the Essex Institute*, lxviii (January, 1932), 65–87.

Bradfield, Thomas, "The Romances of Nathaniel Hawthorne," *The Westminster Review*, cxlii (August, 1894), 203–14.

Brownell, William Crary, "Hawthorne," *Scribner's Magazine*, xliii (January, 1908), 69–84.

Cargill, Oscar, "Nemesis and Nathaniel Hawthorne," *Publications of the Modern Language Association*, lii (September, 1937), 848–62.

Chandler, Elizabeth Lathrop, "A Study of the Sources of the Tales and Romances Written by Nathaniel Hawthorne before 1853," *Smith College Studies in Modern Languages*, vii, no. 4 (July, 1926).

Coleridge, Mary Elizabeth, "Questionable Shapes of Nathaniel Hawthorne," *The Monthly Review,* reprinted in *Littell's Living Age,* CCXLII (6 August 1904), 348–53.

"Contemporary Literature in America, *The Blithedale Romance,*" *The Westminster Review,* LVIII (October, 1852), 592–98.

CONWAY, MONCURE D., "Hawthorne, His Uncollected Tales in The Token," *The New York Times Saturday Review* (8 June 1901), 397–98.

CONWAY, MONCURE D., "My Hawthorne Experience," *The Critic,* XLV (July, 1904), 21–25.

CONWAY, MONCURE D., "The Secret of Hawthorne," *The Nation,* LXXVIII (30 June 1904), 509–10.

COOK, KENINGALE, "'Dr. Grimshawe's Secret,'" *Athenaeum* (London, No. 2878, 23 December 1882), 847–48.

COOKE, ALICE L., "Some Evidences of Hawthorne's Indebtedness to Swift," *University of Texas Studies in English,* No. 3826 (8 July 1938), 140–62.

COXE, REV. ARTHUR C., "The Writings of Hawthorne," *The Church Review,* III (January, 1851), 489–511. In *Notorious Literary Attacks,* edited by Albert Mordell (New York, 1926), pp. 122–37.

The Critic, XLV (July, 1904). The number is devoted to Hawthorne.

CUMMINGS, C. A., "Hawthorne," *Christian Examiner,* LXXVIII (January, 1865), 89–106.

CURTIS, GEORGE WILLIAM, "The Editor's Easy Chair," on the death of Hawthorne, *Harper's New Monthly Magazine,* XXIX (August, 1864), 405.

CURTIS, GEORGE WILLIAM, "The Editor's Easy Chair," on Henry James's Hawthorne, *Harper's New Monthly Magazine,* LXI (November, 1880), 945–47.

DE CASSERES, BENJAMIN, "Hawthorne: Emperor of Shadows," *The Critic,* XLV (July, 1904), 37–44.

DENNET, J. R., "Hawthorne's English Note-Books," *The Nation,* XI (28 July 1870), 59–61.

DOUBLEDAY, NEAL F., "Hawthorne's Hester and Feminism," *Publications of the Modern Language Association,* LIV (September, 1939), 825–28.

DOUBLEDAY, NEAL F., "Theme of Hawthorne's 'Fancy's Show–Box,'" *American Literature,* X (November, 1938), 341–43.

DUTTON, SAMUEL W. S., "Nathaniel Hawthorne," *The New Englander,* V (January, 1847), 56–69.

DUYCKINCK, EVERT A., "Nathaniel Hawthorne," *Arcturus,* I (May, 1841), 330–37.

FIELDS, JAMES T., "Our Whispering Gallery," *The Atlantic Monthly,* XXVII (February, 1871), 246–57.

FULLER, FREDERICK T., "Hawthorne and Margaret Fuller Ossoli," *The Literary World,* XVI (10 January 1885), 11–15.

GRAY, MAXWELL, "Hawthorne the Mystic," *The Nineteenth Century and After,* LXXXVII (January, 1920), 118–25.

GRIBBLE, FRANCIS, "Hawthorne from an English Point of View," *The Critic,* XLV (July, 1904), 61–66.

"Hawthorne on England," *Blackwood's Edinburgh Magazine,* XCIV (November, 1863), 610–23.

"Mr. Hawthorne on England and the English," *The Christian Remembrancer*, reprinted in *Littell's Living Age*, LXXXI (16 April 1864), 99–114.

HAWTHORNE, JULIAN, "Books of Memory," *The Bookman*, LXI (July, 1925), 567–71.

HAWTHORNE, JULIAN, "Hawthorne, Man of Action," *The Saturday Review of Literature*, III (16 April 1927), 727–28.

HAWTHORNE, JULIAN, "Hawthorne's Philosophy," *Century Magazine*, X (May, 1886), 83–93.

HAWTHORNE, JULIAN, "The Salem of Hawthorne," *The Century Magazine*, n.s. VI (May, 1884), 3–17.

HAWTHORNE, JULIAN, "Scenes of Hawthorne's Romances," *The Century Magazine*, n.s. VI (July, 1884), 380–97.

"Hawthorne's Life of Pierce,—Perspective," *Democratic Review*, XXXI (September, 1852), 276–88.

HILLARD, GEORGE STILLMAN, "The English Note-Books of Nathaniel Hawthorne," *The Atlantic Monthly*, XXVI (September, 1870), 257–72.

HILLARD, KATHERINE, "Hawthorne as an Interpreter of New England," *The New England Magazine*, n.s. XII (August, 1895), 732–36.

HILLMAN, MARY VINCENT, "Hawthorne and Transcendentalism," *The Catholic World*, XCIII (May, 1911), 199–212.

HOLDEN, GEORGE H., "Hawthorne Among His Friends," *Harper's New Monthly Magazine*, LXIII (July, 1881), 260–67.

HOLMES, OLIVER WENDELL, "Hawthorne," *The Atlantic Monthly*, XIV (July, 1864), 98–101.

HORWILL, HERBERT W., "Hawthorne's 'America' Fifty Years After," *The Critic*, XLV (July, 1904), 71–73.

HUNGERFORD, EDWARD BUELL, "Hawthorne Gossips about Salem," *The New England Quarterly*, VI (September, 1933), 445–69.

JAMES, HENRY, "Hawthorne's French and Italian Journals," *The Nation*, XIV (14 March 1872), 172–73.

JEPSON, GEORGE E., "Hawthorne in the Boston Custom House," *The Bookman*, XIX (August, 1904), 573–80.

KERN, ALFRED A., "The Sources of Hawthorne's Feathertop," *Publications of the Modern Language Association*, XLVI (December, 1931), 1253–59.

KOUWENHOVEN, JOHN A., "Hawthorne's Notebooks and *Doctor Grimshawe's Secret*," *American Literature*, V (January, 1934), 349–58.

LANG, ANDREW, "An Appreciation of Hawthorne," *Historical Collections of the Essex Institute*, XLI (January, 1905), 63–65.

LATHROP, GEORGE P., "The Hawthorne Manuscripts," *Atlantic Monthly*, LI (March, 1883), 363–75.

LATHROP, GEORGE P., "Poe, Irving, Hawthorne," *Scribner's Monthly*, XI (April, 1876), 799–808.

LEWIN, WALTER, "Nathaniel Hawthorne," *The Bookman*, XXVI (July, 1904), 121–28.

"Literary Notes," on Life of Pierce, *To-day: a Boston Literary Journal*, II (17 July 1852), 42.

LORING, GEORGE B., "Hawthorne's Scarlet Letter," *Massachusetts Quarterly Review*, III (September, 1850), 484–500.

LOWELL, JAMES RUSSELL, "The Marble Faun," *Atlantic Monthly*, V (April, 1860), 509–10.

MABIE, HAMILTON WRIGHT, "Nathaniel Hawthorne," *The North American Review*, CLXXIX (July, 1904), 13–23.

MAYO, AMORY D., "The Works of Nathaniel Hawthorne," *The Universalist Review*, VIII (July, 1851), 272–93.

MILLER, HAROLD P., "Hawthorne Surveys His Contemporaries," *American Literature*, XII (May, 1940), 228–35.

MITCHELL, DONALD GRANT, "Editor's Easy Chair," on Hawthorne as Consul, *Harper's New Monthly Magazine*, VI (May, 1853), 849–50.

MONTÉGUT, ÉMILE, "Un Roman Socialiste en Amérique," *Revue des Deux Mondes*, XVI (1 December 1852), 809–41.

MONTÉGUT, ÉMILE, "Un Romancier Pessimiste en Amérique," *Revue des Deux Mondes*, XXVIII (1 August 1860), 668–703.

MORSE, J. H., "Nathaniel Hawthorne Again," *Century Magazine*, IV (June, 1883), 311.

"Mosses from an Old Manse," *Athenaeum*, no. 980 (8 August 1846), 806–08.

"Nathaniel Hawthorne," *The Dublin University Review*, XLVI (October, 1855), 463–69.

"Nathaniel Hawthorne," *Universal Review*, reprinted in *Littell's Living Age*, LXV, 3rd ser. 9 (23 June 1860), 707–23.

"Nathaniel Hawthorne's Life and Writings," *The London Quarterly Review*, XXXVII (October, 1871), 48–78.

"Nathaniel Hawthorne's Note-Book," *The Spectator*, reprinted in *Littell's Living Age*, C (27 February 1869), 544–46.

NEVINS, WINFIELD S., "The Homes and Haunts of Hawthorne," *The New England Magazine*, n.s. IX (November, 1893), 289–306.

NEVINS, WINFIELD S., "Nathaniel Hawthorne's Removal from the Salem Custom House," *Historical Collections of the Essex Institute*, LIII (April, 1917), 97–132.

"New Englanders and the Old Home," *Quarterly Review*, reprinted in *Littell's Living Age*, LXXX, 3rd ser. 24 (20 February 1864), 346–53.

"Notes," *The Nation*, XVIII (19 February 1874), 125.

OSBORN, JOHN BALL, "Nathaniel Hawthorne as American Consul," *Bookman*, XVI (January, 1903), 461–64.

PEABODY, ANDREW P., "Nathaniel Hawthorne," *The North American Review*, LXXVI (January, 1853), 227–48.

POE, EDGAR ALLAN, "Marginalia," *Democratic Review*, XV (December, 1844), 585–86.

POE, EDGAR ALLAN, "Tale-writing—Nathaniel Hawthorne," *Godey's Magazine*, XXXV (November, 1847), 252–56.

PORTER, JOHN ADDISON, "The 'Dr. Grimshawe' MSS," *The New Englander*, XLII (May, 1883), 339–53.

RANDEL, WILLIAM P., "Hawthorne, Channing, and Margaret Fuller," *American Literature*, X (January, 1939), 472–76.

SAINTSBURY, GEORGE, a review of James's *Hawthorne, The Academy,* XVII (17 January 1880), 40–41.

SCHÖNBACH, ANTON E., "An Estimate of Hawthorne," *Historical Collections of the Essex Institute,* XLI (January, 1905), 66–67.

SCHUYLER, EUGENE, "The Italy of Hawthorne," *The Nation,* XLIX (11 July 1889), 48–49.

SMYTH, ALBERT H., "Critical Studies in American Literature. IV. A Short Story: 'The Great Stone Face.' Hawthorne." *The Chautauquan,* XXXI (April, 1900), 75–79.

STEWART, RANDALL, "Hawthorne and the Civil War," *Studies in Philology,* XXXIV (January, 1937), 91–106.

STEWART, RANDALL, "Hawthorne and Politics. Unpublished Letters to William B. Pike," *The New England Quarterly* V (April, 1932), 237–63.

STEWART, RANDALL, "Hawthorne and *The Fairie Queene,*" *Philological Quarterly,* XII (April, 1933), 196–206.

STEWART, RANDALL, "Hawthorne in England: The Patriotic Motive in the Note-Books," *New England Quarterly,* VIII (March, 1935), 3–13.

STEWART, RANDALL, "Hawthorne's Speeches at Civic Banquets," *American Literature,* VII (January, 1936), 415–23.

STODDARD, RICHARD HENRY, "Nathaniel Hawthorne," *Lippincott's Monthly Magazine,* XLIII (February, 1889), 250–59.

TAPLEY, HARRIET S., "Hawthorne's 'Pot-8-o Club' at Bowdoin College," *Historical Collections of the Essex Institute,* LXVII (July, 1931), 225–32.

THAYER, WILLIAM H., "The Works of Hawthorne," *The American, A National Weekly Journal,* V (31 March 1883), 393–94.

"The Transcendentalists of Concord," on Hawthorne, *Fraser's Magazine,* reprinted in *Littell's Living Age,* LXXXIII, 3rd ser. 27 (15 October 1864), 104–05.

TROLLOPE, ANTHONY, "The Genius of Nathaniel Hawthorne," *The North American Review,* CXXIX (September, 1879), 203–33.

TURNER, ARLIN, "Autobiographical Elements in Hawthorne's 'The Blithedale Romance,'" *University of Texas Studies in English,* No. 15 (8 July 1835), 39–62.

"Unpublished Letters of Nathaniel Hawthorne," *The Critic,* n.s. XII (7 September 1889), 115–16.

WARD, WILLIAM S., "Nathaniel Hawthorne and the Brook Farm," *Letters,* IV, no. 16 (August, 1931), 6–14.

WARREN, AUSTIN, "Hawthorne, Margaret Fuller, and Nemesis," *Publications of the Modern Language Association,* LIV (June, 1939), 615–18.

WARREN, AUSTIN, "Hawthorne's Reading," *The New England Quarterly,* VIII (December, 1935), 480–97.

WEBBER, CHARLES W., "Hawthorne," *The American Review, A Whig Journal,* IV (September, 1846), 296–316.

WOODBERRY, GEORGE E., on the Influence of Puritanism on Hawthorne, *Harper's Magazine,* CVI (February, 1903), 428–29.

"The Writings of Hawthorne," *The Southern Review,* VII (April, 1870), 328–54.

BROOK FARM

The following bibliography contains material not listed elsewhere in conjunction with Hawthorne. It covers the main features of Brook Farm and in particular Hawthorne's personal connection with the enterprise.

A. Manuscripts

Day Book, containing entries of dinner waiters from 3 May 1845 to 4 April 1846. In the Library of the Massachusetts Historical Society.

Brook Farm Records, containing incomplete financial records of the enterprise, as well as heterogeneous material like the original draft of the Constitution and a list of the original stock-holders. Presented to the Massachusetts Historical Society by Miss Effie Ellis.

RIPLEY, GEORGE, *Commonplace Book,* in the Widener Library at Harvard.

B. Memoirs, Letters, Commentary

Brook Farm Association for Industry and Education: Constitution, with an introductory Statement. 2d ed. with the By-laws (Boston, 1844).

BESTOR, ARTHUR E. JR., *Fourierist Socialism in the United States,* an unpublished dissertation (Yale, 1938).

BRADFORD, GEORGE P., "Reminiscences of Brook Farm, by a Member of the Community," *Century Magazine,* XLV, 141–48.

BROOKS, VAN WYCK, "Retreat from Utopia," *Saturday Review of Literature,* XIII, No. 17 (22 February 1936), 3–4, 14, 16, 18.

BROWNSON, ORESTES A., "Brook Farm," *United States Magazine and Democratic Review,* XI, n.s. (November, 1842), 481–96.

BURTON, MRS. KATHERINE (KURZ), *Paradise Planters, the Story of Brook Farm,* (London, 1939).

CODMAN, JOHN T., *Brook Farm: Historic and Personal Memoirs* (Boston, 1894).

CONWAY, MONCURE D., "Concerning Hawthorne and Brook Farm," *Every Saturday,* VII (2 January 1869), 13–18.

COOKE, GEORGE W., "Brook Farm," *New England Magazine,* XVII, n.s. (December, 1897), 391—407.

COOKE, GEORGE W., *John Sullivan Dwight: Brook-Farmer, Editor, and Critic of Music* (Boston, 1898).

CURTIS, GEORGE W., "Hawthorne and Brook Farm," in his *From the Easy Chair,* 1894, ser. 3, pp. 1–19.

EMERSON, RALPH WALDO, "Brook Farm," (in "Life and Letters in New England"), *Lectures and Biographical Sketches,* the Complete Works of Emerson (Boston, 1887), x.

EMERSON, RALPH WALDO, "Fourierism and the Socialists," *Dial,* III (July, 1842), 86–97.

EMERSON, RALPH WALDO, "Man the Reformer," *Dial,* I (April, 1841), 523–38.

FROTHINGHAM, OCTAVIUS B., *George Ripley* (Boston, 1882).

FROTHINGHAM, OCTAVIUS B., *Transcendentalism in New England* (Boston, 1876).

GOHDES, C., "Brook Farm Labor Record," *Philological Quarterly*, bibliog., VII (July, 1928), 299–302.

GOHDES, C., "Getting Ready for Brook Farm," *Modern Language Notes*, XLIX (January, 1934), 36–39.

GOHDES, C., "Three Letters by James Kay Dealing with Brook Farm," *Philological Quarterly*, bibliog. XVII (October, 1938), 377–88.

GORDON, G. H., *Brook Farm to Cedar Mountain in the War of the Great Rebellion* (Boston, 1883).

HARASZTI, ZOLTÁN, "Brook Farm Letters," *More Books: The Bulletin of the Boston Public Library*, XII (February and March, 1937), 49–68, 93–114.

Harbinger, The, Devoted to Social and Political Progress, Vols. I–IV. Published by the Brook Farm Phalanx (New York, Burgess, Stringer and Co.; Boston, Redding and Co., 1845–47).

HECKER, I. T., "The Transcendental Movement in New England," *Catholic Review*, XXIII (1876), 528–37.

HILLQUIT, MORRIS, *History of Socialism in the United States*, Revised Edition (New York and London, 1910).

HINDS, W. A., *American Communities and Co-operative Colonies* (Chicago, 1908).

KIRBY, GEORGIANNA BRUCE, *My First Visit to Brook Farm* (San Francisco, 1870). Reprinted from the *Overland Monthly*, V (July, 1870), 9–19.

KIRBY, GEORGIANNA BRUCE, "Reminiscences of Brook Farm," *Old and New:* (1871) III, 425–38; IV, 347–58; (1872) V, 517–30.

KIRBY, GEORGIANNA BRUCE, *Years of Experience: An Autobiographical Narrative* (New York and London, 1887).

KNORTZ, C., *Brook Farm and Margaret Fuller* (New York, 1886).

LANE, C., "Brook Farm," *Dial*, IV (January, 1844), 351–57.

LANE, C., "Social Tendencies," *Dial*, IV (July and October 1843), 65–86, 188–204.

Letters from Brook Farm, 1844–1847: by Marianne Dwight, edited by Amy L. Reed (Poughkeepsie, 1928).

McGINLEY, A. A., "Brook Farm Today," *Catholic World*, LXI (April, 1895), 14–25.

METZDORF, ROBERT F., "Hawthorne's Suit Against Ripley and Dana," *American Literature*, XII (May, 1940), 235–41.

NORDHOFF, CHARLES, *The Communistic Societies of the United States* (New York, 1875).

PEABODY, ELIZABETH P., "A Glimpse of Christ's Idea of Society," *Dial*, II (October, 1841), 214–28.

PEABODY, ELIZABETH P., "A Plan of the West Roxbury Community," *Dial*, II (January, 1842), 361–72.

Phalanx, The, A Journal of Social Science. Nos. 1–23 (New York, 1843–45). Continued by the *Harbinger*.

RIPLEY, GEORGE, "The Commencement of Association," *The Harbinger*, I (16 August 1845), 159–60.

RIPLEY, GEORGE AND BRADFORD, GEORGE P., "Philosophic Thought in Boston," in *The Memorial History of Boston,* edited by Justin Winsor (Boston, 1881), IV, 295–330.

RUSSELL, AMELIA, "Home Life of the Brook Farm Association," *Atlantic Monthly,* XLII (October, 1878), 458–66, 556–63.

SALISBURY, ANNIE MARIA, *Brook Farm* (Marlborough, Massachusetts; Smith College, 1898).

SAXON, J. A., "Prophecy—Transcendentalism—Progress," *Dial,* II (July, 1841), 83–121.

SEARS, JOHN VAN DER ZEE, *My Friends at Brook Farm* (New York, 1912).

SEDGWICK, ORA GANNETT, "A Girl of Sixteen at Brook Farm," *Atlantic Monthly,* LXXXV (March, 1900), 394–404.

SUMNER, A., "A Boy's Recollections of Brook Farm," *New England Magazine,* XVI (May, 1894), 309–13.

SWIFT, LINDSAY, *Brook Farm: Its Members, Scholars, and Visitors* (New York, 1900).

TARBELL, A. W., "The Brook Farm Experiment," *National Magazine,* VII (1897), 195–203.

INDEX

YALE STUDIES IN ENGLISH

Benjamin C. Nangle, Editor.

41. SMYTH, M. W., Biblical Quotations in Middle English Literature before 1350. (*Out of print.*)
42. MERRILL, E., The Dialogue in English Literature. (*Out of print.*)
43. CLEAVELAND, E. W., A Study of Tindale's Genesis. $2.00.
44. BULAND, M., The Presentation of Time in the Elizabethan Drama. $1.50.
45. JUDSON, A. C. (Editor), Cynthia's Revels, or, The Fountain of Self-Love. (*Out of print.*)
46. ANDREWS, C. E., Richard Brome: A Study of His Life and Works. $1.25.
47. PECK, H. W. (Editor), The Magnetic Lady, or, Humors Reconciled. $2.00.
48. MASON, L. (Translator), Genesis A. $ .75.
49. TUCKER, E. C., The Later Version of the Wycliffite Epistle to the Romans, compared with the Latin Original. $1.50.
50. COOK, A. S., Some Accounts of the Bewcastle Cross between the Years 1607 and 1861. (*Out of print.*)
51. CLARK, E. M. (Editor), The Ready and Easy Way to Establish a Free Commonwealth. (*Out of print.*)
52. CARTER, H. H. (Editor), Every Man in His Humour. $4.00.
53. HARRIS, L. H. (Editor), Catiline: His Conspiracy. (*Out of print.*)
54. HALE, W. T. (Editor), Of Reformation, Touching Church-Discipline in England. (*Out of print.*)
55. ADAMS, E. N., Old English Scholarship in England from 1566 to 1800. $2.00.
56. SELIN, W. E. (Editor), The Case Is Altered. $2.00.
57. BARSTOW, M. L., Wordsworth's Theory of Poetic Diction. $2.00.
58. GOAD, C., Horace in the English Literature of the Eighteenth Century. (*Out of print.*)
59. REA, J. D. (Editor), Volpone. (*Out of print.*)
60. WEDEL, T. O., The Mediæval Attitude toward Astrology, Particularly in England. $2.50.
61. MENNER, R. J. (Editor), Purity. $3.00.
62. McINTYRE, C. F., Ann Radcliffe in Relation to Her Time. (*Out of print.*)
63. COOK, A. S., The Old English Physiologus. $ .80.
64. CARHART, M. S., The Life and Work of Joanna Baillie. $2.00.
65. WITHERSPOON, A. M., The Influence of Robert Garnier on Elizabethan Drama. $2.00.
66. PITMAN, J. H., Goldsmith's Animated Nature. $2.00.
67. PITMAN, J. H., The Riddles of Aldhelm. $1.00.
68. BISSELL, B., The American Indian in English Literature of the Eighteenth Century. (*Out of print.*)
69. MERRILL, L. R., The Life and Poems of Nicholas Grimald. $4.50.
70. CLUBB, M. D., Christ and Satan: An Old English Poem. $2.00.
71. SMITH, H. J., Oliver Goldsmith's The Citizen of the World. (*Out of print.*)
72. SAVAGE, H. L., St. Erkenwald: A Middle English Poem. $2.00.
73. HARRIS, J. H. (Editor), Eastward Hoe. $2.00.
74. BRADNER, L., The Life and Poems of Richard Edwards. $2.00.
75. CASKEY, J. H., The Life and Works of Edward Moore. $2.00.
76. WHITE, H. A., Sir Walter Scott's Novels on the Stage. $2.50.
77. BRINKLEY, R. F., Nathan Field: The Actor-Playwright. $2.50.
78. CROMWELL, O., Thomas Heywood. $2.50.
79. BOLTON, J. S. G., Melanthe. $2.50.
80. BELDEN, M. M., The Dramatic Work of Samuel Foote. (*Out of print.*)
81. DODDS, J. W., Thomas Southerne: Dramatist. $2.00.
82. HARROLD, C. F., Carlyle and German Thought: 1819–1834. $2.50.
83. SMITH, W. H., Architecture in English Fiction. (*Out of print.*)
84. ZUNDER, T. A., The Early Days of Joel Barlow: A Connecticut Wit. $2.00.
85. SMALL, M. R., Charlotte Ramsay Lennox: An Eighteenth Century Lady of Letters. $2.50.
86. HEARSEY, M., The Complaint of Henry, Duke of Buckingham. $2.00.
87. OSBORN, L. B., The Life, Letters, and Writings of John Hoskyns, 1566–1638. $3.50.
88. WAPLES, D., The Whig Myth of James Fenimore Cooper. $2.75.

Orders for volumes in print should be addressed to
YALE UNIVERSITY PRESS, New Haven, Connecticut.